# Praise for

# *The Geography of Bliss*

"Fresh and beguiling...This wise, witty ramble reads like Paul Theroux channeling David Sedaris on a particularly good day... The author vividly renders happily repressed Switzerland, determinedly tolerant and hedonistic Holland, and culturally vibrant Iceland as models of happiness-encouraging environments...But the author's conclusions are hardly the point—as with all great journeys, getting there is at least half the fun."
— *Kirkus Reviews*

"With one single book, Eric Weiner has flushed Bill Bryson down a proverbial toilet, and I say that lovingly...The relationship between place and contentment is an ineffable one, and Weiner cuts through the fog with a big, powerful light. THE GEOGRAPHY OF BLISS is no smiley-face emoticon. It's a Winslow Homer."
— Henry Alford,
author of *Municipal Bondage*
and *Big Kiss*

"Think *Don Quixote* with a dark sense of humor and a taste for hashish and you begin to grasp Eric Weiner, the modern knight-errant of this mad, sad, wise, and witty quest across four continents. I won't spoil the fun by telling if his mission succeeds, except to say that happiness is reading a book as entertaining as this."
— Tony Horwitz,
author of *Confederates in the Attic*

One Grump's Search for
the Happiest Places in the World

# THE GEOGRAPHY OF

# *Bliss*

# ERIC WEINER

TWELVE

NEW YORK   BOSTON

Twelve
Hachette Book Group USA
237 Park Avenue
New York, NY 10017

Visit our Web site at www.HachetteBookGroupUSA.com.

Twelve is an imprint of Grand Central Publishing.
The Twelve name and logo is a trademark of
Hachette Book Group USA, Inc.

Printed in the United States of America

Originally published in hardcover by Hachette Book Group USA.

First International Trade Edition: January 2008
10 9 8 7 6 5 4 3 2 1

ISBN 978-0-446-19963-6 (pbk.)

*for Sharon*

*In these days of wars and rumors of wars, haven't you ever dreamed of a place where there was peace and security, where living was not a struggle but a lasting delight?*

—*Lost Horizon*, directed by Frank Capra, 1937

# Contents

Introduction                                                        1

Chapter *1* The Netherlands                                         5
            Happiness Is a Number

Chapter *2* Switzerland                                            27
            Happiness Is Boredom

Chapter *3* Bhutan                                                 49
            Happiness Is a Policy

Chapter *4* Qatar                                                  97
            Happiness Is a Winning Lottery Ticket

Chapter *5* Iceland                                               141
            Happiness Is Failure

Chapter *6* Moldova                                               185
            Happiness Is Somewhere Else

Chapter *7* Thailand                                              219
            Happiness Is Not Thinking

Chapter *8* Great Britain                                         245
            Happiness Is a Work in Progress

x    *Contents*

Chapter 9  India  275
Happiness Is a Contradiction

Chapter 10  America  307
Happiness Is Home

Epilogue  324
Are We There Yet?

Acknowledgments  327

# THE GEOGRAPHY OF

## *Bliss*

# Introduction

My bags were packed and my provisions loaded. I was ready for adventure. And so, on a late summer afternoon, I dragged my reluctant friend Drew off to explore new worlds and, I hoped, to find some happiness along the way. I've always believed that happiness is just around the corner. The trick is finding the right corner.

Not long into our journey, Drew grew nervous. He pleaded with me to turn back, but I insisted we press on, propelled by an irresistible curiosity about what lay ahead. Danger? Magic? I needed to know, and to this day I'm convinced I would have reached wherever it was I was trying to reach had the Baltimore County Police not concluded, impulsively I thought at the time, that the shoulder of a major thoroughfare was no place for a couple of five-year-olds.

Some people acquire the travel bug. Others are born with it. My affliction, if that's what it is, went into remission for many years following my aborted expedition with Drew. It resurfaced after college with renewed fury. I desperately wanted to see the world, preferably on someone else's dime. But how? I had no marketable skills, a stunted sense of morality, and a gloomy disposition. I decided to become a journalist.

As a foreign correspondent for National Public Radio, I traveled to places such as Iraq, Afghanistan, and Indonesia: unhappy places. On one level, this made perfect sense. Unconsciously, I was observing the first law of writing: Write about what you know. And so, notebook in hand, tape recorder slung over my shoulder, I roamed the world telling the stories of gloomy, unhappy people. The truth is that unhappy people, living in profoundly unhappy places, make for good stories. They tug at heartstrings and inspire pathos.

They can also be a real bummer.

What if, I wondered, I spent a year traveling the globe, seeking out not the world's well-trodden trouble spots but, rather, its unheralded happy places? Places that possess, in spades, one or more of the ingredients that we consider essential to the hearty stew of happiness: money, pleasure, spirituality, family, and chocolate, among others. Around the world, dozens of what-ifs play themselves out every day. What if you lived in a country that was fabulously wealthy and no one paid taxes? What if you lived in a country where failure *is* an option? What if you lived in a country so democratic that you voted seven times a year? What if you lived in a country where excessive thinking is discouraged? Would you be happy then?

That's exactly what I intended to find out, and the result of this admittedly harebrained experiment is the book you now hold in your hands.

I was born in the Year of the Smiley Face: 1963. That's when a graphic designer from Worcester, Massachusetts, named Harvey Ball invented the now-ubiquitous grinning yellow graphic. Originally, Ball's creation was designed to cheer up people who worked at, of all places, an insurance company, but it has since become synonymous with the frothy, quintessentially American brand of happiness.

Ball's cheery icon never worked its magic on me. I am not a happy person, never have been. As a child, my favorite Winnie-the-Pooh character was Eeyore. For most of human history, I would have been considered normal. Happiness, in this life, on this earth, was a prize reserved for the gods and the fortunate few. Today, though, not only is happiness considered possible for anyone to attain, it is expected. Thus I, and millions of others, suffer from the uniquely modern malady that historian Darrin McMahon calls "the unhappiness of not being happy." It is no fun at all.

And so, like many others, I've worked at it. I never met a self-help book I didn't like. My bookshelf is a towering, teetering monument to existential angst, brimming with books informing me that happiness lies deep inside of me. If I'm not happy, they counsel, then I'm not digging deep enough.

This axiom of the self-help industrial complex is so deeply ingrained as to be self-evident. There's only one problem: It's not true. Happiness is not inside of us but out there. Or, to be more precise, the line between out there and in here is not as sharply defined as we think.

The late British-born philosopher Alan Watts, in one of his wonderful lectures on eastern philosophy, used this analogy: "If I draw a circle, most people, when asked what I have drawn, will say I have drawn a circle or a disc, or a ball. Very few people will say I've drawn a hole in the wall, because most people think of the inside first, rather than thinking of the outside. But actually these two sides go together—you cannot have what is 'in here' unless you have what is 'out there.'"

In other words, where we are is vital to who we are.

By "where," I'm speaking not only of our physical environment but also of our cultural environment. Culture is the sea we swim in—so pervasive, so all-consuming, that we fail to notice its existence until we step out of it. It matters more than we think.

With our words, we subconsciously conflate geography and happiness. We speak of searching for happiness, of finding contentment, as if these were locations in an atlas, actual places that we could visit if only we had the proper map and the right navigational skills. Anyone who has taken a vacation to, say, some Caribbean island and had flash through their mind the uninvited thought "I could be happy here" knows what I mean.

Lurking just behind the curtain is, of course, that tantalizing, slippery concept known as paradise. It has beguiled us humans for some time now. Plato imagined the Blessed Isles, a place where happiness flowed like the warm Mediterranean waters. Until the eighteenth century, people believed that biblical paradise, the Garden of Eden, was a real place. It appeared on maps—located, ironically, at the confluence of the Tigris and Euphrates rivers, in what is now modern-day Iraq.

European explorers prepared for expeditions in search of paradise by learning Aramaic, the language Jesus spoke. I set out on my journey, my search for paradise, speaking not Aramaic but another obscure language, the modern liturgy of bliss spoken by the new apostles of the emerging science of happiness. I brush up on terms like "positive affect" and "hedonic adaptation." I carry no Bible, just a few *Lonely Planet* guides and a conviction that, as Henry Miller said, "One's destination is never a place, but a new way of seeing things."

And so, on a typically steamy day in Miami (itself some people's concept of paradise), I pack my bags and depart my home on what I know full well is a fool's errand, every bit as foolish as the one I tried to pull off as a peripatetic five-year-old. As the author Eric Hoffer put it, "The search for happiness is one of the chief sources of unhappiness." That's okay. I'm already unhappy. I have nothing to lose.

# Chapter 1

# THE NETHERLANDS

## Happiness Is a Number

It is a fact of human nature that we derive pleasure from watching others engage in pleasurable acts. This explains the popularity of two enterprises: pornography and cafés. Americans excel at the former, but Europeans do a better job at the latter. The food and the coffee are almost beside the point. I once heard of a café in Tel Aviv that dispensed with food and drink altogether; it served customers empty plates and cups yet charged real money.

Cafés are theaters where the customer is both audience and performer. I find a wonderful one a block from my hotel in downtown Rotterdam. It is simultaneously large and cozy, upscale and run-down. Nice wood floors, but they look like they haven't been polished in years. It's the kind of place where you could spend hours nursing one beer, and I suspect many people here do just that.

Everyone is smoking, so I join in, lighting up a little cigar. Something about the place makes time feel expansive and I become acutely aware of the smallest details. I notice a woman sitting on a bar stool, her legs perpendicular, resting on a nearby banister so that they form a little drawbridge, which she raises and lowers as people pass by.

I order something called a Trapiste beer. It's warm. Normally, I don't like warm beer, but I like this beer. All around me I hear the pleasant chortle of Dutch. It sounds vaguely familiar, though I can't imagine why. Then it dawns on me. Dutch sounds exactly like English spoken backward. I know this because I've heard a lot of backward English. In the predigital era, I'd edit tape for my NPR stories on a reel-to-reel tape deck the size of a TV set. Invariably, this would entail playing segments of the tape backward. As I sit in the café, with my little cigar and my warm Trapiste beer, I wonder if I recorded someone speaking Dutch and played that backward, would it sound like regular English?

As you have no doubt surmised, I am a man with time on my hands. Lots of time. But that is the whole point of a European café: to linger excessively and utterly without guilt. No wonder most of the world's great philosophers came from Europe. They hung out at cafés and let their minds wander until some radically new school of philosophy—existentialism, say—popped into their heads. I have not come here to invent a new school of philosophy. Not exactly. I am engaged in what the French call *la chasse au bonheur,* the hunt for happiness.

Specifically, my prey is a Dutch professor named Ruut Veenhoven: the godfather of happiness research. Veenhoven runs something called the World Database of Happiness. It is no joke. Veenhoven has collected, in one location, the sum of human knowledge about what makes us happy, what does not, and, of particular interest to me, which places are the happiest. If there is indeed a road map of happiness out there, an atlas of bliss, then Ruut Veenhoven will know about it.

I leave the café, reluctantly, and head back to my hotel for dinner. Rotterdam is not a beautiful city. It is gray and dull, with few sights of interest. Still, Rotterdam's mix of native Dutch and immigrants, many of them Muslims, leads to some interesting juxtapositions. The Cleopatra Sex Shop, the window display of which consists of a menagerie of large and alarmingly lifelike dildos, is only one block from the Pakistan Islamic Center. At one point, I catch a whiff of marijuana, the fragrant aroma of Dutch tolerance: secondhand stoke. Two blocks later, I see a man perched on a ladder, hanging a giant yellow clog on a storefront, while below two Middle Eastern men greet each other with symmetrical pecks on the cheek. I don't know exactly where they're from, but some of the immigrants here come from countries where alcohol is illegal and women are covered from head to toe. In their adopted home, marijuana is legal, and so is prostitution. No wonder I sniff tension in the air, mingling with the cannabis.

The hotel dining room is small, cozy. The Dutch do cozy well. I order the asparagus soup. It's good. The waiter clears my bowl and then says, "Now maybe you would like some intercourse."

"Excuse me?"

"Intercourse. You can have intercourse."

I'm thinking, Wow, the Dutch really are a permissive bunch, when it dawns on me that he is speaking of something else entirely. Inter course. As in "between courses."

"Yes," I say, relieved. "That would be nice."

And so I do. I have inter course, right there in the Hotel van Walsum dining room. I enjoy it very much, this unhurried dining experience. I sip my beer, stare into space, and, in general, do nothing—until the waiter brings the grilled salmon, indicating that, for now, my inter course is over.


In the morning, I take the subway to my Holy Grail: the World Database of Happiness, or WDH. Normally, I do not associate the words "happiness" and "database," but this is different. The World Database of Happiness is the secularist's answer to the Vatican and Mecca and Jerusalem and Lhasa, all rolled into one. Here you can, with the click of a mouse, access the secrets of happiness. Secrets based not on ephemeral revelations in some ancient desert but on modern science; secrets inscribed not on parchment but on hard drives; written not in Aramaic but in the language of our times, binary code.

I walk a few blocks from the subway and am instantly disappointed. The college campus where the WDH is housed looks more like a suburban office park than a center of bliss, the repository of humanity's knowledge about happiness. I try to shrug off this feeling. After all, what was I expecting? The Wizard of Oz? Willy Wonka and the Oompa Loompas scurrying around shouting ecstatically, "We've got it, we've got it. The secret to happiness"? No, I guess not, but I had been hoping for something a little less sterile. More happy, less data.

I walk down a nondescript corridor and knock on a nondescript office door. A man with a Dutch accent yells for me to enter. There he is. Dr. Feelgood himself. Ruut Veenhoven is a trim man, in his early sixties, I guess. He has a salt-and-pepper beard and bright, electric eyes. He is dressed in all black—stylish, not morbid black. He looks vaguely familiar, and then I realize why: He looks like a Dutch Robin Williams, with the same coiled energy and slightly impish grin. He springs from his chair and offers his hand and a business card, which reads: "Ruut Veenhoven, Professor of Happiness Studies."

His office looks like that of any professor: books and papers everywhere—not especially messy, but not the neatest office I've ever seen, either. Conspicuously, there is not a smiley face in sight. Veenhoven pours me a cup of green tea. Then he grows silent and waits for me to talk.

I don't know what to say. As a journalist, I've conducted hundreds of interviews. I've interviewed kings and presidents and prime ministers, not to mention heads of terrorist organizations like Hezbollah. Yet sitting here, across from this kindly Dutch professor who looks like Robin Williams, I am stumped. Part of me, the part that desperately craves peace of mind, wants to shout, "Dr. Veenhoven, you've crunched the numbers, you've studied happiness your entire professional life; please give it to me. Give me the damn formula for happiness!"

But I don't say that. I can't shake years of training, which tell me to maintain my distance from my subject and never, ever reveal too much about myself. I'm like the off-duty cop who is out to dinner with his family but can't stop scanning the restaurant for potential shooters.

So instead of unburdening my soul, I resort to an old trick

employed by journalists and women who want to put a date at ease. "Dr. Veenhoven," I finally say, "tell me about yourself. How did you get into the happiness business?"

Veenhoven leans back in his chair, happy to oblige. He came of age in the 1960s. Everyone on his college campus was smoking dope, wearing Che Guevara T-shirts and talking about the good society. Veenhoven also smoked plenty of dope but didn't wear a Che Guevara T-shirt; and as for those "good societies," Eastern Bloc countries, Veenhoven found them wanting. Instead of judging a society by its system, he thought, why not judge it by its results? Were its citizens happy? Veenhoven's hero wasn't Che Guevara but a socially inept nineteenth-century British barrister named Jeremy Bentham. Bentham famously espoused the utilitarian principle, "the greatest happiness of the greatest number." Veenhoven would have gladly worn a Jeremy Bentham T-shirt, had such a thing existed.

Veenhoven was studying sociology—a field that, at the time, meant only the study of sick societies, dysfunctional ones. Its sister discipline, psychology, studied sick minds. But not young Ruut. He was interested in healthy minds and happy places. One day, a bit timid but determined nonetheless, Veenhoven knocked on his advisor's door and asked if he could please study happiness. His advisor, a sober man with solid academic credentials, told him, in no uncertain terms, to shut up and never mention that word again. Happiness was not a serious subject.

Veenhoven left, chastised but secretly pleased. He knew he was on to something. It so happened, though the young Dutch graduate student didn't know at the time, couldn't possibly have known, that around the world social scientists were waking up to a new discipline: happiness studies. Today, Veenhoven is at the forefront of a field that churns out hundreds of research papers each year. There are happiness conferences and a *Journal of Happiness Studies* (which Veenhoven edits). Students at Claremont

Graduate University in California can now earn an MA or PhD in positive psychology—in happiness.

Some of Veenhoven's colleagues still think his old advisor was right, that the study of happiness is misguided, stupid. But they can't ignore him. His research is out there; it's cited in journals, and in the academic world that means it matters.

The contemplation of happiness, of course, is not new. The ancient Greeks and Romans did a lot of it. Aristotle, Plato, Epicurus, and others sweated over the eternal questions. What is the good life? Is pleasure the same as happiness? When are we going to invent indoor plumbing?

Later, the Greeks and the Romans were joined by others, paler-skinned men from lands farther north who spent an inordinate amount of time in cafés, contemplating life's inextricable quandaries. Men like Kant, Schopenhauer, Mill, Nietzsche, and, later, Larry David. They, too, had much to say about happiness.

And then there is religion. What is religion if not a guide to happiness, to bliss? Every religion instructs followers in the ways of happiness, be it in this life or the next, be it through submission, meditation, devotion, or, if you happen to belong to the Jewish or Catholic faith, guilt.

All of this may have been helpful, enlightening even, but it wasn't science. It was opinions about happiness. Learned opinions, no doubt, but opinions nonetheless, and in today's world we have little regard for opinions, except possibly our own and then not always. No, what we respect, pay heed to, is hard science or, failing that, soft science. Most of all, we love a good study. Newscasters know instinctively that the best way to get people's ears to perk up is with these five words: "A new study has found." It matters little what follows next. A new study has found that red wine is good for you / kills you. A new study has found that homework dulls the brain / enlarges it. We especially like studies that lend credibility to our own idiosyncrasies, as in, "A new study has found that people with messy desks are smarter" or "A new study has found that moderate daily flatulence improves longevity."

Yes, if this new science of happiness was to be taken seriously, it needed studies. But first, it needed a vocabulary, a serious jargon. The word "happiness" wouldn't do. It sounded too frivolous, too easily understood. This was a problem. So the social scientists came up with a doozy: "subjective well-being." Perfect. Not only was it multisyllabic and virtually impenetrable to laypeople, it also could be condensed into an even more obscure acronym: SWB. To this day, if you want to find the latest scholarly research on happiness, you need to Google "SWB," not "happiness." Next came other pieces of the jargon puzzle. "Positive affect" is when something feels good; "negative affect" is—you guessed it—when something feels bad.

Next, the new science of happiness needed data. Numbers. For what is science if not numbers, preferably large ones with lots of decimal points. And how do scientists get these numbers? They measure things.

Oh, no. Major roadblock. How can you measure happiness? Happiness is a feeling, a mood, an outlook on life. Happiness can't be measured.

Or can it? Neuroscientists at the University of Iowa have identified the regions of the brain associated with good and bad moods. They do this by hooking up research subjects (college students in need of quick cash) to MRI machines and then showing them a series of pictures. When they show people pleasant pictures—bucolic landscapes, dolphins playing—parts of the prefrontal lobe are activated. When they show unpleasant images—a bird covered in oil, a dead soldier with parts of his face missing—the more primitive parts of the brain light up. Happy feelings, in other words, register in the regions of the brain that have evolved most recently. It raises an intriguing question: Are we, in evolutionary if not personal terms, slouching toward happiness?

Researchers have toyed with other ways of measuring happiness: stress hormones, cardiac activity, and something called "facial coding"—counting how many times we smile, for instance. All of these techniques are promising, and, indeed, one day scientists may be able to "take your happiness" the way a doctor today takes your temperature.

Now, though, the main way researchers measure happiness is through a far more low-tech and, when you think about it, quite obvious technique. They ask people how happy they are. Really. "All things considered, how happy would you say you are these days?" That is the question, more or less, that surveyors have asked people around the world for the past forty or so years.

Ruut Veenhoven and his colleagues claim that the answers are remarkably accurate. "You can have a disease and not know it," Veenhoven tells me, "but you can't be happy and not know it. By definition, if you are happy, you know it."

Perhaps, but man's capacity for self-deception is not to be underestimated. Are we indeed capable of gauging our own happiness? There was this moment, for instance, when I was seventeen years old that I thought I was very happy indeed, completely content, without a care in the world. In retrospect, it turns out I was just extremely stoned at the time. Plus, beer was involved. I think.

Another speed bump on the road to happiness: Different people define happiness differently. Your idea of happiness may not be the same as mine. My favorite definition of happiness sprang from the mind of an unhappy man named Noah Webster. When he penned the first American dictionary, in 1825, he defined happiness as "the agreeable sensations which spring from the enjoyment of good." That says it all. It has "agreeable sensations," the notion that happiness is a feeling. The hedonists would get off on that. It has "enjoyment," which signifies that happiness is more than pure animal pleasure. And enjoyment of what? Of the "good," a word that, I think, Webster should have capitalized. The Good. We want to feel good but for the right reasons. Aristotle would have approved of that. "Happiness is a virtuous activity of the soul," he said. A virtuous life, in other words, is a happy life.

We humans are creatures of the last five minutes. In one study, people who found a dime on the pavement a few minutes before being queried on the happiness question reported higher levels of satisfaction with their overall lives than those who did not find a dime. Researchers have tried to get around this quirk of the human psyche through something called the experience-sampling method. They strap little Palm Pilot–like devices to research subjects and then ping them maybe a dozen times a day. Are you happy now? What about now? Here, though, the Heisenberg principle rears its head. The mere act of observing something alters it. All of that pinging, in other words, might affect the subjects' happiness.

Also, most people want to present a happy face to the world. That explains why people consistently report higher happiness levels when they are asked in face-to-face interviews rather than in mail-in surveys. And we report even higher happiness levels if the interviewer is a member of the opposite sex. Instinctively, we know that happy is sexy.

Happiness researchers, however, are quick to defend their work. For one thing, people's answers are consistent over time. Also, researchers corroborate people's responses by, for instance, checking with their friends and relatives. "Does Joe seem like a happy person to you?" It turns out that these outside assessments tend to jibe with our own degree of perceived happiness. Besides, scientists measure IQ and attitudes toward issues like racism, which are also subjective. Why not happiness as well? Or as Mihály Csíkszentmihalyi, a giant in the field of happiness studies, put it: "When a person says he is 'pretty happy' one has no right to ignore his statement, or interpret it to mean the opposite."

So assuming that these happiness studies are reasonably accurate, what have they found? Who is happy? And how do I join them? This is where Ruut Veenhoven and his database come into play.

Veenhoven leads me to a room as nondescript and soulless as the rest of the campus. Inside is a bank of a half-dozen computers. They are manned by the small, mostly volunteer staff of the

WDH, none of whom looks especially happy. I let this incongruity slide; even an overweight doctor might have some good advice about exercise and diet.

I pause to take in the moment. On these computers, right in front of me, is humanity's accumulated knowledge of happiness. After virtually ignoring the subject for decades, social scientists are now making up for lost time, churning out research papers at a prodigious rate. Happy, you might say, is the new sad.

The research findings are alternatively obvious and counterintuitive, expected and surprising. In many cases, the findings validate the great thinkers of centuries past—as if the ancient Greeks need validation. Here are a few of the findings, in no particular order.

Extroverts are happier than introverts; optimists are happier than pessimists; married people are happier than singles, though people with children are no happier than childless couples; Republicans are happier than Democrats; people who attend religious services are happier than those who do not; people with college degrees are happier than those without, though people with advanced degrees are less happy than those with just a BA; people with an active sex life are happier than those without; women and men are equally happy, though women have a wider emotional range; having an affair will make you happy but will not compensate for the massive loss of happiness that you will incur when your spouse finds out and leaves you; people are least happy when they're commuting to work; busy people are happier than those with too little to do; wealthy people are happier than poor ones, but only slightly.

So what should we do with these findings? Get married but don't have kids? Start going to church regularly? Drop out of that PhD program? Not so fast. Social scientists have a hard time unraveling what they call "reverse causality" and what the rest of us call the chicken-and-egg problem. For instance, healthy people are happier than unhealthy ones; or is it that happy people tend to be healthier? Married people are happy; or maybe happy people are more likely to get married? It's tough to say. Reverse causality is the hobgoblin that makes mischief in many a research project.

What I really want to know, though, is not who is happy but where they are happy—and why. Veenhoven sighs when I ask about this and pours another cup of tea. Here, the calculations get trickier. Can we really say which countries, which peoples, are happier than others? Has my search for the world's happiest places ended before it begins?

All cultures have a word for happiness, and some have many words. But does the English word "happiness" mean the same as the French *bonheur* or the Spanish *felicidad* or the Arabic *sa-haada*? In other words, does happiness translate? There's some evidence that the answer is yes. The Swiss report equal levels of happiness, whether they take the surveys in French, German, or Italian, the country's three main languages.

All cultures value happiness, but not to the same degree. East Asian countries tend to emphasize harmony and fulfilling societal obligations rather than individual contentment; perhaps not co-incidentally, these countries also report lower levels of happiness, what's been called the East Asian Happiness Gap, which sounds to me like some sort of Chinese Grand Canyon. Then there is the "social desirability bias." The concern here is that people answer the happiness surveys not from their heart but in ways that their society would approve of. The Japanese, for instance, are famously self-effacing, afraid to be the proverbial nail that sticks out; they are also, relative to their wealth, not very happy. I lived in Japan for years and never got used to the sight of Japanese women covering their mouths when they laughed or smiled, as if ashamed of their glee.

We Americans, on the other hand, wear our happiness on our sleeves and, if anything, are guilty of inflating our contentment in order to impress. Here is what a Polish citizen living in the United States told the writer Laura Klos Sokol about Americans: "When

Americans say it was great, I know it was good. When they say it was good, I know it was okay. When they say it was okay, I know it was bad."

This is going to be tough. The atlas of bliss, if one exists, won't be easy to read. It's like that crumpled map sitting in your glove compartment. But I was determined to plow ahead, convinced that while we may not be able to differentiate fine shades of happiness among countries, surely we can say that some countries are happier than others.

Veenhoven gives me complete access to his database and wishes me luck, but first he warns me: "You may not like what you find."

"What do you mean?"

The happiest places, he explains, don't necessarily fit our preconceived notions. Some of the happiest countries in the world—Iceland and Denmark, for instance—are homogeneous, shattering the American belief that there is strength, and happiness, in diversity. One finding, which Veenhoven just uncovered, has made him very unpopular with his fellow sociologists. He found that income distribution does not predict happiness. Countries with wide gaps between the rich and poor are no less happy than countries where the wealth is distributed more equally. Sometimes, they are happier.

"My colleagues are not amused," says Veenhoven. "Inequality is big business here in the sociology department. Entire careers have been built on it."

I accept his advice politely but think he must be exaggerating about the dangers that lie ahead. I am wrong. Looking for the world's happiest places can make anyone miserable—or at the least give them a splitting headache. With each click of the mouse, I encounter mysteries and apparent contradictions. Like this: Many of the world's happiest countries also have high suicide rates. Or this one: People who attend religious services report being happier than those who do not, but the world's happiest nations are secular. And, oh, the United States, the richest, most powerful country in the world, is no happiness superpower. Many other nations are happier than we are.

My days in Rotterdam fall into a pleasant routine. I have breakfast at the hotel, perhaps indulge in a bit of inter course, then ride the subway to the World Database of Happiness. There, I sift through the research papers and the data, looking for my elusive atlas of bliss. In the evenings, I go to my café (I never do learn its name), where I drink warm beer, smoke little cigars, and ponder the nature of happiness. It's a routine that involves much contemplation, moderate amounts of intoxicants, and very little actual work. It is, in other words, a very European routine. I'm going native.

For some reason, I decide to start at the bottom of the happiness ladder and work my way up. Which countries are the least happy? Not surprisingly, many African nations fall into this category. Tanzania, Rwanda, and Zimbabwe are near the very bottom of the happiness well. A few African countries, such as Ghana, manage to achieve middling levels of happiness, but that's about it. The reasons seem obvious. Extreme poverty is not conducive to happiness. The myth of the happy, noble savage is just that: a myth. If our basic needs are not met, we're not likely to be happy.

Curiously, I find another batch of nations stuck at the bottom of the happiness spectrum: the former Soviet republics—Belarus, Moldova, Ukraine, Uzbekistan, and a dozen others.

Are democracies happier than dictatorships? Not necessarily. Many of those former Soviet republics are quasi-democracies; certainly they are freer now than in Soviet times, yet their happiness levels have decreased since the collapse of the Soviet Union. Ron Inglehart, a professor at the University of Michigan, has spent most of his career studying the relationship between democracy and happiness. He believes that the causality flows the other way; democracies don't promote happiness, but happy places are more likely to be democratic—which, of course, does not bode well for Iraq.

What about the warm and sunny places, those tropical paradises that we associate with happiness and pay good money to vacation in? It turns out that they are not so happy. Fiji, Tahiti, the Bahamas—they all fall into the middle latitudes of happiness. Happy countries tend to be those in temperate climates, and some of the happiest—Iceland, for instance—are downright cold.

Believe it or not, most people in the world say they are happy. Virtually every country in the world scores somewhere between five and eight on a ten-point scale. There are a few exceptions: The sullen Moldovans consistently score about 4.5, and for a brief period in 1962 the citizens of the Dominican Republic could muster only a 1.6, the lowest level of happiness ever recorded on the planet. But, as I said, these are rare exceptions. Most of the world is happy.

Why does this come as such a surprise? Two types of people, I think, are to blame: journalists and philosophers. The media, of which I am a culpable member, report, as a rule, only bad news: wars, famine, the latest Hollywood couple's implosion. I don't mean to belittle the troubles in the world, and God knows I have made a good living reporting them, but we journalists do paint a distorted picture.

The philosophers, though, are the real culprits—the brooding white guys from Europe. They tended to wear all black, smoke too much, and had trouble getting dates. So they hung out, alone, in cafés, pondered the universe, and—surprise!—concluded it is an unhappy place. Of course it is. That is, if you happen to be a lonely, brooding, pasty-skinned white guy. The happy people of, say, eighteenth-century Heidelberg were busy being happy, not writing long, rambling diatribes intended to torture some not-yet-born college student in Bloomington who needs to pass Philosophy 101 in order to graduate.

Worst of all was Freud. While not technically a brooding philosopher, Freud did much to shape our views on happiness. He once said: "The intention that Man should be happy is not in the plan of Creation." That is a remarkable statement, especially coming from a man whose ideas forged the foundation of our mental-health system. Imagine if some doctor in turn-of-the-century Vienna had declared: "The intention that Man should have a healthy body is not in the plan of Creation." We'd probably lock him up, or at least strip him of his medical license. We certainly wouldn't base our entire medical system on his ideas. Yet that is exactly what we did with Freud.

Still, most people are happy? It doesn't sit right with me. I'm a person, and I'm not particularly happy. Which got me thinking: Where did I fall in Veenhoven's constellation of happiness data? If I am honest, and I might as well be if I'm taking the trouble to write this, I'd say I was a six. That makes me considerably less happy than my fellow Americans, but according to the WDH I'd feel right at home in Croatia.

I'm inclined to agree with linguist and fellow curmudgeon Anna Wierzbicka, who, when faced with this very same claim that most people are reasonably happy replied with one simple question: "Who *are* those reportedly happy people?"

Who indeed. My head hurts. Have I embarked on a futile mission to find the world's happiest places? Then I notice that one country scores consistently high on the happiness scale—not number one but darned close. It also happens to be the country I am visiting at this very moment.

I retire to my café, order a beer, and ponder Dutch happiness. Why should the Netherlands, a flat and nondescript country, be so happy? For starters, the Dutch are European, and that means they don't have to worry about losing their health insurance, or for that matter their job. The state will take care of them. They get a gazillion weeks of vacation each year and, being European, are also entitled to, at no extra cost, a vaguely superior attitude toward Americans. Does smugness lead to happiness? I wonder, sipping my Trapiste beer. No, there must be something else.

Tolerance! This is the original "don't tread on me" nation. A nation where, it seems, the adults are out of town and the teenagers are in charge. Not just for the weekend, either. All of the time.

The Dutch will tolerate anything, even intolerance. In the past few decades they have welcomed, with open arms, immigrants from around the world, including those from nations that don't tolerate things like religious freedom and women who work or drive or show their faces. Dutch tolerance comes at a cost, as the murder of the filmmaker Theo van Gogh by a Muslim extremist highlighted. But Veenhoven's research shows that tolerant people tend to be happy.

What exactly does Dutch tolerance look like, in an everyday way? Three things come to mind: drugs, prostitution, and cycling. In the Netherlands, all three activities are legal. All three can easily lead to happiness, provided that certain precautions are taken. Wearing a helmet while cycling, for instance.

I needed to investigate one of these activities, up close, in order to get at the heart of Dutch happiness. But which one? Cycling is certainly worthwhile, and God knows the Dutch love their bicycles, but it was chilly outside, too chilly to get on a bike. Prostitution? That activity takes place indoors, usually, so the weather wouldn't be a factor. And it clearly makes some people happy. But there was the issue of my wife. She has supported my happiness research, up to a point, and something told me that engaging the services of a Dutch prostitute lies beyond that point.

So drugs it is. Soft drugs, marijuana and hashish, are legal in the Netherlands. They are served in coffee shops, which aren't really coffee shops at all but drug dens. "Coffee shop" sounds more respectable than "drug den," though.

But which one should I try? There are so many to choose from. In Rotterdam, every third or fourth storefront, it seems, is a "coffee shop." I'm tempted by one called Sky High, but the name seems too...obvious. Others look too hip. I haven't gotten high since my junior year in college. I don't want to make a fool of myself.

Then I spot it. The Alpha Blondie Coffee Shop. It's perfect. Besides the irresistible name, the Alpha Blondie also offers ventilation, an open window, which is a definite plus. I press a buzzer then walk up a narrow staircase. Inside, there's a foosball table and a cooler filled with orange Fanta and Coke, as well as plenty of Snickers and M&M's, for the munchies, no doubt. I'm surprised to see an actual coffee machine in this coffee shop, but it looks like it hasn't been used in months. A prop, I conclude.

Bad 1970s music is playing, and a little too loudly. On one wall, I notice a painting that looks like it was done by a talented sixth-grader. In the foreground is a car that has just plowed into a tree, with skid marks trailing off toward the horizon. Underneath is written: "Some roads only exist in drugged minds." I'm not sure if this is meant as a warning about these roads or as an endorsement of them.

Everyone here seems to be a regular, except, of course, for me. I'm instantly transported back to my college dorm room in New Jersey. Trying to be cool, trying to fit in, but failing miserably.

An olive-skinned man comes over to me and, in broken English, explains the menu. Today they are featuring Thai marijuana, he says, as if describing the soup du jour, as well as two types of hashish: Moroccan and Afghan.

I'm at a loss. So I do what I always do when the menu proves overwhelming. I ask the waiter for his recommendation.

"Do you prefer strong or mild?" he asks.

"Mild."

"Then I would definitely go with the Moroccan."

I hand him a five-euro note (about six dollars), and he hands me a baggie with a chalky brown slab the size of a postage stamp.

I have absolutely no idea what to do with it.

For a moment, I'm tempted to call my old college roommate, Rusty Fishkind. Rusty would know what to do. He was always the cool one. Rusty handled a bong the way Yo-Yo Ma handles a cello. I'm sure Rusty is a corporate lawyer now, living in the suburbs with four kids, but still, I bet he would know what to do with this chunk of Moroccan hash.

As if on cue, Linda Ronstadt pipes up. *You're no good, you're no good, baby, you're no good.*

I briefly consider swallowing the hash and washing it down

with a Pepsi but think better of that idea and just fumble with the hash instead, trying to look as helpless as possible, which under the circumstances comes naturally. Finally, a bearded man wearing a leather jacket takes pity on me. Without saying a word, he takes the hash in his hands and crumbles it like feta cheese. Then he unrolls a cigarette, a regular cigarette, and inserts the hash. After a fluent shake, lick, and tap, he hands the now hash-infused cigarette back to me.

I thank him and light up.

A few observations. First of all, I do recommend the Moroccan. It is indeed a smooth smoke. Second, at least half the fun of engaging in illicit activity is the illicit part and not the activity part. In other words, smoking hash legally in Rotterdam is not nearly as much fun as doing it illicitly in your college dorm room with Rusty Fishkind, knowing that at any moment you might get caught.

Still, I am feeling good. No pain. And, as the Moroccan settles into my cerebral cortex, I wonder: What if I stayed like this all of the time? Wouldn't I be happy all of the time? I could end my search for the world's happiest places right here, at the Alpha Blondie Coffee Shop in Rotterdam. Maybe this is the happiest place in the world.

The philosopher Robert Nozick had something to say on the subject. Not about the Alpha Blondie, which I doubt he's frequented, nor about Moroccan hash, which he may or may not have smoked. But Nozick did think long and hard about the relationship between hedonism and happiness. He once devised a thought experiment called the Experience Machine.

Imagine that "superduper neuropsychologists" have figured out a way to stimulate a person's brain in order to induce pleasurable experiences. It's perfectly safe, no chance of a malfunction, and not harmful to your health. You would experience constant pleasure for the rest of your life. Would you do it? Would you plug into the Experience Machine?

If not, argued Nozick, then you've just proved that there is more to life than pleasure. We want to achieve our happiness and not just experience it. Perhaps we even want to experience unhappiness, or at least leave open the possibility of unhappiness, in order to truly appreciate happiness.

Regrettably, I find myself in agreement with Nozick. I would not plug myself into the Experience Machine, and therefore I will not be relocating to the Alpha Blondie Coffee Shop. Which is a shame. Did I mention how smooth the Moroccan hash is?

The next morning, my mind Moroccan-free, I make my daily trip to the WDH. I mention my little experiment to Veenhoven. He approves, of course. In fact, when I had first pointed out that many of the activities that the Dutch engage in regularly, such as prostitution and drugs, would get me arrested in the United States, he just smiled slyly and said, "I know. Enjoy."

Veenhoven says the database might provide some answers to the age-old question: Is pleasure the same as happiness? After a few digital detours, I find a paper that Veenhoven himself wrote. It's called "Hedonism and Happiness." I read the abstract.

"The relation between happiness and consumption of stimulants follows an inverted U-curve. Spoil sports and guzzlers are less happy than modest consumers." In other words, as the ancient Greeks counseled a few thousand years ago, everything in moderation. I read on and learn that "several studies have observed a positive correlation between permissive attitudes towards sex and personal happiness." Presumably, these permissive happy people are not the same happy people who are attending church regularly. As for drugs, a 1995 study found that—no surprise—use of hard drugs tends to decrease happiness over time. But what about soft drugs, like, say, Moroccan hash? It turns out that there has been little research in this area.

How about that, I think, swiveling away from the computer monitor. Last night, at the Alpha Blondie Coffee Shop, on the very first leg of my journey, I was engaged in cutting-edge happiness research. Who knew?

It's my last day in Rotterdam. A forgettable city but one that I will miss nonetheless. It's time to say goodbye to Veenhoven, and I am never good at goodbyes. I thank him for all of his help, for all of his blissful data. Then, almost as an afterthought, I pause at the door and say, "It must be wonderful working in the field of happiness studies."

Veenhoven looks perplexed. "What do you mean?"

"Well, you must have an abiding faith in mankind's capacity for happiness."

"No, not really."

"But you've been studying happiness, analyzing it your entire life."

"Yes, but it doesn't matter to me if people are happy or not, as long as some people are happier than others. I can still crunch the numbers."

I just stand there for a moment, stunned. Here I thought Veenhoven was a fellow traveler, a comrade in the hunt for happiness, but it turns out that, as they say in the South, he has no dog in this hunt. Or, if you prefer, Veenhoven isn't a player in the happiness game; he's the referee, keeping score. And, like any good referee, it matters not one whit to him who wins the game. Happiness or despondency, it's all the same. As long as one side prevails.

That is, I suppose, the whole point of this new, dispassionate study of happiness. Veenhoven and the other blissologists desperately wanted academia to take their discipline seriously, lest they be dismissed as New Age faddists. They have succeeded, but I wonder at what cost. In their world, happiness is reduced to yet another statistic, data to be sliced, diced, parsed, run through the computer, and, ultimately, inevitably, reduced to spreadsheets. And I can't think of anything less happy than a spreadsheet.

I realize that my visit to the WDH was a fine start but an incomplete one. Nowhere among the eight thousand studies and research papers did I find any mention of the happiness a nation derives from its arts, the pleasure accrued by hearing a particularly lovely poem read aloud and well, or by watching a darned good movie, accompanied by a tub of popcorn, no butter. Nor does the database reveal anything about the invisible threads that bind a family. Some things are beyond measuring.

So I construct my atlas of bliss, my road map of happiness, based partly on Ruut Veenhoven's database and partly on my own hunches. Rich or poor, hot or cold, democracy or dictatorship, it matters not. I will follow the happiness scent wherever it leads.

With my atlas in hand, I board the train at Rotterdam Central. As the train begins to roll and the Dutch countryside glides by, I feel an unexpected sense of relief. Freedom even. Freedom from what? I can't imagine. My visit was fine. I drank some good beer, smoked some fine hash, and even learned a thing or two about happiness.

Then it dawns on me. Freedom from all that...freedom. Tolerance is great, but tolerance can easily slide into indifference, and that's no fun at all. Besides, I can't live with so much slack. I'm too weak. I wouldn't know when to stop. If I moved to Holland, you'd probably find me a few months later, engulfed in a cloud of Moroccan hash, a hooker under each arm.

No, the Dutch way is not for me. Perhaps my next destination is the one. I'm heading to a country where the trains run on time, the streets are clean, and tolerance, like everything else, is doled out carefully, in moderation. I am heading to Switzerland.

# Chapter 2

# SWITZERLAND

## Happiness Is Boredom

The first Swiss people I ever met pissed me off like nobody's business. I know what you're thinking. The Swiss? The nice, neutral, army-knife-toting, watch-wearing, chocolate-eating Swiss? Yes, those Swiss.

It was the late 1980s, and I was in Tanzania. My girlfriend and I were on a safari. We were doing it on the cheap, along with four other budget travelers: two easygoing Norwegians and a quiet Swiss couple.

Our driver was a Tanzanian named Good Luck. We thought this was fortuitous. Only later did we learn that his name represented a wish and not a point of fact. But by then it was too late, and things started to go terribly wrong. First, a truck kicked up a rock that came crashing through our windshield, shattering it. Nobody was hurt, but we spent the next two days stopping in every village in Tanzania looking, in vain, for a replacement. Then came the rain, even though it wasn't the rainy season. My girlfriend and I managed to set up our tent, but a few minutes later it collapsed, leaving us drenched, muddy, and miserable. The Norwegians' tent was barely hanging on.

But the Swiss? Their tent was geodesic and as sturdy as the Matterhorn. Unflustered by the driving rain and strong winds, it kept them warm and dry. I bet they were sipping hot chocolate in there. Damn them, I thought at the time, damn the efficient, competent Swiss to hell.

This memory is fresh in my mind as the train from Rotterdam passes through Germany and into Switzerland. I am here for a reason, and that reason doesn't involve revenge, I swear. The Swiss, it turns out, occupy a place near the pinnacle of Ruut Veenhoven's happiness pyramid. Prime real estate. Yes, the Swiss are on to something—the happy, happy bastards.

My train is eighteen minutes late, causing mass consternation in Basel, the border city where I am supposed to catch the train to Geneva. Schedules are thrown into disarray. Passengers, myself included, scramble off the slightly late German train and run to catch our perfectly on-time Swiss train. Amazing, I think, huffing and puffing up a flight of stairs, only the Swiss could make the Germans look sloppy.

Okay, so the stereotype is true. Switzerland is efficient and punctual. Also wealthy and with hardly any unemployment. And, oh, the air is clean. The streets are nearly spotless. And don't forget the chocolate, which is delicious and plentiful. But happy? I saw no joy on the faces of the well-tented Swiss couple in Africa. Only quiet satisfaction, tinged with just a trace of smugness.

To solve this mystery, we turn once again to those dead, white, and unhappy philosophers. None was less happy than Arthur Schopenhauer. If happiness is indeed the absence of misery, as he believed, then the Swiss have every reason to be happy. But if happiness is more than that, if happiness requires an element of joy, then Swiss happiness remains a mystery as deep and dark as a slab of Lindt chocolate.

Why should the Swiss consistently rank higher on the happiness charts than the Italians and the French, two countries that possess oodles of *joie de vivre*? Heck, the French practically invented *joie de vivre*.

All of this is rattling around inside my head as my taxi pulls up to my friend Susan's apartment in Geneva. Susan is a writer from New York. She is a woman who speaks her mind, in English *and* French. Her candor is constantly bumping up against the Swiss reserve. Susan complains that the Swiss are "culturally constipated" and "stingy with information." Even if that information is vital, such as "your train is leaving now" or "your clothing is on fire," the Swiss will say nothing. To speak out would be considered insulting, since it assumes ignorance on the part of the other person.

Susan's in-your-face New York ways do not always endear her to Geneva's diplomatic corps—thousands of well-meaning men and women who fret full-time about the world's problems. They do their fretting well dressed and, whenever possible, over lunch. Or, if extreme fretting is required, at conferences. Europeans love conferences. Get three Europeans together, and chances are quite high a conference will break out. All that's needed are those little name tags and many, many gallons of Perrier.

Geneva has been called a great place to live, but you wouldn't want to visit. There is some truth to that. The Swiss consider Geneva boring, and if the Swiss consider someplace boring, you know it is very boring indeed. It doesn't seem that way to me, though. Susan's apartment overlooks a warren of narrow streets and alleys. Geneva, like most European cities, is built on a human scale, and that makes it intrinsically interesting.

Even Susan isn't all negative. She finds aspects of life here endearing—the civil-mindedness, for instance. The way you'll be riding the bus, and there will be this teenage boy with a Mohawk and combat boots, looking like trouble, who will politely offer his seat to an older woman. "In New York, nobody would move," says Susan, amazed.

I unpack my bags. I have, of course, brought along my Swiss army knife. Mine is an old-fashioned model—these days, they come with flash drives—and I love it. I take it everywhere. If only every army in the world was best known for something like the Swiss army knife. As far as I know, no wars have been waged with Swiss army knives, no international commissions established to discuss their dangerous proliferation.

Spring in this part of Europe arrives late but with a delightful vengeance. Almost instantly, at the first hint of warmth, people begin to disrobe, and before long the Speedos are in full bloom along Lake Geneva. It is indeed a gorgeous day, so Susan and I do the only sensible European thing: We head for a café.

Susan has arranged for me to meet some real-live Swiss. We commandeer a large table and settle in, the way Europeans do, as if we're not merely having a few drinks but moving in for a few months. Beers are ordered, cigarettes lit, cheeks pecked.

At our table is an eclectic bunch. There's Tony, a wealthy banker who describes himself as "culturally English but geographically Swiss." I think but don't say, "What the hell does that mean?" By that measure, I, too, am geographically Swiss since, geographically speaking, I am in Switzerland at the moment. Then there's Dieter, who is Swiss, geographically and in every other sense. He's a doctor, with an abundance of hair and self-confidence. Next to him is his American wife, Caitlin, a former Hollywood agent who has lived in Switzerland for the past ten years. I notice that she is the only one at the table with a BlackBerry, which she thumbs nervously during lulls in the conversation.

Everyone is surprised that my research has taken me to Switzerland. The Swiss happy? There must be some mistake. No, I insist, that's what a Dutchman who looks like Robin Williams told me. And he has studies to back it up, too. I take an informal poll around the table. Overall, how happy are you these days? The results are in: solid eights and nines all around, and a seven from the American. The Swiss at the table look surprised, as if they're thinking, "Hmmm. Maybe we *are* happy. Who knew?"

"So, now that we've determined you are indeed happy, what is the source of Swiss happiness?" I ask.

"Cleanliness," says Dieter. "Have you seen our public toilets? They are very clean." At first, I think he's joking but quickly rule out that possibility, since the Swiss do not joke. About anything. Ever.

He's right. Swiss toilets are indeed clean. I wonder if Ruut Veenhoven and his colleagues have done any studies correlating a nation's happiness and the cleanliness of its toilets. I bet the results would be enlightening.

Not only are the toilets clean in Switzerland, everything else is, too. In some countries, it would be suicidal to drink the tap water. In Switzerland, it is fashionable to do so. Zurich even boasts about the quality of its tap water to tourists.

There are no potholes on Swiss roads. Everything works. Switzerland is a highly functional society, and while that may not be a source of joy or even happiness, it eliminates a lot of the reasons to be unhappy.

So appealing is the image of Switzerland as an affluent, clean, and well-run society that other countries fancy themselves the Switzerland of their particular region. Singapore is the Switzerland of Asia, Costa Rica the Switzerland of Central America. But here I am in what can rightfully be called the Switzerland of Europe. The real deal.

Sometimes, though, even the real deal falls short of its own expectations. Sometimes things don't work so well in Switzerland. Dieter tells me that "if a train is twenty minutes late, people get very anxious." A few years ago, he says, the entire rail system broke down for eighteen hours, hurling the nation into a period of deep existential doubt.

"So what is your source of happiness besides the clean toilets and on-time trains?"

"Envy."

"That's why you're happy?"

No, he explains, the Swiss are happy because they go to great lengths not to provoke envy in others. The Swiss know instinctively that envy is the great enemy of happiness, and they will do anything to squash it. "Our attitude," says Dieter, taking a sip of beer, "is don't shine the spotlight too brightly on yourself or you might get shot."

The Swiss hate to talk about money. They would rather talk about their genital warts than reveal how much they earn. I met a few Swiss people who couldn't even bring themselves to use the "m" word; they would just rub their fingers together to indicate they're talking about money. At first, this struck me as odd, given that Switzerland's economy is based on banking—a profession that, last time I checked, had something to do with money. But the Swiss know that money, more than anything else, triggers envy.

The American way is: If you've got it, flaunt it. The Swiss way is: If you've got it, hide it. One Swiss person told me, "You don't dress or act like you're rich. Of course, you might have a four-thousand-dollar espresso machine in your apartment."

I ask Dieter why the subterfuge.

A rich Swiss person, he explains, doesn't show off his money because he doesn't have to. Everyone knows he's rich, because the Swiss know everything about their neighbors. In fact, if a rich person suddenly starts flashing his money around—buying a fancy new car, for instance—people suspect something is amiss, that he's facing some financial trouble.

In America, the worst thing you can be is a loser. In Switzerland, the worst thing you can be is a flashy winner, *nouveau riche.* "Dreadful thing," one Swiss person told me of the newly monied, as if he were talking about some terrible disease.

The philosopher Martin Heidegger once defined boredom as "the hot breath of nothingness on our necks." In Switzerland that hot breath is pervasive. It's in the air. The Swiss have done for boredom what the French did for wine and the Germans for beer: perfected it, mass-produced it.

The Swiss live attenuated lives. They hum along, satisfied, never dipping below a certain floor but never touching the ceiling, either. A Swiss would never describe something as awesome or super, but only *c'est pas mal,* not bad. Is that the secret to happiness, a life that is *c'est pas mal?* Or perhaps the Swiss really do find many aspects of life awesome but know on some subconscious level that such superlatives diminish the experience. Describe something as awesome, and it ceases to be so.

Happiness researchers have found that, from a statistical point of view, the Swiss are on to something. Better to live in this middle range than to constantly swing between great highs and terrible lows.

No one knows more about Swiss boredom than Jonathan Steinberg, an academic who has spent his entire career studying Switzerland. When he announced to his students that he would be devoting a lecture to the Swiss civil war, half the class got up and left, leading Steinberg to the depressing conclusion that "even a civil war, if it takes place in Switzerland, must be boring."

Not only boring but humorless. Maybe I'm wrong. Maybe Swiss humor operates at an entirely different frequency, undetectable to my non-Swiss ears. And so, with this open-minded attitude, I ask Dieter—diplomatically, of course—if it's true that the Swiss have no sense of humor.

"Define sense of humor," he responds instantly, thus sealing the case.

Swiss humorlessness has a long and serious history. One academic tells me that in the seventeenth century in Basel, there was actually a prohibition on public laughter. There is no longer such a law, of course. That's because there is no need for it. Swiss humorlessness, like most aspects of life here, is self-policing.

The Swiss are as fond of rules as the Dutch are of marijuana and prostitution. In many parts of Switzerland, you can't mow you lawn or shake your carpets on Sunday. You can't hang laundry from your balcony on any day. You can't flush your toilet after 10:00 p.m.

I met a British woman living in Switzerland who has repeatedly run afoul of Swiss rules. Like the time she came home from working the late shift and shared a few laughs and a few beers with some colleagues. Nothing raucous, just your usual after-work decompression. The next day, she found a note pinned to her door. "Please," it said, "no laughing after midnight."

Leave your car dirty in Switzerland and someone will pin a note to it saying "Please wash your car." Not a cute "Wash me" sign that an American might scrawl on it. The Swiss, lacking any detectable sense of irony, mean what they say. Sort your trash improperly, and some nosy neighbor will find the offending item and return it to your doorstep with a curt note attached. This isn't just a nanny state. It's a supernanny state.

Everything is regimented in Switzerland, even anarchy. Once a year, on the May Day holiday, the anarchists break a few shop windows, but it's always exactly at the same time. As one Swiss person quipped, in a rare display of humor, "Yes, we have anarchy. It's in the afternoon."

Let's tally what we have so far. The Swiss are a humorless, uptight nation. Everything works, usually, and envy is squelched, but at a cost: You're always being watched, monitored, judged. Where's the bliss?

"It's simple," says Dieter. "Nature. We Swiss have a very deep connection to nature." I am surprised, not so much by the statement, which I've heard mouthed by many a tree hugger and even by myself on occasion, but by who is saying it. Dieter is about as urbane a city dweller as you'll find, not a crunchy bone in his body.

He's right, though. A Swiss person, no matter how cosmopolitan and seemingly removed from his natural surroundings, never loses his love of the land. Even billionaires in Switzerland see themselves as mountaineers at heart.

You can't understand the Swiss without visiting the Alps, Dieter tells me. So I go.

Susan and I arrive in the kitschy Alpine town of Zermatt. Recorded greetings welcome us in Japanese and four other languages. Little electric cars zip around town. Regular cars are banned, an environmental regulation that the Swiss gladly accept to protect their beloved Alps.

We take a cable car to the top of a mountain adjacent to the famous Matterhorn. It's still ski season, and everyone (except us) is decked out in fashionable ski attire. It's an older crowd, their skin leathery and monied.

The most sublime aspect of this mountainous terrain, I realize as we coast upward, is the light. The hue and intensity is fluid, constantly shifting as the sun ducks in and out of the peaks. The nineteenth-century Italian painter Giovanni Segantini once said that people of the mountains see the sun rise and set as a golden fireball, full of life and energy, while flatlanders know only a tired and drunk sun.

Finally, we reach the peak: 12,763 feet. A sign informs us that this is "Europe's highest mountaintop accessible by cable car." The qualification somehow deflates our sense of adventure. It's snowing lightly. There's a wooden crucifix, which strikes me as odd in such a secular country. Underneath are three words: "Be more human."

A sense of calm sneaks up on me, a feeling so unusual that, at first, I am startled by it. I don't recognize it. But there's no denying its presence. I am at peace.

The naturalist E. O. Wilson gave a name to this warm, fuzzy feeling I'm experiencing: biophilia. He defined it as "the innately emotional affiliation of human beings to other living organisms." Wilson argued that our connection to nature is deeply ingrained in our evolutionary past. That connection isn't always positive. Take snakes, for instance. The chances of encountering a snake, let alone dying from a snakebite, are extraordinarily remote. Yet modern humans continue to fear snakes even more, studies have found, than car accidents or homicide or any of the dozens of other more plausible ways we might meet our demise. The fear of snakes resides deep in our primitive brain. The fear of the Long Island Expressway, while not insignificant, was added much more recently.

Conversely, the biophilia hypothesis, as Wilson calls it, also explains why we find natural settings so peaceful. It's in our genes. That's why, each year, more people visit zoos than attend all sporting events combined.

In 1984, a psychologist named Roger Ulrich studied patients recuperating from gallbladder surgery at a Pennsylvania hospital. Some patients were assigned to a room overlooking a small strand of deciduous trees. Others were assigned to rooms that overlooked a brick wall. Urlich describes the results: "Patients with the natural window view had shorter post-operative hospital stays, had fewer negative comments in nurses' notes...and tended to have lower scores for minor post-surgical complications such as persistent headache or nausea requiring medication. Moreover, the wall-view patients required many more injections of potent painkillers."

The implications of this obscure study are enormous. Proximity to nature doesn't just give us a warm, fuzzy feeling. It affects our physiology in real, measurable ways. It's not a giant leap to conclude that proximity to nature makes us happier. That's why even the most no-nonsense office building includes a park or atrium (in the belief, no doubt, that a happy worker is a productive one).

The biophilia hypothesis is not your run-of-the-mill Berkeley/Al Gore/Eat Your Spinach environmentalism. It does not appeal directly to our sense of stewardship or responsibility. It appeals to a much more base, and common, human proclivity: selfishness. It says, in effect, protect the environment because it will make you happy. For a country like the United States, with the word "happiness" in its founding document, you'd think environmentalists would have latched on to biophilia a long time ago.

I've certainly latched on to it. I feel like I'm floating above the valley below. I read another sign: "Great are the works of the Lord," it says, and I nod my head in silent agreement. I feel pleasantly light-headed and imagine a melodic chirping sound. Am I having a transcendental experience?

No, it's Susan's cellphone, announcing that a text message has arrived. Europe's highest peak accessible by cable car is also, it turns out, accessible by cellphone. My moment of bliss evaporates like snowcaps in July.

Back in Zermatt, I ponder what happened to me up there. One

rational explanation is hypoxia, a lack of oxygen. It can lead to many symptoms (including death, the ultimate symptom), but one of the more common is a sense of euphoria.

It also, I discover, leads to hunger. Susan decides I need a fondue experience. The last time I heard the word "fondue," or thought about it in any way, was 1978. My mother owned a fondue set. I can picture it clearly. It was a sickly orange color, with little indentations for tiny forks. It sat in our dining room for years like some museum piece. I don't remember anyone ever using it.

Our fondue comes in a large bowl, not orange, and it's good. After a few helpings, the euphoria is gone, but I'm feeling, I think, very Swiss. Satisfied. Neutral. Maybe this explains Swiss neutrality. Maybe it's not based on a deep-seated morality but a more practical reason. Fondue and war don't mix.

Back in Geneva, Susan introduces me to Jalil, a young Swiss guy who is in a band. We're drinking wine. His English is a bit rough, so his American girlfriend, a bittersweet blonde from Minnesota, translates. Her name is Anna. She is sweet when sober, but a raw bitterness emerges when she drinks, which I gather is fairly often.

"Why are the Swiss so happy?" I ask Jalil.

"Because we know we can always kill ourselves," he says with a laugh, but he's not joking. Switzerland has one of the world's most liberal euthanasia laws. People travel from all over Europe to die here.

The strangeness of it all sinks in. In Switzerland, it's illegal to flush your toilet past 10:00 p.m. or mow your lawn on Sunday, but it's perfectly legal to kill yourself.

When I told friends I was going to Switzerland as part of my research into happiness, some people replied, "Don't they have a high suicide rate?" Yes, they do, one of the highest in the world. This seems to make absolutely no sense. How can a happy country have a high suicide rate? In fact, it's easily explained. First of all, the number of suicides is still statistically low, so it doesn't affect the happiness surveys very much, since the odds of the research-ers interviewing a suicidal person are quite low. But there's an-other reason. The things that prevent us from killing ourselves are different from those that make us happy. Roman Catholic coun-tries, for instance, tend to have very low suicide rates because of the Catholic prohibition on suicide. Yet that doesn't mean these countries are happy. Good government, meaningful work, strong family ties—these are all major contributors to happiness, yet if you are unhappy, truly despondent, none of them will prevent you from committing suicide.

Part of the problem, perhaps, is that being surrounded by happy people can be a real bummer sometimes. Franz Hohler, a well-known Swiss author, told me: "If I'm not happy, I think, 'Shit, all of this beauty, all this functionality, why the hell am I not happy? What's wrong with me?'"

Every country has its cocktail-party question. A simple one-sentence query, the answer to which unlocks a motherlode of in-formation about the person you've just met. In the United States that question is, What do you do? In Britain it is, What school did you attend? In Switzerland it is, Where are you from? That is all you need to know about someone.

The Swiss are deeply rooted in place. Their passports list the name of their ancestral town. Not their hometown but the town of their roots. Maybe they weren't born there. Maybe they've never even been there. But it is their home. It's said that the Swiss only become Swiss upon leaving the country. Until then, they are Gene-vans or Zurichers, or otherwise defined by wherever they happen to come from.

No wonder it was the Swiss who invented the modern concept of homesickness; they were the first to put a word, "heimweh," to that nagging feeling of dislocation, that feeling of loss we experi-ence when uprooted from the place we call home.

I wonder: Is all happiness, like all politics, local? I'm not sure.

But clearly the Swiss focus on the local makes people feel grounded. There are downsides, though, to this hyperlocalness. As Jonathan Steinberg puts it: "There's an awful lot of ignorance about what goes on next door." That's not surprising in a country with four official languages. Or, as a Swiss friend told me, "We Swiss get along so well because we don't understand each other."

Maybe, but they do trust one another. I was able to book a hotel room without providing my credit-card number. I pumped gas without paying first. A lot of Switzerland works on the honor system, like the little rest huts that dot the Alps. There's food inside. You eat the food and leave some money behind.

John Helliwell, a Canadian economist, has spent many years studying the relationship between trust and happiness. He's found the two to be inseparable. "You can't feel properly engaged if you don't trust the people you engage with on a regular basis. Engagement breeds trust; trust supports engagement. It's a two-way flow; both parts are critical."

Or consider this statement: "In general, people can be trusted." Studies have found that people who agree with this are happier than those who do not. Trusting your neighbors is especially important. Simply knowing them can make a real difference in your quality of life. One study found that, of all the factors that affect the crime rate for a given area, the one that made the biggest difference was not the number of police patrols or anything like that but, rather, how many people you know within a fifteen-minute walk of your house.

I'm in love. The object of my amour is not a woman or even a person. It is the Swiss rail network. I love it. I love the way the trains are whisper-quiet and the way the sliding glass doors between cars open and close so gracefully. I love the way jacketed attendants come around with fresh coffee and croissants, and the dining cars with their gourmet meals served on real china. I love the wood paneling in the bathrooms. I love the leather seats. I love how when it's time to disembark little platforms miraculously appear under your feet. I am, in fact, overwhelmed with the urge to stay on the Swiss trains forever, shuttling among Geneva and Basel and Zurich and wherever. It doesn't really matter. I could be happy here, on the Swiss trains.

But I don't stay on the train forever. I get off in Bern, the sleepy Swiss capital. It is as Anna, a bittersweet American, described it: quaint in the extreme. Yes, there is such a thing as too quaint, I think, as I walk around the old walled city. Then I see that some-one has written on a wall: "Fuck the police." That is not quaint. Anyplace else, I'd find it offensive, disturbing. But in Switzerland I'm just glad to see signs of life.

I visit the Swiss parliament building, a building that manages to be grand and ornate yet at the same time understated. Every nation has its iconic figures, statues that neatly sum up what the nation is all about: the Marines hoisting the flag at Iwo Jima; Lord Nelson, looking regal, in London's Trafalgar Square. The Swiss have someone known as Nicholas the Reconciler. His statue is on display here. He has an arm outstretched, palm facing downward, as if to say, "Calm down, everyone; let's talk about this rationally." It's very Swiss.

Albert Einstein lived in Bern. This is the city where, he says, he had "the happiest thought of my life." That thought was the rev-elation that led to his Special Theory of Relativity. The place was a modest apartment on the city's main shopping street. It's now a small museum. It's been restored to exactly the way it looked when Einstein lived here: a sofa, wooden chairs, a bottle of wine labeled 1893, the carriage for his son Hans, the suit he wore to his job as a clerk at the patent office. There are also several black-and-white photos of a young Einstein, before his hair went wild, posing with his family. His wife and son are looking into the camera, but Ein-stein, in every photo, is looking off into the distance. Was he ru-minating about energy and mass? Or was he thinking, "I've got to get out of this marriage"? (which he eventually did).

I open the French windows, crane my neck, and look down

the street. Except for a few cars, the scene is, I imagine, virtually unchanged from 1905. I close my eyes for a few seconds, then open them again, half believing that I might be transported back in time. Einstein, after all, proved that such a thing is theoretically possible.

Somebody lives upstairs from Einstein's old apartment. A graphic designer. Living in the same building where Einstein lived! At first, I think that would be wonderful. A real thrill. Then, I realize, the pressure would be enormous. Every time I climbed the stairs—the very same stairs Einstein climbed—I'd be disappointed if I didn't come up with something like $E = mc^2$. No, not for me.

Einstein, like myself, found Bern pleasant but boring. And so I wonder: If the Swiss were more interesting, might he never have daydreamed as much as he did? Might he never have developed the Special Theory of Relativity? In other words, is there something to be said for boredom?

The British philosopher Bertrand Russell thought so. "A certain amount of boredom is...essential to a happy life," he wrote. Maybe I've misjudged the Swiss. Maybe they know something about boredom and happiness that the rest of us don't.

Patience and boredom are closely related. Boredom, a certain kind of boredom, is really impatience. You don't like the way things are, they aren't interesting enough for you, so you decide—and boredom is a decision—that you are bored.

Russell had something to say about this: "A generation that cannot endure boredom will be a generation of little men, of men unduly divorced from the slow process of nature, of men in whom every vital impulse slowly withers as though they were cut flowers in a vase."

I'm beginning to think that perhaps the Swiss aren't boring after all. They just appear that way from the outside.


I'm reunited with my love. I'm back on a Swiss train. My next stop is Zurich, a city so clean it makes Geneva look like a slum. I check into my hotel and then have some time to kill. I take a small train to a nearby hilltop. Zurich's public transportation works on the honor system, except that undercover wardens travel the trains, too, and bust people who don't have a ticket. Trust but verify. That's what's happening on my small train. A middle-aged man is being interrogated. He's clearly trying to explain his way out of it. He looks ashen, not with fear but embarrassment. I realize it's not the fine that deters free riders but the public humiliation of getting caught.

On the hilltop, the entire city of Zurich is spread below, like in a Renaissance painting. I feel safe up here, and it occurs to me that maybe that's why we like hilltop terrain. Maybe it goes back to our days as chimps swinging from the trees. From a high vantage point, you could see any potential danger and therefore relax if none was spotted.

It's a beautiful day, the sky a deep blue, the visibility endless. People have brought their lunches and are indulging in impromptu picnics. I see an old man and a woman sitting on a park bench. He's wearing an Italian driving hat and is sitting motionless. Nearby, a woman is walking her two dogs. They are nipping at each other's heels and smiling, I swear. They're not on leashes but don't attempt to run off. They are Swiss dogs.

Well, this is all very nice, I think, but I better get going. It's the kind of thought I'm constantly having and usually don't think twice about, except this time I stop myself cold. And where exactly must you be going? It's 3:00 p.m. on a beautiful spring day in Switzerland. I have no one to see, nowhere to be.

British academic Avner Offer wrote that "affluence breeds impatience and impatience undermines well being." He's right. You don't see many impatient poor people. (They are unhappy for other reasons. More about that later.) And then it dawns on me. The Swiss are wealthy *and* patient, a rare combination. They know how to linger. Indeed, I've been in Switzerland for two weeks now and not a single person has looked at his or her watch—that perfectly synchronized, gold-plated Swiss watch—and said "I have to go" or "I really should be getting back to work." In fact, it is always me, the loafing writer, who is stealing glances at my fifty-dollar Seiko.

With the help of a friend, I had set up a blog to solicit comments from the Swiss about happiness. One in particular caught my eye, and I'm reminded of it now.

"Maybe happiness is this: not feeling like you should be elsewhere, doing something else, being someone else. Maybe the current conditions in Switzerland...make it simply easier to 'be' and therefore 'be happy.'"

So I sit on that hilltop for another twenty minutes. I fidget the entire time. It practically kills me. But I make it without going insane. I consider that a minor breakthrough.

It dawns on me how very un-Swiss I am, and on so many levels. I don't like rules. I am not neat. I am prone to wild mood swings. I do not have any old money, unless you count that crumpled ten-dollar bill in my wallet that I think was printed back in 1981. The one thing we do have in common, the Swiss and I, is our love of chocolate. This is not an insignificant commonality. The Swiss consume mass quantities of chocolate, and there is some credible evidence that chocolate makes us happier.

In order to investigate this link, I visit a chocolate store. It reminds me of an art gallery, an edible art gallery. The clerks lift the truffles with tongs, as if they were handling some rare and precious jewels. There is an entire wall of chocolate, with every type imaginable. Chocolate made with cocoa from Colombia and Ecuador and Madagascar. Chocolate laced with orange and raspberry and pistachio and raisins and cognac and rum and pure malt whiskey. I buy one of each and take them back to my hotel room, feeling quite literally like a kid in a candy store. I lock the door and spread my catch on the comforter. I bite into the Madagascar, and it is good—there is no such thing as bad Swiss chocolate.

But, as I said, this is not mere indulgence. This is research. Scientists have isolated the chemical in chocolate that makes us feel good. Actually, there are several chemicals involved. Tryptophan is what the brain uses to make the neurotransmitter serotonin. High levels of serotonin can produce feelings of elation, even ecstasy. Then there is something called anandamide. It's a neurotransmitter that targets the same regions of the brain as THC, the active ingredient in marijuana. But this chocolate-as-marijuana theory remains just that, a theory, since according to a BBC article on the subject, "experts estimate you would need to eat several kilos of chocolate" in order to feel this effect. Several kilos, huh? What is that in pounds, I wonder, as I get busy with the chocolate spread before me like a banquet.

The relationship between choice and happiness is tricky, and nowhere more so than in Switzerland. We think of choice as desirable, something that makes us happy. That is usually true but not always. As Barry Schwartz has shown convincingly in his book *The Paradox of Choice,* there is such a thing as too much choice. Faced with a surplus of options (especially meaningless ones), we get confused, overwhelmed, less happy.

On the one hand, the Swiss have more choices than any other people on the planet, and not just when it comes to chocolate. Their system of direct democracy means that the Swiss are constantly voting on issues large and small: whether to join the United Nations, whether to ban absinthe. The average Swiss person votes six or seven times a year. The Swiss believe that anything worth doing is worth doing seriously. And so it is with voting. At one point, the Swiss actually voted to increase their own taxes. I can't imagine American voters doing the same.

The system of direct democracy is not perfect. It is truly a democracy of the people, and sometimes the people can be complete morons. For instance, the Swiss didn't give women the right to vote until 1971—in one canton, or state, not until 1991.

Still, Canadian happiness researcher John Helliwell believes that quality of government is the single most important variable that explains why some countries are happier than others. Another researcher, a Swiss economist named Bruno Frey, examined the relationship between democracy and happiness across Switzerland's twenty-six cantons. He found that the cantons with the greatest number of referendums, the most democracy, were also the happiest. Even foreigners living in those cantons were happier, though they couldn't vote. (Their happiness boost, though, was not as great as the voters'.)

Okay, so it seems that the Swiss like choices. Then how to explain the results of an ingenious little experiment by psychologist Paul Rozin of the University of Pennsylvania. He asked a cross-section of people from six countries (the United States, the United Kingdom, France, Germany, Italy, and Switzerland) a simple question: "Imagine that you feel like eating ice cream and that you have the choice between two ice-cream parlors. One offers a choice of ten flavors. The other offers a selection of fifty flavors. Which ice-cream parlor would you choose?"

In only one country, the United States, did a majority (56 percent) of respondents prefer the ice-cream parlor with fifty flavors. The Swiss were on the other end of the spectrum. Only 28 percent preferred the ice-cream parlor with more choices. Choice translates into happiness only when choice is about something that matters. Voting matters. Ice cream matters, too, but fifty flavors of it do not.

On a train again. This time my destination is Saint-Ursanne, which I was told was a "middle-aged town." When I heard this, I imagined an entire town filled with balding, overweight men driving red sports cars. In fact, the Swiss person on the other end of the line had meant a medieval town, as in from the Middle Ages.

His name is Andreas Gross, and everyone said he is someone I should meet. He is a member of the Swiss parliament and a big proponent of direct democracy. He travels the world espousing its virtues. He's most famous, though, for a ballot initiative he brought forth in 1989. Gross wanted to abolish the Swiss army, just get rid of it. Nobody thought the initiative would get more than a tiny number of votes. In fact, 35 percent voted for it. The

Swiss were shocked. The initiative shook up the establishment, and the Swiss army today is half the size it was in 1989.

I go to the dining car. This is not Amtrak. The menu, in four languages, informs me of my choices: penne with fresh mushrooms or a risotto with fresh asparagus. I am in heaven.

The train crosses the linguistic dividing line between German- and French-speaking Switzerland, and I transition seamlessly from Caveman French to Caveman German: "Me want coffee. You have?" The Swiss translate everything into at least three languages. This means that even the simplest sign takes up lots of real estate. I see one that says "Danger: Do Not Cross the Railroad Tracks." By the time you get to the English, at the bottom of the linguistic pyramid, you could be electrocuted.

We arrive in Saint-Ursanne, and Andreas Gross is there to meet me. He's wearing jeans and has a fuzzy salt-and-pepper beard and just the hint of a gut. He looks more like an aging hippie than a distinguished parliamentarian. We head to his institute, which is really just a converted old house.

Andreas makes me a cup of espresso—Italy's contribution to happiness—and we sit down to talk. It quickly becomes apparent that Andreas is not too keen on this whole happiness business. It's not serious enough for him. He wants to talk about direct democracy and plenary sessions, serious Swiss subjects. He quotes Rousseau and says things like, "I would like the Swiss to be more like the Swiss they think they are." I have no idea what he's talking about.

He tells me how Switzerland cares so much about its environment that it's about to spend the equivalent of twenty billion dollars to dig a huge tunnel under the Alps. Trucks that want to cross the country will be put on trains and transported literally through the mountains. He tells me that "human rights are the child of war. All of humanity's great advances have come through war." The Swiss haven't fought a war since 1848.

"So I guess the Swiss need to fight more wars," I say.

"No, no, no," he says, missing my dry humor, as I knew he would. "We need to find other ways to promote human rights."

We talk some more, about postmodernism and democracy and neutrality, before circling back to where I began my Swiss adventure: clean toilets. Andreas, like Dieter, is very fond of them. "Even the tiniest rail station has a clean toilet," he says proudly.

We continue our conversation as Andreas drives me to the train station. We arrive early, and it's raining outside. The air smells sweet. We sit in his musty old Saab and talk awhile longer. He tells me how he once met an aging American activist, an old-timer, a 1960s diehard, a union organizer who went to Nicaragua and stood shoulder to shoulder with the Sandinistas.

The old-timer was impressed with Andreas's idealism and complained that American youth have lost their rebellious spark. Nothing anyone does seems to make a difference in the United States.

"Why don't you fight for proportional representation?" Andreas asked him.

"I don't have time for such procedural stuff," the old-timer snapped.

"So you want to bang your head against concrete for another twenty years?" retorted Andreas.

For Andreas, the problem isn't the banging but the concrete. Change the system, he believes, one boring procedure at a time. It's a very Swiss approach and, in its own quiet way, admirable. It requires patience and a high tolerance for boredom. The Swiss possess both in spades.

I steal one last look at Andreas Gross. In the United States, I realize, he would be relegated to the angry and inert chatter of a Berkeley coffeehouse; here, he is a distinguished parliamentarian who nearly abolished the entire Swiss army. More proof that the Swiss aren't so boring after all.


As I board one more train, the train that will take me out of Switzerland, a sudden twinge of sadness sneaks up on me. I'll miss this place. The Swiss don't piss me off anymore.

But are they happy? Content seems more like it. No, content

isn't quite right, either. Words fail me. We have far more words to describe unpleasant emotional states than pleasant ones. (And this is the case with all languages, not just English.) If we're not happy, we have a smorgasbord of words to choose from. We can say we're feeling down, blue, miserable, sullen, gloomy, dejected, morose, despondent, in the dumps, out of sorts, long in the face. But if we're happy that smorgasbord is reduced to the salad bar at Pizza Hut. We might say we're elated or content or blissful. These words, though, don't capture the shades of happiness.

We need a new word to describe Swiss happiness. Something more than mere contentment but less than full-on joy. "Conjoyment," perhaps. Yes, that's what the Swiss possess: utter conjoyment. We could use this word to describe all kinds of situations where we feel joyful yet calm at the same time. Too often when we say we feel joyful, we're really feeling manic. There is a frenetic nature to our joy, a whiff of panic; we're afraid the moment might end abruptly. But then there are other moments when our joy is more solidly grounded. I am not speaking of a transcendental moment, of bliss, but something less, something Swiss.

We might experience conjoyment when we are doing something mundane, like sweeping the floor or sorting our trash or listening to that old Bob Dylan CD we haven't heard in years. Yes, that's it. The Swiss may not be happy, but they sure know how to conjoy themselves.

# Chapter 3

# BHUTAN

## Happiness Is a Policy

*There came a time, he realized, when the strange-
ness of everything made it increasingly difficult
to realize the strangeness of anything.*

— James Hilton, *Lost Horizon*

The Airbus levels at thirty-seven thousand feet, somewhere over
the Himalayas. The cabin lights glow soft and warm. The flight
attendants glide down the aisle, gracious and attentive.

I am looking out the window, for I have been advised by Those
in the Know that an aisle seat just won't do. Not on this flight.

For a long while I see nothing but a solid blanket of cloud. I
am beginning to question the wisdom of Those in the Know when
suddenly the clouds are gone, and the mountains reveal themselves. Towering, mesmerizing mountains. The Himalayas make
all other mountains look like bunny hills.

People around me are craning their necks, reaching for cameras, ahhhing and ooohing. My thoughts, however, are elsewhere.
I'm thinking of another airplane and another time. The year is
1933, and this airplane is a rickety propeller plane. It, too, is flying over the Himalayas, not far from where I am now, but the
cabin on this plane is cold, the seats hard, the flight attendants
nonexistent. The passengers—three Brits and an American—need
to shout to make themselves heard over the engine noise. The

trepidation in their voices, however, is unmistakable. The pilot, brandishing a revolver, is way off course, flying toward some unknown destination. They are being hijacked.

The destination turns out to be a remarkable place of "sumptuous tranquility." A place of eternal peace where monks meditate, poets muse, and everyone lives impossibly long and satisfying lives. A remote place, cut off from the horrors of the outside world, though not from its tactile comforts.

The place is Shangri-La, the four passengers characters in the book *Lost Horizon*. Shangri-La is, of course, an invented place. James Hilton, the author, never ventured farther than the British Museum in London for his research. But the idea of Shangri-La is very real. Who hasn't dreamed of a place simultaneously placid and intellectually invigorating? A place made for the head and the heart, where both live in happy unison to the ripe old age of 250.

When the book and the movie came out in the 1930s, *Lost Horizon* captured the imagination of an American public in the grips of the Great Depression, reeling from one world war and bracing for another. Franklin D. Roosevelt named his presidential retreat Shangri-La (later renamed Camp David). Hotels, grand and fleabag alike, called themselves Shangri-La, hoping to bask in its utopian glow.

Shangri-La contains all of the classic ingredients of paradise. First of all, it is difficult to reach. Paradise, after all, is not paradise if you can take a taxi there. Furthermore, there must be a clear demarcation between paradise and ordinary life, separated by a netherworld that only a few fortunate souls can traverse. Paradise, in other words, is a selective club. Just like business class, which owes its pleasures, in no small way, to the presence of other travelers less fortunate than yourself, back there in coach gumming rubbery chicken and fishing in their pockets for exact change (which is always appreciated) to anesthetize themselves with miniature bottles of vodka. You can't see these poor souls—that's what the curtain is for—but you know they are there, and that makes all the difference.

And so Shangri-La's enigmatic High Lama proclaims: "We are a single lifeboat riding the seas in a gale; we can take a few chance survivors, but if all the shipwrecked were to reach us and clamber aboard we should go down ourselves." As would an airliner, no doubt, should the curtain fail and the unwashed masses stream forward, toward business class.

Though invented more than seventy years ago, James Hilton's Shangri-La is a very modern kind of paradise. It contains the accumulated wisdom of the east, yes, but also the accumulated plumbing of the west (bathtubs from Akron, Ohio). Not to mention a reading room with leather-bound volumes of the great books. Comfortable accommodations. Food that is plentiful and delicious. Shangri-La, in other words, was the first soft-adventure destination. Paradise lite.

The thing about paradise, though, is we don't always recognize it immediately. Its paradiseness takes time to sink in. In *Lost Horizon*, most of the kidnapped foreigners plot to escape Shangri-La. They are desperate to return to "civilization" and are suspicious, justifiably so, of the excuses proffered by the lamas. Bad weather. Not enough supplies. But one of the group, a misfit British diplomat named Conway, is enthralled by Shangri-La and chooses to stay. When I first read *Lost Horizon,* I related to Conway and would have given anything to trade places with him.

*Lost Horizon* spoke to me, but I didn't speak back for many years. Not until I heard about Bhutan. I was living in India at the time, the early 1990s, as a correspondent for National Public Radio. I was the network's first correspondent in that country; the path was unbeaten. Monkeys occasionally wandered into my apartment. Snake charmers dropped by. I was having the time of my life.

The countries I was assigned to cover—my patch, as it were—included Bhutan. I could hardly believe my luck. Here was a country that, in my mind, was the closest thing going to Shangri-La. Bhutan had the mountains, towering peaks that touched the heavens. It had the requisite idiosyncrasies—a benevolent king, for instance, with four wives, all of them sisters. It had lamas and mystics and an actual government policy of Gross National Happiness.

My editors in Washington, D.C., didn't share my enthusiasm. You want to go where? It will cost how much? No one had much interest in a tiny Himalayan nation with a polygamous monarch and a happiness fixation.

The years passed. I moved on to another posting in Jerusalem, then Tokyo, all the while pining for Bhutan. For me, a place unvisited is like an unrequited love. A dull ache that—try as you might to think it away, to convince yourself that she really wasn't the right country for you—just won't leave you in peace.

"Your first time?"

I swivel my head, caught off guard. "Beg your pardon?"

"Is this your first time going to Bhutan?"

The words are spoken by a Bhutanese businessman sitting next to me on the Airbus. He's wearing a brown suede jacket and looking me in the eye.

"Yes, my first time."

"Your timing is perfect," he says. "You'll be there for the *tsechu,* the big festival. You'll see things you've never seen before. Amazing things."

The Airbus dips. We've begun our descent. The captain's voice comes on the PA in that reassuring everything-is-under-control tone that they must teach pilots somewhere.

"For those flying into Paro for the first time, if you see mountains closer than you've ever seen them before, do not be alarmed. That is our standard approach."

Sure enough, the Airbus banks steeply—first right, then left, then right again—and with each turn a mountain appears large in my window, close enough to touch, it seems. Finally, clear of the peaks, the Airbus drops abruptly and, with a squeak of tires, we're on pavement. The flight attendants swing the door open. The air is bracing, the sky deep blue.

In most countries, your arrival is staggered, your transition into a new environment eased by the familiarity and hermetic sameness of Airport World. But in Bhutan there is no Airport World. There is, truth be told, barely an airport. Just a tiny hut of a terminal, which, with its carved woodwork and swirls of deep reds and blues, looks more like a Buddhist temple than an airport.

Every visitor to Bhutan is assigned a guide. You pay his salary out of the two hundred dollars a day you must shell out to a Bhutanese tour company for the privilege of being in Bhutan—part of the country's effort to keep out the sort of straggly-haired backpackers who have infiltrated neighboring Nepal. This makes me more than a little apprehensive. On reporting assignments to Iraq during Saddam Hussein's time, our guides were called minders. They were oily-haired men in ill-fitting suits who were there, supposedly, to "facilitate" the work of foreign journalists. In fact, they were there to facilitate the work of the *mukhabarat,* Saddam Hussein's secret police. They were spies. Everybody knew that. We knew that. They knew that we knew.

The young man waiting outside the airport for me doesn't look like a spy. He looks more like a Bhutanese Boy Scout, if they had Boy Scouts in Bhutan. Olive-skinned, with a shiny, freshly scrubbed face, he is wearing a dark brown *gho,* the traditional Bhutanese dress for men. A *gho* looks something like a bathrobe, only much heavier and with cavernous pockets. Bhutanese men have been known to pull all manner of objects from their *gho*s: cups, cellphones, small farm animals. In a pinch, the *gho* can do double duty as a blanket or curtain. (It's a good thing the *gho* is so handy, because all Bhutanese men are required to wear one during business hours. Bhutan is the only country in the world with a dress code for men.)

"Welcome to Bhutan, sir," says the young man in the *gho,* looping a white scarf around my neck. He introduces himself as Tashi, then shakes my hand. It's not like any handshake I've ever experienced. Two hands cupped over one of mine, head lowered in a half bow. It is a very deliberate, present action. At first, I find it off-putting. I'm just shaking hands with you, Tashi, we're not going steady or anything. Later, though, I would learn to appreciate the Bhutanese handshake and, come to think of it, the way they do nearly everything—cross the street, wash dishes—so deliberately, so attentively.

"Attention" is an underrated word. It doesn't get the...well, the attention it deserves. We pay homage to love and happiness and, God knows, productivity, but rarely do we have anything good to say about attention. We're too busy, I suspect. Yet our lives are empty and meaningless without attention.

My two-year-old daughter fusses at my feet as I type these words. What does she want? My love? Yes, in a way, but what she really wants is my attention. Pure, undiluted attention. Children are expert at recognizing counterfeit attention. Perhaps love and attention are really the same thing. One can't exist without the other. The British scholar Avner Offer calls attention "the universal currency of well-being." Attentive people, in other words, are happy people.

Tashi carries my bags to our car. Given the reputation of the roads in Bhutan, I was hoping for something muscular like a Toyota Land Cruiser. It is a Toyota but no Land Cruiser. We pile into a beat-up 1993 Corolla. It's 8:00 a.m., and I didn't sleep a wink on the overnight flight.

"Where would you like to go, sir?"

"To anyplace that serves coffee, Tashi."

We drive to a small café, although calling it a café is a stretch. It is a concrete building with a few wooden tables and chairs. They serve only instant coffee. As a coffee lover, I find this deeply disturbing, but I drink it and don't complain.

Tashi is gracious and eager to please. He also possesses, I soon discover, an impressive knack for the obvious. He says things like "We have arrived at our destination, sir," when clearly we have or "It's raining, sir," when we're dripping wet.

His mannerisms are courtly, like those of an eighteenth-century nobleman. He holds doors open for me, carries my bag, and hovers like a chopper over an L.A. car chase. If he could carry me, he probably would.

He does all of this, though, in a dignified rather than syco-phantic way. The Bhutanese were never colonized, never conquered, so their hospitality is served straight up, devoid of the gratuitous def-erence and outright ass-kissing so common in this part of the world.

Tashi's English is rough and peculiar. It's not just his accent, which is heavy, but his vocabulary. He says things like "Shall we take some vestigial food, sir?" At first I have no idea what he is talking about—some Bhutanese delicacy perhaps?—then I realize he means leftovers. "Vestigial" as in "vestige" as in "no longer needed." I explain to him that this word is not commonly used. He still uses it, though, and eventually I stop trying to correct him.

"Okay, Tashi, let's head to Thimphu." That's the capital of Bhutan and my home for the next week or so.

"We can't go, sir."

"Why not?"

"The road is closed."

"How long will it be closed?"

"For some time."

In this part of the world, For Some Time is the last thing you want to hear. Fortunes have been won and lost during For Some Time. Empires have risen and fallen during For Some Time. The problem is that For Some Time can mean five minutes or five days or five years. It matters not what you are waiting for—the next bus to Bombay or a kidney transplant—For Some Time will not arrive until it does. Unless it doesn't.

"What about taking an alternative route," I suggest, helpfully. Tashi and the driver find this extremely funny. I surmise this by their peals of laughter and knee slapping. Alternative route! Good one sir, ha ha, alternative route, ha ha.

There is no alternative route. There is barely a route. Bhutan's generously named National Highway is the only road in the coun-try—and barely a road at that, only wide enough for one car.

So we sit and wait. This is fine, I think, all Buddha-like. It gives me a few minutes to catch my breath, at this elevation no easy feat, and take stock of where I am.

Why am I here? Where does Bhutan fit into my atlas of bliss? Yes, the country resembles Hilton's Shangri-La, superficially at least, and that I find enormously appealing. Happiness is even in the country's national anthem: "As the doctrine of Lord Buddha flourishes, may the sun of peace and happiness shine on the people." And then there is Bhutan's policy of Gross National Happiness. In a nutshell, Gross National Happiness seeks to measure a nation's progress not by its balance sheet but rather by the happiness—or unhappiness—of its people. It's a concept that represents a profound shift from how we think about money and satisfaction and the obligation of a government to its people.

I have my doubts, though. Is Bhutan really "a laboratory of human betterment"? as one observer put it. Or is it just another shithole, to use the foreign correspondent's inelegant term for countries where the government is corrupt, the roads slow, and the coffee instant.

I can't answer any of these questions yet and instead find solace in the words of Conway, who tried to calm his uppity companions, stranded in Shangri-La. "We're here because we're here; if you want an explanation I've usually found it a soothing one."

Finally, after waiting For Some Time, the road to Thimphu reopens, and we pile into the Toyota. I quickly discover that driving in Bhutan is not for the meek. Hairpin turns, precipitous drop-offs (no guardrails), and a driver who firmly believes in reincarnation make for a nerve-racking experience. There are no atheists on Bhutan's roads.

Fortunately, I sleep for most of the trip, waking to find us chugging up a steep hill. Bhutanese schoolkids, gabbing and laughing as they walk from school, part for our Corolla like the Red Sea for Moses. They do so without snide remarks or dirty looks. Something else that is here—or rather not here. No billboards or neon signs; there is hardly any advertising in Bhutan, and neon signs were banned until a few years ago. However, I do spot this hand-painted sign, propped up by two pieces of wood on the side of the road.

When the last tree is cut,
When the last river is emptied,
When the last fish is caught,
Only then will Man realize that he can not eat money.

I am pondering those words as the Corolla pulls up to a guest-house at the top of the hill. I am greeted like visiting royalty by the entire staff. Another white scarf is lassoed around my neck, and then I'm led upstairs to my room. The proprietor, a hand-some woman named Sangay, informs me that Richard Gere once stayed in the very same room. "I remember it clearly," she says. "He said—how did he put it?—that the room had 'a million-dollar view.'"

The view is indeed wonderful; the city of Thimphu, with its white- and green-roofed houses, is visible directly below, moun-tains and wispy clouds off on the horizon. But "million-dollar view" strikes me as not quite the right term to describe it, not here in Bhutan, a country determined to diminish the importance of money in our lives.

Exhausted, I flop down on the mattress. I close my eyes and try to imagine Richard Gere, *the* Richard Gere, lying on this very same bed. I don't like the images this conjures and think of base-ball instead. It's not personal. I have nothing against Richard Gere. Indeed, I can honestly say that were he a better actor, I might not be married today. On my first date with my now-wife, we went to see a Richard Gere movie in Greenwich Village. It was called *Mr. Jones* and was so profoundly bad, on so many levels, that we spent the rest of the evening dissecting its badness and forming a deep and abiding bond that endures to this day. So now that I have the chance, I'd like to say: thank you, Richard Gere, thank you.

My sleep is restless, my dreams disturbed, due to the altitude, I suspect. I wake the next morning to sounds of hooting and hol-lering off in the distance. An insurrection? A coup d'état?

"No, that's probably an archery match you hear," says Sangay, as I eat runny eggs and toast for breakfast. Archery is the national sport in Bhutan. It is played with vigor and noise. Bhutanese pray quietly; everything else they do raucously.

Afterward, I have some time to kill before Tashi picks me up, so I decide to do something that was not possible in Bhutan, would have been unthinkable, until very recently. I watch television. Bhutan was the last country in the world to get television, in 1999. It has quickly become an indispensable—and controversial—part of life. Bhutanese teenagers, for reasons not entirely clear, developed a taste for *Wrestlemania*. The government banned the channels that carried it. That worked. For a while. Then other channels picked up the wrestling matches. After centuries of isolation, Bhutan finds itself invaded by the likes of Hulk Hogan.

Sangay Ngedup, a former prime minister, expressed a concern shared by many Bhutanese. "Until recently, we shied away from killing insects and yet now we Bhutanese are asked to watch people on TV blowing heads off with shotguns," he told the British newspaper *The Guardian*.

The newscast on BBS—the Bhutan Broadcasting Service—is smartly produced. The anchor, wearing a *gho*, reads the news with that mix of authority and chumminess that American anchors have mastered. Behind him is a shot of Thimphu's Dzong, the Bhutanese equivalent of the White House. Underneath, I can just barely make out squiggles. Wait a minute. The squiggles are moving. What's going on? I inch my chair closer to the screen. Good God, they have the crawl! Only seven years of television and already they have the crawl. And so it goes with Bhutan's headfirst leap into the twenty-first century. There are now Internet cafés and cellphones and, that ultimate sign of civilization, at least civilization circa 1973, discos. Keep in mind that this is a country that until 1962 didn't have a single road, school, or hospital. It didn't even have a national currency.

Tashi arrives at the hotel and announces with great fanfare: "I have arrived, sir." I have decided that Tashi is not a spy. He's not smart enough. Either that, or he's an extremely good spy. No, Tashi is more of a guide or, in journalistic parlance, a fixer. A fixer

arranges interviews, interprets, ferrets out information from reluctant officials, provides juicy anecdotes, takes photos, gets coffee,
and sometimes writes articles. In other words, fixers do most of the
correspondent's work for no credit and little pay. Some might find
this unfair, even unethical. Perhaps, but the fixer/correspondent
relationship has a long and proud tradition. And I am not about to
mess with tradition.

I'm concerned, though, that Tashi might not be a good fixer.
His English is too rough, and he is clearly new at this, as green as
an avocado. I must have let my concerns slip to someone at the
hotel because I get a call from Tashi's boss, Sonam, manager of the
tour company organizing my trip.

"I understand you are not happy with Tashi," she says flatly.
Wow, I'm thinking, this *is* a small country.

"Nooo," I lie, embarrassed by my indiscretion, "I'm perfectly
happy with him." She persists, offering to assign another guide. I
could have agreed, could have dumped Tashi right there and then,
but for reasons I still don't fully understand, I decide to stick with
him.

Word of my unease, however, has clearly reached Tashi. He
has interpreted my criticism to mean he is not hovering closely
enough, not opening enough doors or carrying enough bags, so he
redoubles his efforts.

We drive down the hill to Thimphu. Every trivia buff who
visits the city loves to point out that it is the world's only capital
city without a single traffic light, so I will do so here. Thimphu is
the world's only capital city without a single traffic light. Instead,
at the main intersection, a policeman wearing white gloves directs
traffic with precise, almost comical gestures. A few years ago, they
tried replacing the cop with an actual traffic light, but the king
didn't like it, and—the king being pretty much like the pope; that
is, infallible—everyone agreed it was a bad idea, and down came
the traffic light.

Thimphu is a likable city, about the size of Burlington, Vermont. The skyline is a tangle of power lines and prayer flags.

Life in Thimphu reminds me a lot of James Hilton's description of the inhabitants of Shangri-La: "They were good-humored and mildly inquisitive, courteous and carefree, busy at innumerable jobs but not in any hurry over them."

Thimphu has just the right amount of bustle and chaos: Indian workers trading gossip on their day off; cheap hotels; satellite dishes sprouting from rooftops like wild mushrooms; a sign thanking me for not spitting; dingy Internet cafés; rickety bamboo scaffolding; tourists in sneakers and sunburns, their guides shadowing them like Secret Service agents; Bhutanese women carrying umbrellas to shield themselves from the midday sun.

And stray dogs. Lots of stray dogs. They lie in the sun or, if the mood strikes, cross the street. They do this with an air of invincibility. They know no one would dare hit them. In Bhutan, dogs are the kings of the road. The last time I saw such arrogance from an animal was in India, where the cow, smug in her holiness, has developed a serious attitude problem. Cows loiter in the middle of roads, chewing their cuds and daring—just daring!—drivers to go ahead and hit them. Enjoy your next life as a warthog, buddy.

In my next life, I want to come back as a Bhutanese dog. They have it made. Why? Surely, the Buddhist respect for all sentient beings has something to do with it. But this belief, while surely noble, isn't quite as altruistic as it seems. If you believe in reincarnation, then you also believe you might come back in your next life as a horse or cow, and if so you'd want to be treated well as a horse or cow. This is how Ringzin Dorji, quoted in Barbara Crossette's book on the Buddhist Himalayan kingdoms, describes this phenomenon: "Today my mother may be human. But when I die I may be reborn as a dog and then my mother may be a bitch. So, therefore, you have to think that all living things are my parents. My parents are infinite. Let my parents not suffer."

When I first read that passage, it made a big impression on me. Not just the dubious proposition that "my mother may be a bitch," but the more profound notion that our parents are infinite. That we are all related.

I pick up a newspaper, the *Bhutan Observer*. A headline jumps out at me: "Sneak sales on the street, in the dark." Oh, no, I think, Bhutan has a drug problem or, worse, a brisk trade in contraband firearms. I read on: "The main items sold here are fruits, vegetables and fresh and pure milk products." The vendors, it turns out, can't sell all of their wares during the sanctioned weekend market, so they stick around Thimphu on Monday and make clandestine sales of zucchini and asparagus before traveling back to their villages.

Apparently, this is what passes for crime in Bhutan. But the police are worried. They know that it's a slippery slope; black-market sales of zucchinis and asparagus can easily lead to more hard-core vegetables.

Clearly, Bhutan's low crime rate—murder is almost unheard of—contributes to the overall happiness here. Not surprisingly, places with high crime rates rank low on the happiness scale. (Though there are outliers, Puerto Rico, for instance, is both crime ridden *and* happy.) The reasons are less obvious than you might think. Someone who has been robbed or assaulted, of course, is not likely to be happy, but crime victims still make up a tiny part of the population (in most countries at least). It's not the crime per se that makes places unhappy. It's the creeping sense of fear that permeates everyone's lives, even those who have never been—and probably never will be—victims of crime.

In the last few decades, Bhutan has made tremendous strides in the kind of metrics that people who use words like "metrics" get excited about. Life expectancy has increased from forty-two to sixty-four years (though it is still well short of the 250 years in Shangri-La). The government now provides free health care and education for all of its citizens. Bhutan is the world's first nonsmoking nation; the sale of tobacco is banned. There are more monks than soldiers. The army, such as it is, produces most of Bhutan's liquor, including Red Panda beer and my favorite, Dragon Rum. Imagine if all of the world's armies got into the alcohol business. "Make booze not war" could become the rallying cry for a whole new generation of peaceniks.

*    *    *

I wanted to find out more about Bhutan's policy of Gross National Happiness, which aims to supplement the more traditional measure of progress, gross national product. Is this for real? Everyone with even a passing knowledge of Bhutan advised me to see Karma Ura. He runs Bhutan's most important think tank, which also happens to be Bhutan's only think tank. I look forward to meeting him partly because he is such an intellectual force in this country, a man who has thought long and hard about the nature of happiness and partly because I have never met someone named Karma before.

Tashi and I drive to the outskirts of Thimphu, not far from where the king lives, and pull up to an old building. I'm directed to a conference room a few yards away. I walk along a wood beam, balancing over a pit of mud. My expectations for the "conference room" are low, but when I open the door I'm surprised to find a smartly designed space bisected by a long wooden table. Bhutan bucks the trend in most developing countries, where money is poured into appearances—a glitzy airport terminal surrounded by slums, hotels with extravagant lobbies but shabby rooms. In Bhutan, what's on the inside is often more impressive than what's on the outside.

I hand Karma the white scarf that Tashi gave me, circular giving, and he responds with the trace of a smile. He's wearing a checked *gho* and has a lean, handsome face. He speaks slowly, deliberately. It's not that he thinks before he speaks. He thinks *as* he speaks and does so in a measured, synchronous way. Silence makes me uncomfortable—all of that nothingness drives me nuts—and I have to restrain my urge to fill the empty spaces in our conversation.

The way Karma Ura sees it, a government is like a pilot guiding an airplane. In bad weather, it must rely on its instruments to navigate. But what if the instruments are faulty? The plane will certainly veer off course, even though the pilot is manipulating the controls properly. That, he says, is the state of the world today, with its dependence on gross national product as the only real measure of a nation's progress. "Take education," he says. "We are hooked on measuring enrollment, but we don't look at the content. Or consider a nation like Japan. People live a long time, but what is the quality of their life past age sixty?" He has a point. We measure what is easiest to measure, not what really matters to most people's lives—a disparity that Gross National Happiness seeks to correct.

I feel myself slipping into my old, coolly professional style of interviewing and realize it's time to get personal.

"Karma, are you happy?"

"Looking back at my life, I find that the answer is yes. I have achieved happiness because I don't have unrealistic expectations."

This strikes me as an odd explanation. In America, high expectations are the engines that drive us, the gas in our tanks, the force behind our dreams and, by extension, our pursuit of happiness.

"My way of thinking is completely different," he says. "I have no such mountains to scale; basically, I find that living itself is a struggle, and if I'm satisfied, if I have just done that, lived well, in the evening I sigh and say, 'It was okay.'"

"Do you have bad days?"

"Yes, but it's important to put them in the perspective of insignificance. Even if you have achieved great things, it is a sort of theater playing in your mind. You think it so important, but actually you have not made such a difference to anyone's life."

"So you're saying, Karma, that both our greatest achievements and our greatest failures are equally insignificant?"

"Yes. We like to think we really made a difference. Okay, in the week's scale it may have been interesting. Take another forty years, I'm not so sure. Take three generations, and you will be forgotten without a trace."

"And you find this a source of comfort? I find it terribly depressing."

"No, as we say in Buddhism, there is nothing greater than compassion. If you have done something good, then in the moment you should feel satisfaction. I used to kill many flies and mosquitoes every day because they give me some fear of malaria, but sometimes I don't do that. I have a moment of pause and think, 'Well, he is not harming me, not directly threatening me. He is defenseless. Why am I crushing it?' So then I release it, and there is a moment—it is an insignificant act, I know—but there is a moment of genuine peace. I just let it go."

Then I decide to do something out of character. I talk about myself. Really talk. Why, I'm not sure. Maybe it is the gentleness of this man, or the fact that he's named Karma, or the disorienting nature of Bhutan, but for whatever reason, I tell Karma a story, one that unfolded in Miami a few weeks before I began my search for the world's happiest places.

"Wake up," I hear the doctor say, impatiently, eyes fixed downward, as he swings open the door to the examination room.

"I am awake," I say.

"No," chides the doctor. "I'm talking to my computer." Of course. Now I can see the microphone—the size and shape of a gumball, hovering in front of his mouth—and the glowing tablet in his hands.

This strange sight distracts me briefly before I remember why I am here. The numbness in my hands and feet. The shortness of breath. These symptoms have grown worse in recent weeks, keeping me up at night.

And so it came to pass that at the pivotal, no-turning-back, life-is-half-over age of forty-three, I find myself sitting in a cold examination room, with a doctor who talks to his computer, awaiting the MRI results that I know, just *know*, will provide grim confirmation of my inoperable brain tumor. Or maybe, if I'm lucky, Lou Gehrig's disease. Two weeks earlier, lying prone in the sarcophagus-like tube, the machinery invisibly clicking and whirring around me, I could practically hear the technicians behind the glass partition muttering to each other. "Poor bastard, he doesn't have long."

So as I await the official results, my life clicks before my eyes like a bad PowerPoint presentation. Final slide. Death. Thanks for attending our seminar. Coffee and bagels are available outside.

"Well, I have the MRI results here," the doctor says.

Yes, I know you do. I can see them in the palms of your cold, merciless hands. Give it to me, Doc. I can take it. Actually, I can't. But give it to me anyway.

"And we have your blood work."

Yes, my blood work, I know. How long do I have?

"And...we found..."

"Nothing. They found nothing," interjects Karma, flatly, without a hint of doubt.

I am floored. He's right. The numbness in my hands and feet was caused by erratic breathing and inconsistent oxygen flow; in other words, a panic attack. Just another brush with hypochondria.

"How did you know, Karma?"

Karma pauses one of his pauses and then answers with a suggestion, a prescription. "You need to think about death for five minutes every day. It will cure you, sanitize you."

"How?"

"It is this thing, this fear of death, this fear of dying before we have accomplished what we want or seen our children grow. This is what is troubling you."

"But it sounds so depressing, thinking about death every day. Why would I want to do that?"

"Rich people in the west, they have not touched dead bodies, fresh wounds, rotten things. This is a problem. This is the human condition. We have to be ready for the moment we cease to exist."

It is only then that he tells me about his cancer. The diagnosis. Chemotherapy. Surgeries in hospitals far from home. Finally, remission.

Now I am the one who is silent.

We say our goodbyes, and I make a point of asking to see him once again, before I leave Bhutan. Then I walk back across the wooden plank, and get back into the Corolla. We're driving back to the hotel, something Tashi feels compelled to announce, and I'm thinking about this remarkable man I have just met. A happy man. He is an academic who studied at Cambridge and can riff about regression analysis along with the best of them, but the next second he's talking about Buddha and the cancer that nearly killed him. Seamlessly. Karma Ura's life is integrated. Organic. Not a series of silos—work, love, family—like most people's I know. Like mine.

When we arrive at the hotel—which Tashi points out by declaring, "We have arrived at the hotel, sir"—I am in no mood for small talk with the staff, so I carry a chair to the balcony outside my room and sit. Just sit. My head is spinning. Karma Ura has thrown me for a loop. Happiness is low expectations? How do I reconcile that with my driving ambition, which has served me so well in life? Or has it? And what he said about compassion being the ultimate ambition. What was *that* about?

Then I see it. About two feet from me. A bug. It is lying upside down, its tiny legs flailing futilely. I look away. But my eyes are drawn back to this tiny creature in such a pathetic state.

I consider my options. Option One: I can squash it and put it out of its misery. The main advantage of Option One is that it ends suffering, the bug's and mine. Option Two: I could ignore it, which is how I usually respond when faced with the suffering of others. Don't get involved. Be a good journalist. Remain neutral at all costs. But this is not a news story. There will be no "Bug Dies in Himalayas. Family Distraught. Footage at 11:00."

There is, I realize, an Option Three. I could intervene and save a life—an insect life, true, but still a life. I take a tentative step toward the bug and give it a gentle kick. Only it's not quite as gentle as I intended, and the bug slides a good ten feet across the patio, still upside down, legs still flailing. Okay, another failed humanitarian intervention. The United States—with all of its resources—couldn't save Somalia or Iraq, so why should I feel bad that I couldn't save one bug?

I go downstairs and order a Red Panda beer. When I return

to my room a half hour later, out of morbid curiosity I peek out on the patio and see that the bug is still flailing, though losing steam. Why the hell should I care? I hate bugs, damn it. But all this Buddhist talk of loving-kindness has gotten to me. What the heck, I give the bug one more kick, this time more gently, and in an instant it is right-side up, scampering away. Not thanking me, but that's okay. It feels good. I saved a life. I got involved.

A postscript. When I stepped out on the patio later that evening I found a bug, the very same bug I'm sure, on its back again. I couldn't believe my eyes. This time, I did nothing. I slept easily that night, though. Nobody, not even Karma Ura, I bet, can save a dumb bug from itself.


Bhutan is an upside-down place. Here the number thirteen is considered lucky. Children greet you with "bye-bye." The king wants to abolish himself.

Or take marijuana. In Bhutan, they have a novel use for it. They feed it to pigs. This makes the pigs hungry and therefore fat. The first time I heard this, I couldn't help but imagine an entire barnyard of pigs with the munchies. They're marching to a 7-Eleven, a pig 7-Eleven, and buying goopy chicken burritos and now—I can see it so clearly—they're trying to heat them in the microwave, but their pudgy pig paws get stuck in the microwave door so they start squealing wildly, as pigs are wont to do, until the clerk, a pig himself, waddles over and asks them, in pigspeak, to please keep the racket down because this is, after all, a 7-Eleven and not a barnyard or something.

These are the kind of thoughts I find myself having in Bhutan. It might be the altitude, but I think it's something more than that. This place gives license to my imagination. Most of the time I keep my imagination on a leash. In Bhutan, it runs wild, messing up the freshly mowed lawn and sometimes pooping where it shouldn't but also rewarding me in unexpected ways.

For all of these reasons, traveling in Bhutan requires a serious suspension of disbelief. Reality and fantasy live side by side. Sometimes they are indistinguishable.

I'm sitting at the hotel drinking tea, when Sangay, the hotel owner, says out of the blue, "My husband is the brother of the Dalai Lama."

"Really," I say, "he's the Dalai Lama's brother? I didn't know the Dalai Lama had a brother."

"No, not brothers now but in a previous life. My husband is the twelfth incarnation of a Tibetan lama."

This sort of confusion happens all the time in Bhutan. This life, a previous life, a next life. They all blur together, happily. Or take this exchange I had with one of the sweet young girls who works at my hotel.

"There has been so much rain lately," I say, making conversation.

"Yes, sir, that is because of Blessed Rainy Day. It's a festival we have every year to mark the end of the rainy season. After Blessed Rainy Day, there will be no more rain." She says this with utter certainty, as if she were explaining to a dullard that the sun always rises in the east.

The next day, the rain stopped.


Tashi and I decide to visit the weekend market, where every manner of vegetable and craft is sold: apples the size of your head and Buddhas by the bushel. Sitting at the entrance to the market is an astrologer. "Very good, very famous man," says Tashi. The man is squatting on the ground, a blanket spread out in front of him. It is then that I notice he is a leper. He is missing all of his fingers, only stubs remain. Yet he manages to hold a deck of fortune cards, each about the size of a bumper sticker.

He asks me to pick three cards. Then I roll three dice. The verdict: "What you're doing now is fine, everything will turn out fine. All your dreams will come true." I wonder if my favorable fortune has anything to do with the small fee I paid. I mention this to Tashi, who reassures me that the fortune-teller is "very good man, very respected." Later that evening, reading about the adventures in Bhutan of the British explorer Lord Ronaldshay, I discover that he encountered the same good fortune a century ago. "I was invited to make offerings to the deity and to throw the dice. I did so, and curiously enough threw three 'ones.' A throw which was immediately proclaimed by the presiding lama to be supremely lucky!"

The next morning, I wake after another fitful night's sleep and more disturbing, hazy dreams—it *is* the high altitude, I'm sure—and stumble downstairs for breakfast. I'm slurping up my runny eggs when I hear a deep baritone "Good morning." For a moment I think it's the TV, but when I spin around in my chair I am greeted by a smiling man with a shiny bald head and meaty cheeks. He's wearing a red vest and bright yellow shirt. He looks like the Dalai Lama's younger brother.

He is Barba Tulku, Sangay's husband, otherwise known by the honorific Rinpoche, which means "precious one." He's an expressive man, with kind eyes and a ferocious laugh. When he talks, his whole body shakes and wiggles. He hunches over to make a point, then springs up, then hunches again. Hunching and springing, he tells me his story.

A few days before he was born, several respected lamas visited his home. "Suddenly, springwater appeared in the garden, very white water, like milk. All the pots and pans filled with it. Then, a round rainbow appeared above the house." These are the classic signs, he says, that an incarnate was about to be born.

As a child, he began speaking Tibetan, even though he never studied the language, and the Bhutanese language is quite different from Tibetan.

He traveled to India when he was eighteen years old and met the Dalai Lama.

"The Dalai Lama took me aside and said, 'You are very special. Where did you learn Tibetan?' I told him I just knew it. He said, 'Come tomorrow morning.'" It was at that morning meeting when the Dalai Lama concluded the young man, the man with the ferocious smile, was a reincarnated lama from eastern Tibet.

The Dalai Lama took him under his wing, inviting him to study in the Indian town of Dharamsala, the capital of the Tibetan government in exile.

"It was a great opportunity to get the oral transmission; you can read and read the text to get some ideas, but you can be misled by written words. It is best if it is done orally."

I'm not sure what to make of this man with the soft eyes and convulsive laugh. Back home, stories of miracles and reincarnation and milky-white springwater would strike me as fanciful, possibly psychotic. I decide to change tacks.

"Are the Bhutanese people happy?"

He pauses a good long while before saying "Maybe" and laughs hard, his body shaking and convulsing so much I wonder if he's having some sort of seizure. I decide not to pursue the matter any further. I listen as he tells me more things, crazy things. About a hidden land where spiritual treasures are buried. About how he once meditated for three years, three months, and three days.

Then he tells me about someone who lived in Bhutan five hundred years ago, someone known as the Divine Madman. His name was Drukpa Kunley, and he was the Howard Stern of Tibetan Buddhism. A holy man unlike any other.

"He was an amazing man. He would go to wineshops and tease women. His mother would say, 'Kunley, why can't you be like your elder brother, who is always praying? He has a look of such concentration on his face.'

" 'No, Mother,' Kunley replied. 'My elder brother is looking for a toilet. That's why he is always making that face.' " Kunley was right, as he was about most things. His elder brother was constipated, not consecrated. The moral of the story, the Rinpoche explains: "We can not judge by action, only by motivation."

This is the first I had heard of Drukpa Kunley, the Divine Madman, but it was not the last. In fact, I was told you can't really understand Bhutan without understanding Drukpa Kunley. Mention his name, and people break into laughter. But it is no ordinary laughter. It is reverential laughter, if such a thing is possible.

Kunley belongs to a spiritual school of thought known as crazy wisdom. Every religion has its branch of crazy wisdom. The Christians have their Fools for Christ. The Muslims have their Sufi Mast-Qalanders. The Jews have Woody Allen. Yet none is as crazy, or as wise, as Drukpa Kunley.

I was determined to find out more about him. In an overstuffed bookstore in Thimphu, I found an English translation of his collected works. Some parts are ribald even by the raunchy standards of today. In one passage, Kunley "breaks wind like a dragon." On many occasions, he drops his drawers and employs his "flaming thunderbolt of wisdom." (Yes, it is what you think it is.) Drukpa Kunley was a womanizer extraordinaire, with a preference for virgins. Or, as he put it, "The best *chung* wine lies at the bottom of the pail / And happiness lies below the navel."

There was a point to Kunley's escapades. His outrageous behavior was meant to shock the Bhutanese people out of their stupor. Keith Dowman, who translated Kunley's adventures into English, says the point was that "emotion, particularly desire, is not to be suppressed, it is to be purified." In other words, the ancient Greeks turned upside down. Everything in excess, nothing in moderation.

I am late for my afternoon coffee with Linda Leaming, an American who has lived in Bhutan for the past nine years. Asia has attracted its share of spiritual seekers, or lama lickers as they're sometimes called, but Bhutan was closed to outsiders until the 1970s. Even after that, it was not an easy country to get to. You had to want it.

Linda Leaming wanted it. She sold everything she owned and moved from New York in order to teach English in Bhutan. As she tells it, she fell in love with Bhutan and then fell in love with a Bhutanese. She's been living here ever since.

She recommends a place called the Art Café, a new addition in Thimphu. It is light and airy, with overstuffed cushions and blond wood floors. We could be in any U.S. college town. I notice that the woman behind the counter is reading *The Tibetan Book of Living and Dying*. Like I said, we could be in any U.S. college town.

Linda flounces in, wearing a patterned scarf and buzzing with energy. Apparently, she's starved for fluent English conversation, and her words fly out rapid-fire.

"Spirituality is everywhere here," she says, tucking into a brownie. "It's in the rocks, it's in the trees." It's one of those comments that I would snicker at anywhere else. But not in Bhutan. As one writer put it: "There is no such thing as an inanimate object in Bhutan." Everything is imbued with a spirit. This comes less from their Buddhist beliefs and more from an animist faith called Bon. I always associated animism with a primitive sort of faith, but if you think about it, all things are animated with a life force, and that sounds rather progressive.

"Geography dictates life here," Linda continues. "Isolation has made Bhutan what it is."

"Is that a good thing or bad thing?"

"It's a good thing. The mountains, the isolation slow everyone down. The attitude is 'What to do, *la*.'"

Bhutan is the land of *la*. The monosyllabic word serves as all-purpose affirmation, honorific, and verbal tic. Mostly, it is a softener, appended to almost everything. *La* means "sir" but also "ya know." I like the way it sounds and, during my weeks in Bhutan, use it myself, but always self-consciously, never finding the right rhythm.

"What about you, Linda? Do you believe in all this Tantric mumbo jumbo?"

"Oh, yeah. I'm gone," she says. "I've made the leap of faith. When I first came here, I was the typical neurotic woman, pushing forty, and I said, 'I don't want to get old and bitter before my time.' Bhutan has calmed me down, slowed me down."

Then there it is again: death. A subject that, oddly, comes up an awful lot in my search for happiness. Maybe we can't really be happy without first coming to terms with our mortality.

Linda tells me how she had never really seen a dead body until she came to Bhutan. "I've seen a lot of death and suffering here," she says, her tone of voice signaling that this is not necessarily a bad thing. "Here, you think about death more often. People die more tragically, more openly. Dead bodies hang around for days." Then there is the discomfort of life in Bhutan. "I am cold; in the winter, I need to wear a coat inside my house. The strange thing is, it makes you feel alive."

Many Bhutanese men, Linda explains, go on three-year meditation retreats, like the Rinpoche did. For three years, three months, and three days, they do nothing but meditate. They don't even cut their hair. "And for three years they don't talk." That is a deal breaker for me. The longest I've ever gone without talking is nine hours. And I was asleep at the time.

The government strings electrical lines up to the places where the men meditate, in little wooden huts perched on the edge of a cliff. "What other country would spend $100,000 to wire this tiny place in the mountains? They would say, 'No, you come down here.'"

And that is the thing about Bhutan. They do things that don't make economic sense. Like forsaking millions of dollars in tourist revenue or refusing to sell valuable timber. The Bhutanese, poor as they are, do not bow to the gods of efficiency and productivity.

When I was leaving for my trip to Bhutan, a colleague wished me well. "I hope you have a productive trip," he said. At the time I thought nothing of it, but here in Bhutan it strikes me as absurd. A productive trip? Why not an enjoyable trip or a good one?

Finally, Linda grows silent. We sit in this silence for what seems like forever but is probably only about thirty seconds. Then, Linda looks at me and says: "You know, if you stay here long enough, you lose touch with reality."

"In a good way or a bad way?"

"I'm not sure. You decide."

I'm at breakfast the next morning when the Rinpoche drops by. He's holding something spherical, wrapped in newspaper. He unfurls it with a flourish. It is an apple. The biggest apple I've ever seen, the size of a Nerf basketball.

He hands it to me. I thank him, then ask him about his work as a faith healer. Apparently, people come from all over the world to see him. Western doctors do a lot of good, he says, but it would be better if they understood that not everything can be cured by medicine. He invites me to see him at work one day, and I eagerly accept.

"You see, everybody has a personal deity, every person, every child has a guru, and your guru shakes you to your own reality," and with this he shakes the chair next to him so hard I'm afraid it will break. He must have picked up on my skepticism. "You don't believe me, do you?"

I ask him how he knows all this to be true, since there is no proof of these things.

"You see this light?" he asks, gesturing toward a lamp over-head.

"Yes, I see it."

"But you cannot prove it. If you were born blind, you cannot see it. If you want proof, you will never be enlightened."

In America, few people are happy, but everyone talks about happiness constantly. In Bhutan, most people are happy, but no one talks about it. This is a land devoid of introspection, bereft of self-help books, and woefully lacking in existential angst. There is no Bhutanese Dr. Phil. There is, in fact, only one psychiatrist in the entire country. He is not named Phil and, I am sad to report, does not even have his own television show.

Maybe Plato was wrong. Maybe it is the examined life that is not worth living. Or, to put it another way, and to quote another dead white man: "Ask yourself if you are happy and you cease to be so." That was John Stuart Mill, the nineteenth-century British philosopher who believed that happiness should be approached sideways, "like a crab." Is Bhutan a nation of crabs? Or is this whole notion of Gross National Happiness just a clever marketing ploy, like the one Aruba dreamed up a few years ago. "Come to Aruba: the island where happiness lives." In other words, have I been scammed?

I don't think so. For starters, the Bhutanese aren't that sophisticated. They suffer from an excess of sincerity, a trait anathema to good marketing. The Bhutanese take the idea of Gross National Happiness seriously, but by "happiness" they mean something very different from the fizzy, smiley-face version practiced in the United States. For the Bhutanese, happiness is a collective endeavor.

The phrase "personal happiness" makes no sense to them or, as Karma Ura told me, "We don't believe in this Robinson Crusoe happiness. All happiness is relational."

A quick quiz. What do the following events have in common? The war in Iraq. The *Exxon Valdez* oil spill. The rise in America's prison population. The answer: They all contribute to our nation's gross national product, or what's now referred to as gross domestic product, or GDP, and therefore all are considered "good," at least in the dismal eyes of economists.

GDP is simply the sum of all goods and services a nation produces over a given time. The sale of an assault rifle and the sale of an antibiotic both contribute equally to the national tally (assuming the sales price is the same). It's as if we tracked our caloric intake but cared not one whit what kind of calories we consumed. Whole grains or lard—or rat poison, for that matter. Calories are calories.

GDP doesn't register, as Robert Kennedy put it, "the beauty of our poetry or the strength of our marriages, or the intelligence of our public debate." GDP measures everything, Kennedy concluded, "except that which makes life worthwhile." Nor does GDP take into account unpaid work, the so-called compassionate economy. An elderly person who lives in a nursing home is contributing to GDP, while one cared for by relatives at home is not. Indeed, he may even be guilty of reducing GDP if his caregivers are forced to take unpaid leave from work. You have to give economists credit. They have taken a vice—selfishness—and converted it into a virtue.

Recent research into happiness, or subjective well-being, reveals that money does indeed buy happiness. Up to a point. That point, though, is surprisingly low: about fifteen thousand dollars a year. After that, the link between economic growth and happiness evaporates. Americans are on average three times wealthier than we were half a century ago, yet we are no happier. The same is true of Japan and many other industrialized nations. Think about it as Richard Layard, a professor at the London School of Economics, has: "They have become richer, they work much less, they have longer holidays, they travel more, they live longer, and they are healthier. But they are no happier."

Enter Gross National Happiness, an idea first floated by Bhutan's King Wangchuk in 1973. It didn't really catch on, though, until a smart young journalist named Michael Elliott interviewed the king in 1986 for the *Financial Times*. The headline of the story couldn't have said it any plainer: "Bhutan King: Gross National Happiness More Important than Gross National Product."

Conventional economists probably thought that the king was suffering from a lack of oxygen up on his Himalayan perch. Or perhaps he was nibbling on the pig feed again. You can't measure happiness, and even if you could, how can a government have a happiness policy? It is absurd.

And yet the idea caught on with other developing countries and even among a few rich industrialized ones. Papers were written. Conferences were held. Praise was sung. "Bhutan is the first nation to officially say 'No' and the first to challenge the idea that money alone is absolutely good," writes Jeff Johnson in the compendium *Gross National Happiness and Development*.

John Ralston Saul, the Canadian philosopher, describes Gross National Happiness as a brilliant trick. "What it does is go 'Snap!' and changes the discourse. Suddenly you're talking about something else. You're not trying to amend the old discourse—you're

introducing a new discourse from the core; that's what's so important and clever about GNH."

Drukpa Kunley, the Divine Madman and trickster extraordinaire, would have loved Gross National Happiness. It is so absurd,
so outlandish, that it shakes us out of our stupor.

But what exactly is Gross National Happiness? What does
it look like? The best explanation I heard came from a potbel-
lied Bhutanese hotel owner named Sanjay Penjor. GNH, Penjor
told me, "means knowing your limitations; knowing how much
is enough." Free-market economics has brought much good to the
world, but it goes mute when the concept of "enough" is raised. As
the renegade economist E. F. Schumacher put it: "There are poor
societies which have too little. But where is the rich society that
says 'Halt! We have enough!' There is none."

Wealth is liberating, no doubt. It frees us from manual labor,
working in the fields under a merciless midday sun or flipping
burgers, the modern-day equivalent. But wealth can also stymie
the human spirit, and this is something that very few economists
seem to recognize. As Schumacher said, "The richer the society,
the more difficult it becomes to do worthwhile things without
immediate payoff." That is a radical and profound statement. In
a wealthy, industrialized society, one where we are supposedly
enjoying a bountiful harvest of leisure time, we are discouraged
from doing anything that isn't productive—either monetarily or in
terms of immediate pleasure. The Bhutanese, on the other hand,
will gladly spend a day playing darts or just doing nothing. For
yet another parallel with Shangri-La, witness this exchange in the
book between the British missionary, Miss Brinklow, and Chang,
Shangri-La's inscrutable host.

"What do lamas do?" she asks.

"They devote themselves, madam, to contemplation and the
pursuit of wisdom."

"But that isn't doing anything."

"Then, madam, they do nothing."

Albert Einstein once said, "No problem can be solved from

the same level of consciousness that created it." Economics is long overdue for the kind of radical shift in thinking that Einstein brought to his field of physics. Does Gross National Happiness represent such a breakthrough? Is it the elusive answer that so many of us have been looking for? Not necessarily, at least not yet, but it reframes the question. That matters more than you might think.

With Gross National Happiness the official policy of the government of Bhutan, every decision, every ruling, is supposedly viewed through this prism. Will this action we're about to take increase or decrease the overall happiness of the people? A noble aim, no doubt, but is it working? In order to find out, I needed to speak with someone from the government.

Easier said than done, it turns out. Considering they run a blip of a nation, a smudge on world maps (assuming it appears at all), Bhutanese officials play awfully hard to get. Never mind the king, revered as a living god and just about as accessible. I was aiming for the home minister, a man who doubles as roving happiness ambassador.

Alas, I was told the Honorable Home Minister was too busy to see me, so I do what any self-respecting journalist would do. I crash his party. The party is, to be precise, an event called "Feel GNH." It is sponsored by a group of Japanese do-gooders living in Bhutan. The home minister is the guest of honor. I take a seat in the first row. Everyone stands when the home minister enters. He is a trim man, late fifties I guess, with gray in all the right places and a dignified manner.

On the stage is a giant paper crane and a sign that says, "Love, emotion, feeling." Oh, no. I brace myself for an onslaught of mushiness. The Japanese do-gooders show a film about the American bombing of Nagasaki. Horrible images flash across the screen. Children with skin peeling off their bodies like a layer of clothing. Men whose eyes are dangling from their sockets. People in the audience steal glances at me, the only American present, as if I personally dropped the bomb.

I'm not sure what any of this has to do with happiness, other than underscoring the rather obvious point that a nuclear bomb dropped on a city will probably suppress happiness levels in said city. This is the problem—one of many—with Gross National Happiness. It is a fuzzy concept, easily co-opted by anyone with a cause—a good cause, perhaps, but still a cause. Once that happens, Gross National Happiness becomes just another slogan and not a new economic template, not a new way to live our lives.

The film is over, and everyone breaks for an intermission. I tail the home minister, who has made a beeline for the buffet table outside. He is balancing a plate of *momos* in one hand and a glass of apple juice in another when I make my move.

"What does Nagasaki have to do with Gross National Happiness?" I ask. Surprise flashes across his face. He is unhinged by my ambush—just for a moment, though, before finding his diplomatic footing.

"I truly believe that a country that is committed to happiness will not be bellicose; if we don't pursue a sustainable way of life, we will be fighting for resources. Not just for oil, and not necessarily between nations. It might be a fight for water between San Diego and Los Angeles."

He's moving back into the conference hall now. I tuck in behind him. Doesn't adopting a policy of national happiness place a burden on his small nation, a presumption of felicitousness that might be hard to live up to? I ask.

"Bhutan has never said we are a happy people," he parries. "What we are saying is we are committed to this process of Gross National Happiness. It is a goal."

"But many people in Bhutan, those in the villages, haven't even heard of Gross National Happiness," I counter.

"No, but they are living it."

Good answer. Maybe only clever, maybe more than that. I'm not sure. We chat for a few more minutes. Him picking at his *momos,* me leaning on the edge of my chair. Him, a tremendously important person from an insignificant nation. Me, an insignificant person from a tremendously important nation. Somehow, these two converse facts cancel each other out, creating an odd symmetry between us.

He talks about his trips to America, where he's greeted like a rock star in predictable places like Berkeley. ("It's amazing, packed halls everywhere.") He talks about the need to create happiness indexes. ("Governments only respond to data.") Now, he seems to have plenty of time for me, a little too much time, I think, considering he is the third-most powerful man in Bhutan. Finally, he finishes his last *momo*, and I take this as an excuse to say goodbye.

The Feel GNH event ends a while later with a traditional Bhutanese folk dance. Everyone forms a circle—the circle being the universal geometry of folk dances—and sways in unison to the melodic music. I'm on the sidelines when someone grabs my arm, and next thing I know I've transitioned from observer to participant. Normally, participation in pretty much anything that makes me queasy, but there is something inexplicably nice—there's no other word for it—about this simple folk dance. Arms up. One, two. Step to the right. Three, four. I was somewhere between five and six when I noticed the home minister swaying along with everyone else. Why, I wonder, is he doing this? Is this the Bhutanese equivalent of a politician yucking it up for the cameras at a softball game? Nope. There are no cameras. It occurs to me then that the home minister, the third-most powerful man in Bhutan, is dancing because everyone in Bhutan dances. Nothing more, nothing less.

As the music winds down and people begin to file out of the hall, I find myself thinking about home. American politicians were probably like this, long ago, before the consultants and the focus groups drained the sincerity from their veins. Before we confused form and substance.

The next morning, I wake early, shaken again by another bad dream that I can't remember. Today is a big day. I'm due to see the Rinpoche at work. After breakfast, I'm led up a muddy pathway to a door. I remove my shoes. (Given the amount of mud in Bhutan, this is pragmatic more than anything else.) There are two rooms in the house. One for spiritual healing, the other for TV viewing. The latter has overstuffed chairs and a large-screen Panasonic, blaring an Indian film.

I'm guided from TV room to healing room and told to sit and observe quietly. The room is a blaze of colors: deep blues and yellows. It looks like a Tibetan curio shop after an explosion. There is stuff everywhere. *Thangkas* and other paintings, musical instruments. Mostly, though, offerings from grateful (or hopeful?) patients. Money, of course, but also fruit, biscuits, and big plastic bottles of Coke and Fanta. On the wall hang necklaces—more offerings—and what looks like an Olympic gold medal. I later learn it is indeed an Olympic medal, a token of appreciation from an American swimmer suffering from Parkinson's disease.

Four or five men are in the room, sitting quietly. They have a court hearing later in the day and are here to better the odds of a ruling in their favor. It doesn't strike me as a particularly noble cause, but I keep my thoughts to myself. The men are kneeling and facing the Rinpoche, who is sitting on a kind of wooden altar, legs folded, eyes closed. He is chanting quietly and has a slightly pained look on his face, as if he were constipated. The men rise, as one, and the Rinpoche dribbles water on their foreheads. Then they leave. That's it.

I am now alone in the room with the Rinpoche, but he doesn't acknowledge me for a few minutes. He is still chanting, eyes closed. Suddenly, he speaks.

"This is Vaseline," he says, holding up a small jar for me to see. I wonder where he is going with this. "Before, we used to use cow's butter to spread the blessings. But this works much better. It's especially good for diseases, wounds and all."

I ask him to explain what is actually happening during a healing, what is going on in his head. "I am concentrating on a deity, not the Buddha, but the totality deity. It's like a reflection in the mirror. We dissolve, the deity and me, and we become one."

A middle-aged woman enters the room. She has a giant sore on one leg, which she props up on a bench. The Rinpoche, eyes closed tightly, chanting, blows in the direction of her leg. Then he gives her water, which she swishes in her mouth. He is still chanting when she places her offering, apples and biscuits, on the altar.

I am again alone with the Rinpoche. He opens his eyes. "You know, for these people I am a last resort. First, they prefer hospitals and the highest technology. They go to hospitals in Bangkok and America. Then, they come to me." He tells me the woman with the swollen leg used to be much worse before she started seeing him. "You see, I have to experience my own actions, if not in this life then the next," he says enigmatically. I'm about to ask him what he means by this when I hear a strange chiming sound. I've never heard anything quite like it. It's coming from the altar, near the Rinpoche's feet, and it's getting louder every second.

"Sorry," he says, reaching down and switching off his cellphone. "Where were we?"

"You were talking about experiencing your own actions."

He tells me a story. It's about a man who referred to his servant as a monkey—"Get me some tea, you monkey; take out the trash, monkey." In the next life, the man was reborn as—you guessed it—a monkey.

I like the story, but I'm not sure what it means beyond the obvious point that we reap what we sow. I decide to broach a sensitive subject. I ask the Rinpoche if he ever has any doubts about this healing business.

"No, I don't. I have helped thousands of people. I helped and that has brought me true joy and happiness." I'm jotting down his comments in my small black notebook when he looks at me and says, "You are always writing, writing in your notebook. You need to experience. Really experience." I'm getting every word—"always writing...need to experience"—when the irony dawns on me. I stop writing and look up. I mumble something lame about old habits dying hard.

"You see, everything is a dream. Nothing is real. You will realize that one day." Then he laughs and returns to his quiet chanting.

*     *     *

Thimphu may not have any traffic lights—or fast-food joints or ATMs—but it is still a capital city. A road trip is in order. The next morning, Tashi and our driver load up the Toyota and we head east. Our destination is Bumthang province, about two hundred miles from the capital. It's a journey that in most parts of the world would take five or six hours. In Bhutan, it takes two days.

The word "travel" stems from the same root as "travail" does. There's a reason for this. For centuries, traveling was equated with suffering. Only pilgrims, nomads, soldiers, and fools traveled.

Traveling in Bhutan still has that element of travail, of suffering. Even more so, that is, than economy class on the red-eye from L.A. to New York. In Bhutan, the roads don't subdue nature but are subdued by it, bend to its whims, curving and snaking around the mountains in a series of endless switchbacks. I find this meditative. For about ten minutes. Then, I find it nauseating. Now I know how a pair of socks feels on tumble dry. No wonder they abscond.

Then there are the animals. Bhutan's roads rival the best zoos in the world. We pass cows, wild boars, goats, horses, monkeys, and too many dogs to count.

At times, the journey is exhilarating. The sheer drop-offs make me feel like we are flying along the ridgelines, a feeling amplified by the birds that occasionally shadow us, like dolphins frolicking in the wake of a boat.

A few miles out of Thimphu, I encounter my first penises. Alarmingly lifelike, painted on the side of a house. There would be more penises, many more. Colorful penises. Monochromatic ones. Large ones, small ones. Penises dangling from rafters of a building, others swinging from the end of a bar like party favors. I say something to the effect of, "What's up with the penises, Tashi?"

Tashi explains that they are designed to ward off evil spirits. As

the owner of a penis myself, I can think of no body part less quali-
fied to ward off evil spirits than the penis. Penises stray and are
notoriously unreliable. They are vulnerable to injury and do not always rise to the occasion. Indeed, if anything, penises tend to attract
evil, not repel it. Better, I think, the Bhutanese use wooden thumbs
or toes or elbows—anything, for God's sake, except penises.

All of these penises, though, again remind me of Drukpa Kunley, the Divine Madman. It turns out that a temple devoted to
Kunley is nearby. It is popular with infertile couples.

We pull the Toyota into a small village. From there, Tashi
and I walk on a muddy path that takes us through rice paddies,
neatly arranged and impossibly yellow. We pass an old man with
a mouthful of betel juice. It's turned his lips ruby red. Leaves pro-
trude from his mouth. He looks like he's swallowed a rooster.
Tashi has a conversation with the man, but I can't imagine how,
given the explosion of colors and textures in his mouth.

Rooster man gives us directions to the temple, and we walk
on. We pass a sign that says "Happy Visit." A feeling of peace
washes over me, and I'm thinking this is it, this is happiness, when
I hear Tashi yell, "Stop, sir! Stop!" I'm about to say, "What is it
now, Tashi? Can't you see I'm enjoying a rare moment of bliss?"
when an arrow whizzes a few feet in front of me.

The Bhutanese love archery. They also love drinking. They
tend to combine their two passions, and this is worrying. I apologize to Tashi, and once the archer has moved on we continue our
trek up a muddy incline. Then there it is: the Divine Madman's
temple. It's nothing fancy, as Drukpa Kunley would have insisted.
We walk inside the temple, and Tashi prostrates himself several
times, touching his forehead to the ground, then springing to his
feet, then back down again. Buddhist calisthenics. At the altar, offerings of money, nuts, and Kit Kat bars are piled high. I meet the
abbot, a rotund man, with a not-unpleasant smile.

"Yes, it's true," he says, when I ask about the temple doubling
as a fertility clinic. "Many women have come here to be blessed.
Women who could not bear children were then able to conceive."

He tells me of one American woman, forty-five years old, who was able to conceive only after being blessed by the Holy Dildo. That's what I call it. A fourteen-inch-long wooden phallus carved with impressive detail. Colorful pendants dangle off one end—the end that would be attached to a real man, if real men were endowed with fourteen-inch wooden penises.

The abbot shows me photos—smiling couples (some foreign, some Bhutanese) with their bundles of joy. Cards, too.

"Thank you for blessing us with the greatest joy of our lives...our son," signed Barbara Banks-Alterkruse.

I'm thumbing through the pile of cards when a couple of Bhutanese women show up. One by one, and with great gentleness, the priest touches the Holy Dildo to the crown of their heads. They seem pleased with the treatment and leave soon after.

Tashi asks if he can take time from his guide duties to have his fortune read by the abbot. I say sure. Tashi holds three dice to his forehead then rolls them. The abbot looks at the dice for a long second then tells Tashi that his wish will be granted. I roll the dice and am told that my wish, too, will be granted. Walking out of the temple, I ask Tashi if it is possible to get a bad fortune in Bhutan. "Oh, yes, sir, very much so."

Nearby, an old man is sitting on the ground, twirling beads in his hands and every now and then pushing a giant prayer wheel beside him. It's huge, the size of a refrigerator, and it takes a good heave to get it going. I ask him how long he's been doing this.

"I always do this," he says.

"Nothing else?"

"No, nothing else." It doesn't strike me as a well-rounded life, but who am I to question faith?

We stop for the night in the nearby town of Wangdue. The guesthouse is surprisingly nice. They even serve real coffee. I'm sitting on the terrace, overlooking a fast-moving river. It's a beautiful setting, and instinctively I reach for my notebook and camera. But I stop myself. The words of the Rinpoche echo in my head. Experience. You need to experience. He's right. Recording life is a poor substitute for living it. So for the next twenty minutes I sit on that terrace, listening to the roar of the river and doing nothing. Absolutely nothing. No notebook, camera, or tape recorder. Just me and life. And a vicious swarm of killer Bhutanese mosquitoes. That's enough experience for now.

We press on, driving farther east into the Bhutanese heartland. Something—or someone—is blocking the road. A dozen or so creatures with white bodies and dark faces scurry as our car approaches. Langur monkeys, Tashi tells me. He says that spotting them is a good sign.

"Is anything a bad sign in Bhutan, Tashi?"

"Yes, sir, the brown monkeys. If you see them, it is a bad sign."

The monkeys eventually tire of loitering on the road, and we continue. Every now and then we pass a hand-painted sign that says, simply, "Thanks." Thanks for what? The sign doesn't say, but I appreciate the thought nonetheless.

I can't take the hairpin turns anymore and ask the driver to stop. He pulls the Toyota over, and Tashi and I walk. Tashi confesses that he doesn't enjoy walking like this in the dark.

"Because of the bears, Tashi?" Sonam, the tour operator, had warned about them.

"No, sir, because of the demons. I am more afraid of the demons than the bears. From birth, we are taught to fear the demons."

Can this be healthy? I wonder. All of these demons running amok in the Bhutanese mind.

We're back in the Toyota, climbing and climbing to ever higher elevations. More than ten thousand feet. The road is only wide enough for one car at a time. Passing is negotiated through a series of elaborate, poetic hand gestures, and I'm reminded of what one Bhutanese told me back in Thimphu: "There is no room in

Bhutan for cocky assholes." He's right. Everything in this country requires cooperation. Harvesting the crops. Passing another car on the road.

In the west and in the United States especially, we try to eliminate the need for compromise. Cars have "personal climate controls" so that driver and passenger need not negotiate a mutually agreeable temperature. That same pair, let's say they're husband and wife, need not agree on the ideal firmness of their mattress, either. Each can set their own "personal comfort level." We embrace these technologies. Why shouldn't everyone enjoy their own personal comfort level, be it in a car or in a bed? I wonder, though, what we lose through such conveniences. If we no longer must compromise on the easy stuff, like mattresses, then what about the truly important issues? Compromise is a skill, and like all skills it atrophies from lack of use.

We arrive in Trongsa, a smidge of a town built along a hillside. The guesthouse is simple, just shy of fleabag. It's run by a rotund divorcée with a big smile. I ask her if she's happy, and she bursts into an even bigger smile and says, "Yes!" She reminds me of a laughing Buddha.

On the wall, a row of clocks shows the time in Tokyo, New Delhi, New York, and Bangkok. I am amused. No one in Trongsa cares what time it is in Trongsa, let alone in New York.

The next day, more driving. At one point, Tashi and I decide to get out of the Toyota and walk to a local temple. The sun is strong, but after two days on the road it feels good to be out of the Toyota.

"Sir," asks Tashi, "is it true that cowboys are very respected in your country?" I try to explain to him that there are not many cowboys left in my country. He seems a bit disappointed. Tashi asks if I want to hear a poem he learned to recite in school. I say okay.

"Climbing on the hillside beneath the shadow trees..."

I can barely understand the words—"beneath" sounds like

"bequeath"—but Tashi is proud. "If we didn't recite it properly, the teacher would beat us mercilessly," he says, shadowboxing to underscore his point. I suspect Tashi was hit many times, and I wonder if it explains a few things about him. I ask Tashi if this sort of thing still happens in Bhutan. "Only in the rural areas, sir." I find this little solace; 80 percent of Bhutanese live in rural areas.

As we walk, silently, toward a nearby monastery, I realize how fond I have grown of Tashi. His annoying habits now seem endearing. Has he changed, or have I?

The next morning, I am walking alone along a ridgeline. The air is bracing and fresh. I feel good. Then I remember Sonam and her warning about bears. I no longer feel so good. When did I become so afraid of nature? Why do I feel safer in the frenzy of Tokyo or New York than here in the Himalayan foothills, among the fir trees and chirping birds? I am shaking my head, bemused by my childish trepidations when I see an object, a very large object, moving off in the distance. I can't make it out completely, a tree is blocking my view, but I'm not about to find out. I spin on my heels and start walking briskly in the opposite direction. Oh, heck, I'm not walking briskly. I'm running, damn it!

After a few dozen yards, I turn around and see that I have been running from a large and ferocious...cow. I decide to give myself a time-out. I walk toward a nearby monastery, sit on a ledge, and close my eyes. Karma Ura is right. There is a theater in my mind. Only it is Off-Off-Broadway. The critics have panned it. It is, I know, time to close the show, but I don't know how.

I'm more successful in taking Karma Ura's advice in another matter. I decide to visit the village where he grew up, as he had suggested. His family home is a solid house, with sturdy wood floors. There is virtually no furniture, though, except for a knee-high table called a *chokse*. Karma Ura's mother, seventy-nine years old, is sitting at the table, a dark wool blanket draped on her lap, a book open in front of her. She had been praying.

Her skin is lined but retains an elasticity. She is missing more than a few teeth. She welcomes us warmly and gestures for me to take a seat on a cushion on the floor. Unlike her son, she doesn't speak a word of English. Tashi offers to translate. Which is a good thing, for Mrs. Ura turns out to be a talker.

"I moved to this village when I was twenty years old. As a child, we traveled by horse. We would journey for miles, twice a week, to get basic supplies like salt. Now we have cars and a paved road and electricity."

"Was there anything better about life back then?" I interject.

"No," she says, as if I were a dolt. "Life is better now. Except for television. That is both good and bad."

I ask about the king's plans to introduce democracy in Bhutan. Is she ready for it?

"It can't be good for the people. There will be corruption and violence. I've seen the TV pictures from Nepal and India, people throwing stones at the police, and the police shooting at the people, police firing tear gas and worse. Nothing productive, nothing good, will come of this democracy. We are begging our king, please, we don't want democracy." A few months later, back in Miami, I would read a small news item in *The New York Times:* The king had abdicated to his son. Mock elections were held. Real ones weren't far off. I thought of Mrs. Ura, who surely wouldn't be pleased.

She lifts herself up, with a nimbleness that surprises me, and offers tea. I decline, but she insists. "What would my son say if I didn't offer you tea?" Mothers are the same everywhere, I think.

Back in the Toyota, heading back toward Thimphu, Tashi tells me a story. In 1999, six boys went hiking at a lake. They threw rocks and litter into the lake. Suddenly, a fog appeared, and the boys lost their way. Three survived, three died. Tashi is convinced it's because they had disturbed a deity, the lady of the lake.

"Many people believe it. You're not supposed to pollute lakes."

"What about rivers?"

"Rivers are different, sir."

We stop for one last night. Our travels and travails are nearly over. After dinner, I'm savoring a Red Panda when I hear a familiar accent. American. Suffolk County, Long Island, to be precise. A small group of American tourists. Terri and her husband, Marty, invite me to join them. I tell them that I am writing about happiness in Bhutan, and everyone perks up. I tell them about the government's policy of Gross National Happiness. Marty is skeptical. "How can you measure happiness? It's what you believe that makes you happy, and you can't measure beliefs."

The conversation turns to the huge economic disparity between the United States and Bhutan. The average American earns nearly a hundred times more than the average Bhutanese. "Remember that house we saw on Long Island?" Marty says to his wife. "That woman had an entire walk-in closet just for her shoes. Here, some people don't even have a single pair."

"Yes, but they seem to be happy," says Terri. "Even those women with a baby strapped to their backs, breaking rocks on the side of the road, they seem happy. They smile when we drive by."

I don't have the heart to tell Terri that those women are neither Bhutanese nor happy. They are Indian laborers imported to do the jobs the Bhutanese don't want to do. But her point is valid. People in Bhutan do seem happy.

"So maybe we don't need as much as we think we do in order to be happy," I suggest.

"No, these people just don't know any better," she says. "If you took them to America, they would see what they're missing."

I tell her that of the Bhutanese who study abroad, 90 percent return to Bhutan, forsaking western-style incomes for life here in Bhutan. Terri is silent, clearly confused. Finally, she says, "Now, why would they do a thing like that?"


We're back in Thimphu. The Toyota pulls up to the guesthouse. I rest for a few minutes, but I'm in a hurry. I only have two more days in Bhutan, and there are some people I need to see again, some questions I need answered.

Karma Ura lives high in the hills overlooking the capital. When I asked directions on the phone, he said, "Just ask anyone where I live. They will know." He was right, and a few minutes later the Toyota glides up to a walled compound. A servant leads me through a corrugated-tin gate into a large yard, where two young girls are bouncing on a trampoline. I'm then directed to a room enclosed in floor-to-ceiling glass. The room is sparse; other than the Dell laptop in one corner, it's no different, really, from the room in the village where I met Karma's mother.

Karma is wearing slacks and a vest, no *gho* today, and is sitting on the floor with a wool blanket draped across his lap. He looks pale, and I wonder if he is not well. He offers me walnuts, which he expertly cracks open with a hammer.

We make small talk, then I ask him about the story Tashi told me, about the lady of the lake. Do people really believe that?

"Yes, they do," says Karma. "And it is a good thing." The way he sees it, these deities—"greenhouse deities," he calls them— represent the highest form of environmentalism. People in the United States don't pollute in part because they fear they will be fined. People in Bhutan don't pollute because they fear the greenhouse deities. Is one way of thinking really better than the other?

Karma is on his feet now. He nimbly catches a fly in his palms and carries it outside, where he releases it. He's still talking. He must have picked up on my skepticism, for he tells me a story about the surgery to remove the tumors in his stomach. "The surgery went well; they removed the tumors, but for two years my stomach wouldn't function properly. The doctors attributed it to 'postsurgical complications.' What does that mean? It means they don't know what the problem is, haven't a clue. But they need to call it something, so they give it a name. Postsurgical complications. Is that really so different from people believing that there are deities living in lakes?"

He asks me to stay for dinner. We sit on the floor eating rice and green beans that he grew in his backyard. I ask the question that Bhutan demands: Can money buy happiness?

Karma answers quickly (or so it seems; either his speech has speeded up or my tolerance for silence has grown): "Money sometimes buys happiness. You have to break it down, though. Money is a means to an end. The problem is when you think it is an end in itself. Happiness is relationships, and people in the west think money is needed for relationships. But it's not. It comes down to trustworthiness." I'd heard the same thing in Switzerland. Trust is a prerequisite for happiness. Trust not only of your government, of institutions, but trust of your neighbors. Several studies, in fact, have found that trust—more than income or even health—is the biggest factor in determining our happiness.

That's not to say that money is irrelevant. A little money can buy a lot of happiness up to a point, as I said. The problem is that Bhutan has not yet reached that point. It is still on the upslope of the happiness/income curve. If the social scientists are right, the most efficient way to make someone from Bhutan happy is to give them more money, at least until they're earning about fifteen thousand dollars a year.

But by then a way of life has taken hold, and it's difficult to shift gears—not only for Bhutan but for all of us. Running after money has brought us happiness in the past, so we assume that it will do so in the future. That's like saying to a starving man, "Here, eat this hamburger, you'll feel better. That was good, yes? Now, here, eat another and another and another."

The next day Linda invites me to dinner at her apartment. She, too, lives in the hills overlooking Thimphu. She lives near the four queens but, as she is quick to point out, not like a queen. Her apartment is small but comfortable. She introduces me to her husband, Namgay. "I married the noble savage," she says affectionately.

Over dinner, she recounts Namgay's first visit to a Sharper Image store in the United States. He was blown away. Here was a store stuffed with wondrous things designed to fulfill needs that Namgay didn't even know he had. He would pick up each item—say a combination juicer/shiatsu massager—and study it with genuine awe. "But the thing is," says Linda, "he had no desire to buy anything, to possess anything. He was perfectly content to admire it, then put it down and walk away."

We are lounging now on big, comfortable chairs, drinking very bad Indian wine and admiring the view of a temple and Thimphu below. Linda is telling me about the two things she misses most about life in America, the First Amendment and working toilets, when suddenly she shifts gears and asks me point-blank: "So, are you happy here?"

This catches me off guard. Am *I* happy here? Though I've had some happy moments, I hadn't really asked myself that question. I'd been too busy running around trying to ascertain if the Bhutanese are happy. I answer yes, but without any real conviction. I'll need to think about this.


But first there is drinking to be done. My last evening in Bhutan, and I've convinced Tashi to join me for a beer. After a few sips of Red Panda, Tashi turns red and, uninhibited, confesses that not all of his guests are equally wonderful. The German tourists are the worst. Big complainers. More confessions: Tashi is worried about his future. He's twenty years old and not married yet. In Bhutan, that's old. He's also worried about the future of his country, with more hotels going up all the time and the smell of money in the air. Good for business, Tashi concedes, but not necessarily happiness. As we say good night, Tashi hands me a gift: a cylindrical package wrapped in plain brown paper.

Lying in bed that night, I wonder if I have fallen too hard for Bhutan, if my journalist's critical eye has gone fuzzy. Have I, dare I say, become a lama licker?

I recall the words of another Bhutanese tour guide I met one day. "People here say they're happy, but they're not. They have problems. They are only telling you 50 percent of the truth." I'm thinking 50 percent happy is not so bad when I remember Tashi's gift. It's long and shaped like a dog bone. Why would Tashi give me a dog bone? I unwrap it and discover it is not a dog bone but a phallus, fourteen inches long, complete with testicles. In any other country, if my guide bought me a giant wooden phallus as a souvenir I would be concerned. In Bhutan, I am touched.

The next morning, I wake before dawn and meet Tashi downstairs. A few minutes later, our driver pulls the Toyota up to the tiny terminal building and Tashi announces, "We have arrived at the airport, sir."

I'm going to miss this guy. We shake hands goodbye. I use two hands, one cupped over the other, and make a point of prolonging the moment. I pay attention.

I clear customs and security quickly and find myself with plenty of time on my hands before my flight. It's raining outside, and I wonder if it's safe to take off in this weather, with the mountains so close, so high.

I think about plane crashes more than most people. I know how to fly planes, small ones, and while you'd think this would be a source of great reassurance, for me it has the opposite effect. Every shake or bump or something not quite right strikes fear in me. Is that flap extended properly? Are we descending too rapidly? Doesn't that left engine sound funny?

Yet sitting here in this airport terminal that looks like a Buddhist temple, watching an archery match on a small TV screen and drinking bad instant coffee, I am overwhelmed with a feeling that is alien to me: calm. Not hashish- or alcohol-induced calm, but the real thing. I take out my pen and write the following words in my notebook, using large letters, scrawling across an entire page so that when they find my body in the wreckage it will be easier to spot.

I would not have done anything differently.

All of the moments in my life, everyone I have met, every trip

I have taken, every success I have enjoyed, every blunder I have made, every loss I have endured has been just right. I'm not saying they were all good or that they happened for a reason—I don't buy that brand of pap fatalism—but they have been right. They have been...okay. As far as revelations go, it's pretty lame, I know. Okay is not bliss, or even happiness. Okay is not the basis for a new religion or self-help movement. Okay won't get me on *Oprah*. But okay is a start, and for that I am grateful.

Can I thank Bhutan for this breakthrough? It's hard to say. Bhutan is not Shangri-La, of that I am sure, but it is a strange place, peculiar in ways large and small. You lose your bearings here, and when that happens a crack forms in your armor. A crack large enough, if you're lucky, to let in a few shafts of light.

# Chapter 4

# QATAR

## Happiness Is a Winning Lottery Ticket

Something strange was happening. It was late 2001, and a reclusive Arab sheikh was jetting around Europe from one art gallery to another, scooping up masterpieces—and paying top dollar. By some accounts, he spent $1.5 billion in just a couple of years. If the sheikh showed up at an auction, other collectors didn't bother to place a bid. They knew they didn't stand a chance. "For him, the sky was the limit," bemoaned one collector.

Who was this mystery sheikh?

His name, it turned out, was Saud bin Mohammed al-Thani, a member of Qatar's royal family. His buying spree signaled that Qatar, a flyspeck of a nation, had arrived. Qatar was loaded.

As a student of happiness, I followed the sheikh's profligate ways with interest. Maybe the Bhutanese had it all wrong. Maybe the secret to happiness *is* money. Lots of money. And if money can buy happiness, or at least rent it for a while, then surely Qatar, by some measures the wealthiest country in the world, must also be the happiest. The clincher was that the word "Qatar," when written in Arabic script, resembles a sideways smiley face. Sort of, if you squint a little. Anyway, I decided to book a ticket to Doha, Qatar's capital.

Little did I know how the trip would shake my perceptions of happiness. I would leave Qatar a few weeks later with a very expensive pen, an intense appreciation for swim-up bars, and two unexpected conclusions: taxes are good, families are bad. But I get ahead of myself.

If you're going to investigate the relationship between money and happiness, it would be intellectually dishonest to do so on the cheap. I fly business class. I'm surprised to find myself alone in that section of the plane. Where are the Qataris? Certainly they can afford business class. Later, I discovered the Qataris were ensconced in the front of the plane, in first class; no Qatari would deign to fly mere business class.

With the entire section to myself, I am the center of attention. The flight attendants practically fall over one another proffering hot towels or serving me macadamia nuts warmed to the perfect temperature or inquiring whether Mr. Weiner would care for another glass of Brut. Why, yes, Mr. Weiner would.

The service on Qatar Airways is so fawning—borderline pornographic, really—that the pleasure of the experience, like all of my pleasurable experiences, is stained with a thin, filmy layer of guilt. Down there, a mere six miles below, are the less fortunate, lugging pails of well water, and if they are eating macadamias at all, they're probably served at room temperature. The horror!

I press a button on my infinitely adjustable Personal Seating System and swivel so I can peer at these poor souls. I see only desert. Sand, no people. A wave of relief washes over me. My guilt fades, though it doesn't disappear entirely. It never does.

Curiously, none of the flight attendants on Qatar Airways is from Qatar. Instead, they possess that ambiguously ethnic look prized by global news networks and international modeling agencies. The entire crew is from Someplace Else, but exactly which Someplace Else I couldn't say. That, I suspect, is the idea. Qatar Airways swaddles you in a fluffy bathrobe of luxury, hoping you don't reach the uncomfortable, inevitable conclusion: Qatar has outsourced its own airline.

It works. I couldn't care less that hardly any Qataris work

for Qatar Airways—an airline where no frill is too frivolous, no expense too expensive. Or silly. When we land in Doha, I am ferried from plane to terminal, a distance of about a hundred yards, in a BMW sedan that smells brand-new. I barely have time to sink into the leather seat and caress the wood trim when it's time to get out again. Why bother? Ahh, I was asking the wrong question. In Qatar, nobody asks why. Why? Because you can. That's why.

I clear customs and step outside the terminal building. I immediately run smack into a wall of heat. Heat has velocity. Anyone who managed to stay awake during high school physics knows that heated molecules move more quickly than cooler ones. But Qatari heat also has mass. It is a solid, a thing, that presses down on you. Much like gravity, only not as pleasant.

The heat, it turns out, is the only solid thing in Qatar. The rest of the nation is ephemeral, gaseous. Which makes perfect sense. Qatar is a nation built on gas. Underneath the sand, and in the warm waters of the Persian Gulf, lie the world's third-largest reserves of natural gas, enough gas to heat every home in America for the next hundred years.

Outside the terminal, waiting for a taxi, I am confronted by a collage of faces, in every hue imaginable: ruby red, pitch-black, ghost white, sunburned. Some faces are invisible, covered by a veil of black cloth. Qatar, like Saudi Arabia, follows the severe branch of Islam known as Wahhabism, and nearly all Qatari women cover themselves, in public, from head to toe. The Qataris, though, are quick to point out that they practice "Wahhabi-lite" and have considerably more fun than the Saudis. The women in Qatar, for instance, can drive and even vote.

The collage of faces is accompanied by a jumble of tongues: the singsong of Tagalog, the jackhammer rhythm of Tamil, and one that I find particularly misplaced—a New Jersey baritone. It's an off-duty U.S. soldier yucking it up with his pals. They are here as a respite from the war in Iraq. I can't help but feel sorry for them. Qatar is no Bangkok, the R-and-R spot for GIs during the Vietnam War. I see other westerners: pasty-skinned white guys in shorts, with bellies that jut out over their belts like shelves. Oil and gas workers or, as it's universally pronounced, oilngas.

I'm staying at the Four Seasons Hotel. If one is serious about researching the nexus of money and happiness, one needs to be consistent. I step into the lobby, which is built with the scale and grandeur of a cathedral or, I suppose, a mosque. I make it only a few yards before I'm accosted by a small army of eager attendants, impeccably dressed in cream-colored blazers. They are cloyingly polite, escorting me to reception as if leading a bride down the aisle.

The attentiveness extends to the bathroom, where an attendant turns on the water for me and hands me a towel. Then he thanks me. For what? For urinating? It was no trouble, really. I do it all the time.

I decide to check out the hotel bar, which is called, imaginatively, Bar. I'm attended to by a waiter—Indonesian, I think, but can't be sure—whose movements are a study in efficiency and grace. Nothing is wasted.

I order a Scotch and the gazpacho. A few minutes later, he brings three crystal flutes, arranged in a sort of three-tiered, wedding-cake deal. I'm about to point out his mistake when I realize that, wait a second, this *is* my gazpacho.

As I eat—no, drink—my soup, I ponder the nature of happiness. We equate happiness with comfort, but is there really any connection? Is there a point where excess comfort actually dilutes our contentment? More prosaically, is it possible for a hotel to be too nice? And is it considered uncouth to slurp one's gazpacho through a straw?

The big question, though, is: What happens to a person's soul when he or she indulges in excessive, obscene—truly obscene— amounts of craven luxury? I didn't know the answer to that question, but my American Express card and I were determined to find out.

Ours is not the first era to equate money and happiness. The ancient Greeks, while contributing much to civilization, were not above some good old-fashioned avarice. "The early Greeks spoke of the gods as...blessed or happy—not least because of their material prosperity," writes Darrin McMahon in his excellent history of happiness. And so it went. Throughout the ages and around the world, people paid lip service to that old saw about money not buying happiness and then proceeded to act precisely as if it does.

If you were to devise an experiment to study the relationship between sudden wealth and happiness, you would need to invent something like Qatar. Take a backward, impoverished spit of sand in the Persian Gulf, add oodles of oil, dollops of natural gas, and stir. Or imagine that you and your extended family are rich. Wildly rich. Now double that amount. Next, imagine that your family has its own country somewhere in the Arabian peninsula. That fairly describes Qatar. It is, in effect, less of a country and more of a family. A tribe with a flag.

Like all wealthy families, the Qatari family squabbles over money and privilege. Except instead of who gets the house in the Berkshires, it's who gets the palace in Doha and who gets to be foreign minister this year.

Qatar is roughly the size of Connecticut. Unlike Connecticut, though, there is no old money in Qatar. Only shiny new money. Fifty years ago, Qataris eked out livings diving for pearls and herding sheep. Today, the only pearls they encounter are the million-dollar ones wrapped around their necks, and the only sheep they come across are the sheepskin seat covers on their new Mercedeses. Rarely before in history has one nation grown so wealthy so quickly.

By many of the measures we typically use to gauge human progress, life in Qatar has improved by leaps and bounds. People live longer, healthier lives—although obesity is an increasing problem. They are better educated and can afford to travel abroad (first class, of course) whenever they want. But these objective measures are not the same as the subjective measure we call happiness. Here the verdict is far from clear.

Qataris, like all *nouveau riche*, possess a strange mix of arrogance and insecurity. What they crave, most of all, is validation. Qatar is using money to accomplish this goal. Doha resembles one giant construction site. They are building forty-one hotels, 108 skyscrapers, and fourteen stadiums. And that is just in the next couple of years. No wonder the country suffers from a cement shortage.

I'm sitting in the lobby, staring at the domed ceiling. Blazered attendants of indeterminate nationality hover nearby, discreetly, just in case I might need something. Adrift in a faraway land, there is nothing quite as reassuring as the hermetic comfort of a five-star hotel. Long driveways, modern-day moats, separate you from the country out there. Once inside the sliding glass doors, life is air-conditioned in every sense of the word. The message is clear: Why leave this palace when everything you need is right here? Within the hotel compound, you can eat, drink, exercise, fax, e-mail, get married, have a massage, hold meetings, play tennis, go swimming, shop, get divorced, receive medical attention, book an airline ticket, and so much more. In the developing world, what we used to call the Third World, hotels serve as meeting grounds for the local elite. In Manila, I once reported an entire story for NPR without leaving my hotel. Everyone I needed to interview was in the lobby, sitting in high-backed chairs, sipping lime juice, smoking cigars, and trading gossip.

Yet here in this oh-so-nice hotel, where my every need is attended to instantly, sometimes before I even know I have such a need, I am not happy. What's wrong with me? After a while, a word pops into my head, and given my surroundings, it's an unexpected word. "Tomb." Yes, that's it. The hotel is a very nice, tastefully appointed, climate-controlled tomb. Tombs are for dead people. And I'm not dead yet.

I decide to call Lisa, an American who's been living in Qatar for the past year. She works for a major American university that has set up a Doha campus, part of something called Education City. It is based on a simple and logically irrefutable premise: Why send Qataris to American universities when you can send the American universities to Qatar? Students get the same education and earn the same degree they would in the United States only without the frat parties or the theater groups or, for that matter, any fun at all.

I'm waiting for Lisa to pick me up. From my hotel window, I have a good view of the traffic below. You can tell a lot about a country by the way people drive. Getting someone behind the wheel of a car is like putting them into deep hypnosis; their true self comes out. *In vehicle veritas*. Israelis, for instance, drive both defensively and offensively at the same time, which is, come to think of it, the way Israelis do pretty much everything. A policeman in Israel once pulled me over. I couldn't imagine why. Was I speeding? No, he explained, I was driving too slowly. Not ridiculously slowly, mind you, just too slowly for a nation of maniac drivers. Miami is no better. (I seem to be drawn to places with bad driving.) Driving there is like driving a bumper car, and as for using your turn signal, don't. As humorist and Miami resident Dave Barry once quipped, it's "a sign of weakness." Miami drivers aren't passive-aggressive. They're aggressive-aggressive. Or take the Swiss. Normally, they are upright and boring but get them behind the wheel of a car and they become...upright and boring. Oh well. Sometimes people are exactly the way they seem.

Qataris, however, are in a league of their own. The State Department issues travel advisories for Americans venturing overseas. Normally, these warnings are reserved for dangers like terrorism and civil war, yet the State Department flags the driving in Qatar, which it describes as an "extreme sport."

A Qatari driver indicates he wants to pass you by getting within six inches of your rear bumper, flashing his high beams repeatedly, and honking loudly until you relent. If you still don't get the idea, he might rear-end you. Why? Because he can. The Qatari passport is like a get-out-of-jail-free card. One expatriate told me that she was sitting at a traffic light when a Qatari rear-ended her. The judge deemed her to be at fault—again, mind you, she wasn't moving at the time. In Qatar, the foreigner is always at fault.

Foreigners living in Qatar react to the atrocious driving by either complaining constantly or by going native. Lisa, I soon learned, went native.

She's moving at a fast clip when she maneuvers her Audi up the hotel driveway. I step out of the Tomb and into the heat. I sweat, just for an instant, and it feels good. Physiological confirmation that I am indeed still alive.

Lisa is happy to see a new face. Doha, despite its wealth, remains a small town and suffers from the claustrophobia that afflicts all small towns.

"Have you noticed something about Doha?" asks Lisa, accelerating the Audi to an alarming rate of speed.

"You mean besides the absurd amount of money, the oppressive heat, and the bad driving?"

"No 7-Elevens," she says, cryptically. "Think about it. Where are the 7-Elevens?"

She's right. Doha has plenty of Starbucks and designer clothing stores but not a single 7-Eleven or any of the other convenience stores found in most affluent countries. Lisa has a theory. Doha has no 7-Elevens because Qataris have no need for the convenience of a convenience store. The servants—every Qatari has at least one—do the shopping, and, being servants, their convenience isn't anyone's concern.

Or take the case of a professor, another foreigner, who was teaching a class on business and the environment. One day, he told his students about hotels that have begun using ecofriendly laundry detergent. He was met with a sea of blank faces. Not only did the students fail to comprehend "ecofriendly," they were stumped by "laundry detergent" as well. They had never seen the stuff, barely heard of it. Laundry was something the servants did.

Most people who live in Qatar are servants, Lisa explains, as she nearly sideswipes an SUV. There is a clearly defined hierarchy of servitude. At the bottom of the ladder are laborers from Nepal: ruby-skinned men with scarecrow bodies and a knack for scaling scaffolding without safety cables. You see them toiling in the brutal midday sun, not complaining one bit because, hey, it's better than being in Nepal. Next come the Indians. Darker skinned, they drive taxis and don't complain much either. Then, there are the Filipinos who, with their English-language skills, work in hotels and restaurants. "I'm also a servant," confides Lisa, accelerating through a red light. "Just a higher grade of servant."

Lisa and I arrive at the restaurant. I'm a bit shaken by her driving but think it best not to mention anything. We step out of her air-conditioned car into the solid heat, sweat for a few seconds, then enter the über-air-conditioned restaurant.

Life in Qatar is a continuous series of air-conditioned moments, briefly interrupted by unair-conditioned intervals. It is crucial that these intervals, otherwise known as the outdoors, be kept to an absolute minimum. Qataris accomplish this in imaginative ways. They are capable, for instance, of converting any store into a drive-through. It works like this: A Qatari drives up to a store, any store, and honks his horn repeatedly and forcefully. Within a matter of seconds, a Pakistani or Indian or Sri Lankan worker scurries outside into the blazing heat and takes the Qatari's order, then returns a few minutes later with the merchandise. The entire transaction takes place without once breaching the sanctity of the air-conditioned environment. At least for the Qatari driver, that is.

I read somewhere that Qatar is 98.09 percent desert. I wonder what the other 1.91 percent is. Mercedes, perhaps. The sand dunes can reach heights of two hundred feet and, due to the winds, are constantly migrating. Qatar, in other words, is never exactly the same from one moment to the next. No wonder people here feel so rootless. The ground—the sand—is literally shifting beneath their feet.

Deserts are not considered happy places. We speak of cultural deserts, deserts of the soul. Deserts are empty places, harsh and unforgiving. Then again, wonderful, unexpected things sometimes bloom in the desert. Two of the world's great religions—Islam and Judaism—took root in the desert. Arab literature, in particular, is replete with homages to desert life. Ibn Khaldoun, the great Arab intellectual of the fourteenth century, wrote lovingly of desert people: "The desert people who lack grain and seasoning are healthier in body and better in character than the hill people who have everything." Khaldoun believed that the great curse of civilization is not war or famine but humidity: "When the moisture, with its evil vapors ascends to the brain, the mind and body and the ability to think are dulled. The result is stupidity, carelessness and a general intemperance." An accurate description, too, of the inhabitants of New York City during the dog days of August.

Over lunch, Lisa drops hints of a troubled past. I suspect alcohol and drugs, possibly in tandem and certainly to excess, but it seems rude to pursue it. I wouldn't be surprised, though. Places like Qatar attract people running away from something: a bad marriage, a criminal record, an inappropriate e-mail sent companywide, and other sundry unhappiness. Conventional wisdom tells us this doesn't work. We take our baggage with us. I'm not so sure. Travel, at its best, transforms us in ways that aren't always apparent until we're back home. Sometimes we do leave our baggage behind, or, even better, it's misrouted to Cleveland and is never heard from again.

After lunch, Lisa drops me off at the Tomb. I am immediately accosted by a platoon of jacketed attendants, inquiring about my day and whether I need anything, want anything, or anticipate needing or wanting anything in the near future. That's it. I do need something. I need to check out, and I need to check out now. I'm sure at some point down the road—when I am, say, dead—I will find a tomb very appealing indeed. But not now. Not yet.

I pack my bags and hand the well-dressed man at reception my credit card.

"Was everything satisfactory?" he asks, noting that I am checking out several days early.

"Oh, much more than satisfactory," I say. "Much, much more."

He gives me a slightly perplexed look before reverting to his corporate smile. A few minutes later, I'm checking into another hotel—no fleabag, mind you, but not a tomb, either. No one greets me at the lobby entrance. A good start. I notice that the ceiling paint is beginning to peel. There's a small crack in one wall. A wave of relief washes over me.

My new hotel, though, does possess one brilliant luxury: a pool with a swim-up bar. If there is any invention that makes one feel more decadent, more thoroughly leisured than a swim-up bar, I have yet to find it. As I dog-paddle up to this particular swim-up bar, I find myself speculating on the genesis of such a brilliant thing. I can picture the meeting, the young hotel executive's voice cracking, "And we could put a bar right in the pool and people, you see, could swim up to the bar and order drinks, right there, in the water." Then that painfully awkward moment, with the other young execs at the table eyeing the boss who says nothing for a really long time but eventually blurts out: "Brilliant. I love it." Yes, I'm sure that's the way it happened.

I'm sipping my Corona, waist-deep in water that is blissfully cool. Surprisingly cool, given that it's 120 degrees outside. It turns out that the water is cooled to a pleasant temperature. Even the swimming pools in Qatar are air-conditioned.

I'm letting the enormity of that concept sink in when I realize that Qatar seems oddly familiar, as if I've seen many Qatars before. Was I a desert nomad in a previous life? No, that's not it. Then it dawns on me. The entire nation of Qatar is like a good airport terminal: pleasantly air-conditioned, with lots of shopping, a wide selection of food, and people from around the world.

In transit. If two sweeter words exist in the English language, I have yet to hear them. Suspended between coming and going, neither here nor there, my mind slows, and, amid the duty-free shops and PA announcements, I achieve something approaching calm. I've often fantasized about living in Airport World. Not one airport, mind you, like the Tom Hanks character in that movie, but a series of airports. I would just keep flying around the world, in a state of suspended aviation. Always coming, never arriving.

But here, in this airport lounge of a nation, my fantasy is less appealing. Humans, even nomadic ones, need a sense of home. Home need not be one place or any place at all, but every home has two essential elements: a sense of community and, even more important, a history. I had asked a Swiss man what the glue was that held his country together, given the linguistic, if not ethnic, diversity. Without hesitation he answered: history. Can history really do that? Is it that powerful?

Space and time, the two dimensions that we humans inhabit, are closely linked. "Landscape is personal and tribal history made visible," wrote the geographer Yi-Fu Tuan in his book *Space and Place*. What he means, I think, is that places are like time machines. They transport us back to years past. As Rebecca Solnit observes in her lovely, lyrical book *A Field Guide to Getting Lost*, "Perhaps it's true that you can't go back in time, but you can return to the scene of a love, of a crime, of happiness, and of a fateful decision; the places are what remain, are what you can possess, are what is immortal."

That's why we feel so disoriented, irritated even, when these touchstones from our past are altered. We don't like it when our hometown changes, even in small ways. It's unsettling. The playground! It used to be right here, I swear. Mess with our hometown, and you're messing with our past, with who we are. Nobody likes that.

Qatar has a past, of course, but not much of one. One thousand years of history, roughly from A.D. 650 to 1600, are unaccounted for, simply missing. The country's more recent past is better documented, but it's quickly being erased by an unstoppable juggernaut of chrome and cement.

Stephen Ulph, a British academic, told me something that made me think about how the past shapes our lives, our happiness. Ulph is an expert on the Arab world. He speaks Arabic fluently and travels to the Middle East often. He always enjoys his visits to the region's ancient cities—Cairo, Damascus, Beirut. But the oil-rich nations of the Persian Gulf leave him feeling empty.

"I visited Dubai, and all of the buildings seemed so new, like they were made of cardboard, barely there. Then I went home to London. And I never thought I'd say this about London—the weather is dreadful, you know—but I felt so much better. The buildings look solid, as if they go underground six stories."

Is that solidness a prerequisite for happiness? Does it ground us, keep us from floating off into the ether, into despair? Before we condemn the Qataris—or, for that matter, the Chinese, another nation that is quickly bulldozing its past—as uncouth *nouveau riche* with no regard for history, I want to tell you a story. It's about a temple I visited in Japan. It was a very old and beautiful temple. More than one thousand years old, my guide told me. How remarkable, I thought. I'd never seen such an old structure so perfectly preserved. The wood had hardly any splinters, and not a log was out of place. I read a plaque mounted on a small stand in front of the temple and, sure enough, the temple was built in the 700s. But then, I noticed a few more words, in smaller print. "Temple rebuilt in 1971."

What was going on? Were the Japanese trying to pull a fast one on unsuspecting tourists, pretending the temple was 1,200 years old when in fact it was fewer than forty years old? Not exactly. In many Asian cultures, what matters is not the age of the physical structure but the spirit of the place. Temples in Japan are routinely destroyed and rebuilt, yet people still consider them as old as the day they were first built.

This is not a semantic sleight of hand. It says a lot about how a culture relates to its past. It might even explain, for instance, why so few Chinese seem to mind that old neighborhoods in cities like Shanghai are being razed at a prodigious rate to make room for yet one more skyscraper (another reason, of course, being pure greed). The essence of the original structure remains, even if the physical building does not.

And while the Chinese may not venerate their old temples and houses, they do honor their dead. Ancestor worship is the Chinese way of staying connected to the past. Who are we to say that worshipping dead people is any better or worse than worshipping dead buildings?

Either way, an important ingredient in the good life, the happy life, is connecting to something larger than ourselves, recognizing that we are not mere blips on the cosmic radar screen but part of something much bigger. For some, a Victorian building, with its creaking staircases and tarnished molding, provides this connection. For others, it's giving a new cellphone, gift wrapped, to Uncle Wen who died twenty years ago but is still part of the family.

Bertrand Russell, the British philosopher, concludes his book *The Conquest of Happiness* by describing a happy person thus: "Such a man feels himself a citizen of the universe, enjoying freely the spectacle that it offers and the joy that it affords, untroubled by the thoughts of death because he feels himself not really separated from those who will come after him. It is in such a profound instinctive union with the stream of life that the greatest joy is to be found."

That's an awfully transcendental statement for a self-declared atheist. It reminds me of what Jonas Salk, inventor of the polio vaccine, said when asked what the main aim of his life had been: "To be a good ancestor." A comment like that can only come from a man profoundly aware of his place in the universe.

I'm no Jonas Salk, and half the time I can't find where I parked my car let alone my place in the universe, but lately I've been thinking a lot about this. If we view our lives as merely the seventy or eighty years (if we're lucky) we putter about on this planet, then they are indeed insignificant. But if, as that Buddhist scholar put it, "our parents are infinite," then maybe we are, too.


It occurs to me that I've been in Qatar for several days now and have yet to meet any Qataris. This is a problem. My journalistic instincts, honed over two decades, tell me that in order to probe the Qatari soul it might be helpful to speak with actual Qataris. But where? The usual journalist's trick of interviewing the cabdriver wasn't working. He was invariably from India. Nor could I interview my waiter (Filipino) or the manager at hotel reception (Egyptian). No, I needed an introduction, an entrée into this tribal society.

I had a lead. A phone number for one Sami. He is a friend of a friend and works at Al Jazeera, the controversial Arabic TV network that's based in Qatar. Sami is not Qatari, but I bet he knows some. We agree to meet where everyone in Qatar meets: the mall.

Sami is dressed impeccably in a crisp suit and tie. We sit down at a café on the mezzanine level. I order a lime juice. Sami, tea.

Sami is ethnically Arab but raised in Britain and educated in the United States. He can swim equally well in both rivers, Arab and western. He is the kind of person, I know from experience, who holds the key to understanding a place. He is a cultural interpreter.

I ask Sami about tribal culture. It's a term that we in the west use often and not in a flattering way. Though we never quite say it, tribal culture is considered backward culture.

That's not the case here, says Sami. "Tribe" is just another word for family—a large, extended family. That term sticks in my mind. I wonder: Can a family be overextended? And, if so, is this just as painful as overextending your knee? Our families are our greatest source of love and support. They are also the ones who are, statistically, most likely to kill us. As Yi-Fu Tuan points out, "We cinch both our enemies and lovers." And so it is with families. They are our salvation and our ruin.

"Tribal values are like family values," continues Sami. Something to rally around during good times and bemoan the loss of during difficult times. And just as families distrust outsiders— don't talk to strangers, our parents warned us—so, too, tribes are wary of outsiders. You're either a member of the tribe or you're not. There's no in-between.

Tribal and corporate culture are actually very similar, Sami tells me. Both honor loyalty above all else and reward it generously, be it with stock options or belly dancers. Both deal harshly with traitors, be it through layoffs or beheadings.

The American CEO is just like a Middle Eastern tribal leader, explains Sami: "If you worked at Time Warner, you wouldn't go to the CEO with a small problem. You know your place." And so it is with the country of Qatar. Everyone has access to the ruling emir—his palace door is always open—but they use that access judiciously.

"But why are the Qataris so gruff? Even rude at times?"

"You have to understand, Eric. These are desert people. Life was tough back then. If you hiked for miles through the desert and you finally found someone with water, you wouldn't say, 'Excuse me, dear sir, but could you possibly spare some water?' You would just blurt out, 'Give me water, damn it, I'm dying of thirst!' " That's why, explains Sami, the contemporary Qatari barks at the Starbucks barista when ordering a grande latte. It's because of the desert.

It's not such a far-fetched theory. We are shaped not only by our current geography but by our ancestral one as well. Americans, for instance, retain a frontier spirit even though the only frontier that remains is that vast open space between SUV and strip mall. We are our past.

I take a sip of lime juice and ask Sami if he could help me meet some Qataris. You would think I had asked Sami if he could arrange lunch with the queen of England, rather than asking to meet the citizens of the very country I happen to be visiting at the moment. Sami brushes a speck of invisible dust off his shoulder before speaking.

"This is going to be tough, Eric. Let's see what we're dealing with. First of all, you're an American. Strike one. Also, you're a journalist. Strike two. And your name sounds awfully Jewish."

"Three strikes. I'm outta here?"

"I'll see what I can do. Give me some time." Then he gets up to leave.


The heat is growing worse every day. By 8:00 a.m., the sun glows bright orange in the sky and presses down on me mercilessly. By noon, it is physically painful to stand outside for longer than a minute or two. The heat is just as debilitating as a blizzard. Only fools and foreigners venture outside.

I fit at least one of those categories, possibly both, and so I brave the midday sun to visit the souks in the old part of Doha, the not-yet-bulldozed part of town. One of the rare examples where Qataris value the old.

Inside the souk, the floors are pearly white. Everything is white, including the heat. I notice a McDonald's, which has been designed to blend in architecturally with its surroundings. It looks like...wait...yes, it looks like a mosque. A McMosque. I imagine a sign out front: Over one billion saved! I find this very, very funny. Yes, the heat is definitely getting to me.

I wander through a maze of shops, all run by foreigners. The names of the stores reflect the proprietor's home county: Mother India Tailors, Manila Barber Shop. I suppose this lends an international feel to the city, yet there is something undeniably wistful about it, a longing for home. The expatriates are the worker bees of the Qatari economy. They live here for twenty, thirty years— maybe they were even born here—but they'll never become Qatari citizens. It is a trade-off they readily accept, though it seems like a lousy one to me. Most leave their families back home until, finally, they retire, return home triumphantly, and build a large house. Just in time to die.

I stop for tea. A hot drink cools you more efficiently than a cold one, another one of the ironies of desert life. I pick up the local newspaper, the *Peninsula Times*. There's a picture of the emir meeting the outgoing Nepali ambassador. The newspapers carry the same picture every day, taken in the same ornate room, with the same gold-plated tissue box, only with a different official sitting across from the emir, looking uncomfortable as hell, while the emir, a man of not-insignificant girth, slumps in his chair, just hanging out. I turn the page. There's a story about a serious air-conditioner shortage. It's written in the same urgent, breathless manner that one might write about, say, a shortage of antibiotics.

The call to prayer, the Middle Eastern sound track, ricochets across the white marble. How many times have I heard this sound and in how many different countries? It's a beautiful thing, really; you don't have to be Muslim to appreciate the vocal talent of a good *muezzin*. These days, though, after the September 11 attacks, I find the beauty tinged with menace.

Muslims pray five times a day. This is what the Koran ordains. Why five times? Why not four or six? Only Allah knows, but when Islam sprouted in the Arabian desert some 1,400 years ago, one function the new religion served, intentionally or not, was to bring people together. The mandatory prayer got people out of their own tents and into bigger, communal tents and, eventually, mosques.

Some 1,300 years later, the French existentialist Jean-Paul Sartre metaphorically spat on the notion of communal bliss by declaring, "Hell is other people."

Sartre was wrong. Either that, or he was hanging out with the wrong people. Social scientists estimate that about 70 percent of our happiness stems from our relationships, both quantity and quality, with friends, family, coworkers, and neighbors. During life's difficult patches, camaraderie blunts our misery; during the good times, it boosts our happiness.

So the greatest source of happiness is other people—and what does money do? It isolates us from other people. It enables us to build walls, literal and figurative, around ourselves. We move from a teeming college dorm to an apartment to a house and, if we're really wealthy, to an estate. We think we're moving up, but really we're walling off ourselves.

My taxi driver has no idea where the Qatar National Museum is located and has to stop three times to ask directions. A sign, I think, that Lisa is right. She had claimed, over breakfast one day, that the Qataris had no culture.

I felt compelled to defend the Qataris, though I'm not sure why.

"That seems a bit extreme. Every country has a culture."

"Okay," she said. "They have no cuisine, no literature, and no arts. To me, that means no culture."

"But they have a Ministry of Culture."

"Yeah, they also have a Ministry of Justice. That doesn't mean they have justice."

She had a point. The only culture in Qatar, Lisa claims, is the kind that arrives on an airplane: artists and authors flown in fresh daily, the cultural equivalent of lobsters from Maine.

"Okay," I said, not ready to concede. "They have a museum. I've seen it on the map. If they have a museum, they must have a culture."

Lisa just smiled coyly and said, "Have you seen the museum?"

So here we are, at the museum. The first thing that strikes me about this squat concrete building is that it must be the only unair-conditioned building in the entire country. Is this, I wonder, an effort to simulate the hardship of Qatari life before the days of air-conditioning? The heat inside the concrete rooms is unbearable. Within seconds, rivulets of sweat form on my forehead and drip into my eyes, stinging.

Fortunately, there is little reason to linger. The exhibits are, in a word, pathetic. Lisa spots a glass case that houses a collection of what looks like camel toenail clippings. There's an exhibit of folk medicine, with the emphasis on the folk. A placard reads: "Cups were used to relieve high blood pressure, the symptoms of which are headaches and fainting." It's not clear if these symptoms were caused by the high blood pressure or the "cupping." A picture shows an old man, with giant ladles attached to his head and blood emptying into plastic cups. I believe in medieval times this was known as bloodletting.

One of the more interesting exhibits is a series of aerial photos of Doha, the same view taken in 1947, 1963, and 1989. In each successive photo you can see the city spreading like an ink stain.

We meander in the courtyard, where an alleged breeze stirs up the hot air. Maybe it's the heat or maybe it's the sad museum, but

it is here where Lisa tells me about her past. It is, in fact, much like
Qatar's past: troubled, mercurial—and with large swaths of time
unaccounted for. As Lisa unreels, I can't help but wonder: What
if everyone had their own personal museum, actual buildings devoted to telling our stories?

The Museum of Lisa would be a bit depressing, much like the
Qatar National Museum, only with air-conditioning and probably
without the camel toenail clippings. One exhibit would feature the
dusty plastic tumbler from which Lisa imbibed her first drink. Underneath, a plaque would read: "This is the authentic cup in which
Lisa, age ten, mixed together Scotch, rum, and gin, acquired from
her parents' liquor cabinet." Another exhibit would feature the actual bright-orange Pontiac LeMans convertible she hopped a ride
in to run away from home at age fifteen. And look, over here—an
exact replica of the rehabilitation center in Columbus, Ohio, that
Lisa entered at age nineteen.

Next, if you walk this way, mind the bong, please, we enter the
Early Tunisian Period. Lisa has sobered up and joined the Peace
Corps. They send her to the North African nation of Tunisia. All
is well but…oh, no…what's this? A picture of Lisa with a bottle
of beer in each hand, a cigarette dangling from the corner of her
mouth. We must have entered the Relapse Era. The placard tells
us that Lisa has fallen off the wagon and fallen hard. She's mede-
vaced to Amsterdam, en route home, but she doesn't want to go,
and Lisa never, ever does anything she doesn't want to do, so she
resorts to one of her old tricks from the Street Urchin Era. She
acts crazy. Roll the grainy video of Lisa at Amsterdam's Schiphol
Airport. "Excuse me, do you know the world is coming to an
end?" she is saying, again and again to anyone who will listen and
even to those who won't. The Dutch authorities lock her up in a
psychiatric hospital. They give her medication, which Lisa deftly
"cheeks," only pretending to swallow, another old trick from her
runaway days. Finally, the Dutch give up and put her on a flight
home to America. On the plane, she has sex in the lavatory with a
long-haired guy she just met.

Hopefully, you leave the Museum of Lisa feeling the way I do about Lisa: warm and fuzzy and wishing her well as she heads toward a Golden Age replete with yoga classes and AA meetings. May Lisa be as lucky as Qatar. May she find huge reserves of natural gas deep beneath her sands.

As we walk back to the car, I wonder: What would my museum look like? I'm drawing a blank, and this disturbs me very much. Is the arc of my life so indiscernible, so amorphous, that no curator could tell my story under one roof?

"So was I right, or what?" asks Lisa.

Yes, I concede, she is right. Qataris have no culture. Frankly, I can't blame them. If you spent a few thousand years scraping by in the desert, fending off the solid heat, not to mention various invading tribes, you wouldn't have time for culture, either. Back then, life was too harsh for culture. Today, it is too comfortable for culture. "Creative cities, creative urban milieux, are places of great social and intellectual turbulence, not comfortable places at all," observes British historian Peter Hall.

The emir of Qatar, ruler of the land, is determined to do something about his country's missing culture. In true Qatari fashion, he plans to buy a culture and, while he's at it, some history as well. It sounds like a sensible plan. But there's a hitch. While it's true that money talks, it talks only in the future tense. Money is 100 percent potential. You can build a future with money but not a past.

This hasn't stopped the emir from trying. He will soon open several new multimillion-dollar (and presumably air-conditioned) museums, celebrating Qatar's recently constructed past. I can imagine the billboards: "Your Cultural Heritage. Coming Soon!"

The emir of Qatar is not your typical Arab leader. He came to power in a family coup d'état, which seems fitting for a country that is basically a family business. He immediately established himself as a new kind of Arab ruler. A soft and cuddly authoritarian.

The emir is expert at playing a double game. Qatar is home to one of the largest U.S. military bases in the world—the United

States ran the 2003 invasion of Iraq from here. Qatar is also home to Al Jazeera, the fiery satellite TV channel that is best known for airing tapes of Osama bin Laden. Thus, the emir manages to be both pro- and anti-American at the same time. No easy feat.

The emir is, if nothing else, generous. He shares Qatar's vast oilngas wealth among his subjects. In fact, this is the ultimate welfare state. Gasoline sells for fifty cents a gallon, cheaper than water. Well, that's not quite true. Water in Qatar is free. So is electricity and health care and education. The government even pays a small salary to Qatari college students. When a Qatari man gets married, the government gives him a plot of land to build a house, an interest-free mortgage, and, to boot, a monthly allowance of roughly seven thousand dollars. And unlike in European welfare states, Qataris aren't burdened with high taxes. In fact, they aren't burdened with taxes at all. No income tax. No sales tax. Nothing.

You might think this is a wonderful thing, as I did at first. But a study conducted recently at the University of Oregon suggests otherwise. Researchers gave nineteen volunteers one hundred dollars and then had them lie on their backs and watch the money disappear, through a series of financial transactions that flickered across a computer screen. At the same time, the researchers scanned the participants' brain activity with an MRI machine.

In one experiment, the participants actively chose a good cause to donate their money to. When they did, two of the more primitive parts of the brain—the caudate nucleus and the nucleus accumbens—lit up. The truly surprising finding, though, is that even when the participants were forced to give up their money (to a good cause, they were told) the parts of the brain associated with altruism still fired. Not as much as when the choice was made voluntarily, but most economists would not have predicted any brain activity at all, at least not of the positive variety, when someone was forced to cough up money involuntarily—in other words, pay taxes.

What to make of this study? Should we wire everyone to an MRI machine to determine their appropriate tax bracket? I don't think so, and the experiment had its shortcomings. In the real world, taxes aren't always seen as fair, and how they're spent is sometimes questionable. But clearly paying taxes is good. Mind you, I'm not saying that *high* taxes are good. I'm just saying that the concept of taxation is good, is necessary, for a healthy democracy. "Tax" is another word for vote. If a public worker is goofing off on the job, Qataris can't chastise him with that old standby, "Hey, I pay your salary, buddy." No, you don't. Qataris have neither taxation nor representation, and that's not a happy thing.

A call from Sami. Good news. He has arranged for me to meet a few Qatari friends at the Al Jazeera offices. I hop a cab and meet him outside the headquarters building. Except for the small mosque near the entrance, this could be any TV station. We head for the employee cafeteria. I'm impressed. Blond wood floors, Scandinavian furniture, and, mounted on the wall like a piece of modern art, a flat-panel TV. Al Jazeera is the emir's child, and the emir treats his children well.

Sami introduces me to his friends, all wearing white *dishdashas,* the long, flowing robes worn by Persian Gulf Arabs, with the standard accessories: cuff links, expensive watches, and Mont Blanc pens tucked into their breast pockets. Since the *dishdashas* are generic clothing, these accessories are the only way that Qatari men can flash their wealth. Their procurement is a vital part of life here.

Hands are shaken, coffee served, cigarettes lit. I decide to open the conversation by asking about the driving in Qatar. Why is it so bad?

There's a long pause.

"Next question," says one of the men, and everyone laughs.

"Actually," says another, "it's your fault, you Americans. We learned to drive by watching Hollywood films, car chases and whatnot. It's a macho thing."

Okay, enough chitchat. I screw up my courage and blurt out the big question.

"Are you happy?"

There is an uncomfortably long silence. Finally, one man says, an edge of irritation in his voice, "Why do you ask such a question?"

That question—are you happy?—the question we Americans chew on every day, every hour, is not entirely appropriate in a Muslim country like Qatar. I've noticed that people cringe slightly when I ask and politely try to change the subject. That's because happiness, bliss, is in the hands of Allah, not man. If we are happy, it is God's will and, likewise, if we are miserable it is also God's will. Are you happy? I might as well have asked these guys if they shaved their legs. I want to slink away.

"Okay, if you insist, yes, I am happy," one man finally says.

"There's no such thing as complete happiness," says a third man, puffing away on a cigarette.

"If you want to know true happiness, you should become a Muslim," says a fourth. "You should believe and know that everything is in the hands of God. You will get what Allah has written for you. Yes, you should become a Muslim if you want to know happiness."

The link between religion and happiness is a subject that could fill many bookshelves, and, indeed, it has. I will dip my big toe into this deep, deep reservoir by pointing out one statistic to emerge from the young science of happiness. People who attend religious services report being happier than those who do not. Why? Is it because of some transcendental experience, the religious part of the religious service? Or is it the service part, the gathering of like-minded souls, that explains this phenomenon? In other words, could these happy churchgoers receive the same hedonic boost if they belonged to a bowling league or, for that matter, the local chapter of the Ku Klux Klan?

I don't think so. Consider this finding: People who say they agree with the statement "God is important in my life" report being significantly happier than people who disagree with that statement, irrespective of their participation in organized religion. A happiness bonus—to put it in earthly financial terms—equivalent to a doubling of their salary.

I can hear the howls of protests from atheists. If belief in a delusional, dogmatic religion makes you happy, then it is not a happiness I want any part of, thank you very much. The atheists might be on to something. For one thing, the happyologists fail to take into account the moral underpinnings of happiness. A pedophile who reports high levels of happiness—say, a nine out of ten—counts exactly the same as a social worker who also reports being a nine on the happiness scale. Likewise, a suicide bomber, firm in his belief in Allah, might very well score higher than either the pedophile or the social worker. He might be a ten, just before blowing himself up and taking a few dozen innocents with him. Aristotle would clear up this moral confusion in an Athenian minute. Happiness, he believed, meant not only feeling good but doing good. Thus, the pedophile and the suicide bomber only *thought* they were happy. In fact, they were not happy at all.

Perhaps it is not the belief in God that makes us happier but belief in something, anything. How else to explain the fact that the happiest countries in the world—Denmark, Iceland, Switzerland, the Netherlands—are hardly religious at all? The citizens of these countries, though, clearly believe in something. They believe in six weeks of vacation, in human rights, in democracy, in lazy afternoons spent sitting in cafés, in wearing socks and sandals at the same time. Beliefs we may admire or, in the case of the sock-and-sandal combo, find utterly abhorrent. But they are beliefs nonetheless.

"So all I need to do is believe in Allah?" I'm careful to keep my tone nonconfrontational with the men from Al Jazeera. I am treading on treacherous, holy ground here. "I don't need to do anything else to be happy?"

"You need to make effort, but it is effort that matters, not result," says one man.

Islam, like other religions, maintains that if you want to be happy, put great effort into living a virtuous life and expect nothing, absolutely nothing. Divorce your actions from their results, and happiness will flow like oil.

The conversation winds down, and the men, one by one, start to fiddle with their Mont Blanc pens and glance at their diamond-encrusted watches. We say our goodbyes, and they leave me with these parting, slightly ominous words: "Religion is like a knife. If you use it the wrong way you can cut yourself."

A major turning point in human history occurred in the Dutch region of Flanders in the year 1445, though you won't read about it in most history books. Flanders is where the first lottery took place. The prize wasn't much—a goat's head and a date with a comely lass of virtue true, I presume—but the event marked a major shift, what I might call a paradigm shift if I were the kind of person who used terms like "paradigm shift." For the first time in history, a member of the unwashed masses could become instantly rich and without lifting a finger. Just like the landed gentry. Legalized prostitution and now this. The Dutch, once again, were on to something.

Lotteries have been popular ever since. Today, dozens of countries around the world have them. Who has not fantasized about winning the jackpot? Who hasn't imagined the exact moment when you walk into your boss's office on Monday morning and very politely, without a hint of malice, tell him to kindly fuck off and die? You don't work there anymore. You don't work *anywhere* anymore. You travel. You shop. You eat Doritos and watch *Seinfeld* reruns.

You wouldn't be one of those selfish lottery winners, though. Oh, no, you'd spread the wealth. Buy your mom that condo in Florida, your brother that sports car, and even throw a few thousand to some worthy cause. Darfur, maybe. You wouldn't be one of those squanderers, either. No, sir, you'd be responsible. You'd invest. Eventually, after a few years, you might even do some work again. On Tuesdays. In the afternoon. Maybe. Yes, if you won the lottery, you would be, in a word, happy.

That's what Qatar thought, too. It has won the oilngas lottery, and it's no longer working at the doughnut shop. Like other lottery winners, Qatar spends a lot of time pampering itself and fielding calls from long-lost cousins and old high school buddies, only this time it's the United Nations high school. "Qatar, how the heck are you, it's your old pal Somalia. It's been tooooo long. We must do lunch."

So end of story. Qatar is loaded and therefore happy as well.

Not so fast.

In 1978, psychologist Philip Brickman studied two groups of people. One group had just won the lottery and was now wealthy. Another group had been in accidents and was now paralyzed. Not surprisingly, shortly after these events, the lottery winners reported increased happiness, while the accident victims were less happy. But as Brickman tracked the groups, something wholly unexpected happened. The lottery winners soon returned to the same happiness levels as before they struck it rich. The paralyzed accident victims, meanwhile, rebounded to happiness levels only slightly lower than before their accident.

What was going on? Brickman surmised that, in the case of the lottery winners, they now derived significantly less pleasure from ordinary events like buying clothes or talking to a friend. What was once enjoyable was no longer so. Psychologists call this the "hedonic treadmill." Much like a regular treadmill, the hedonic treadmill makes you sweat and should be avoided at all costs. Unlike a regular treadmill, however, the hedonic variety is definitely not good for your health. It will drive you nuts, this infinite cycle of pleasure and adaptation. Interestingly, there are two notable exceptions to the hedonic treadmill. Noise and big breasts. Studies have found that we never really get used to loud noises, despite prolonged exposure. Another study found that women who get breast implants never tire of the enjoyment it brings them, and presumably their companions feel the same.

Aristotle was right when he said, "Little pieces of good luck (and likewise of the opposite kind) clearly do not disturb the tenor of our life." And if the Brickman study is right, then big pieces of luck don't disturb the tenor of our life, either. Nothing does. Which invites the inevitable question: Why bother getting out of bed in the morning?

To answer that question, we need to step back. Lotteries are not really about money. They're about the intersection of luck and happiness. It's a busy intersection, prone to accidents. The ancient Greeks believed that happiness required a measure of good luck. Even Aristotle, who preached the need to lead a virtuous life, also believed in the necessity of luck: "For a man is scarcely happy if he is very ugly to look at, or of low birth, or solitary and childless, and presumably less so if he has children or friends who are quite worthless, or if he had good ones who are now dead."

Don't just take Aristotle's word for it, though. In every Indo-European language, the word for happiness is tied to the word for luck. The English word "happiness" comes from the old Norse word "hap," or luck. When we have a mishap, we've had a spell of bad luck. In modern German, the word "glück" means both "happiness" and "luck." In Aristotle's time, luck was bestowed by the gods. Today, that job falls to the good people at Powerball.

But, as the studies of lottery winners show, what at first looks like good luck may turn out to be its opposite. I recently came across this short article from a Pakistani news service.

Multan, March 16: A prisoner Haq-Nawaz, 70, died in New Central Jail Bhawalpur last evening when he was told that court has suspended his imprisonment and ordered to release him. When the jail authorities informed him that he was going to be released on Thursday, he could not control the happiness and his pulses [*sic*] stopped due to over-excitement. Haq-Nawaz's body was handed over to his relatives for burial.

I've hung that article on my refrigerator. A daily reminder to myself: Happiness can kill.

That evening, Lisa and I have dinner at the hotel's Indian restaurant. It is delicious and extremely authentic, which is not surprising given the fact that the entire staff probably arrived from Bombay yesterday.

We attempt to make some chitchat, but Lisa's fierce honesty streak gets in the way. And so, between the papadam and the biryani, she asks me, point blank, if I am happy in Qatar.

"Actually," I say, "I feel sad. Very sad. I can't explain it."

"That's because you need it, you love it."

"Love what?"

"Sadness. You are addicted to sadness."

She doesn't say it like it is some harebrained theory. She says it like it is fact. The earth is round. I'm addicted to sadness. Is such a thing even possible? I wonder. What sane person would crave something like sadness?

If it's true, if I am indeed addicted to sadness, I absolve myself of blame. Responsibility rests firmly with my brain. It is a flawed design. Worse than the 1975 Ford Pinto and just as dangerous.

Neuroscientists have discovered that the parts of the brain that control wanting and the parts that control liking are separate; they operate independently of one another and involve different chemicals. Neuroscientists know this the way they know everything else about how our brains work: by doing strange and often sadistic things to rats.

In the 1950s, Canadian researchers planted tiny electrodes

inside rats' brains and electrically stimulated a part of the brain known as the lateral hypothalamus. The rats loved it. The scientists then gave the rats tiny rat-sized levers to push that would allow them to stimulate their lateral hypothalamus all by themselves. The rats loved this even more. "Working for this reward, they [the rats, not the scientists] will ignore sexually receptive members of the opposite sex, food, or even water, in their single-minded quest for the hit," writes Daniel Nettle in his book *Happiness: The Science Behind Your Smile.*

A bit strange, you might think, but still within the realm of the explainable. Whatever those electrical currents are doing to the rats' lateral hypothalamus, it must be something awfully good, something the rats like a lot and therefore will do anything to repeat.

That's probably what the scientists thought, too, when they devised another experiment. They stimulated the rats' hypothalamus while they were eating. The results were surprising. The rats ate more food but, judging by their body language, weren't enjoying it—clear evidence, says Nettle, that "you can crave for something very much but take little or no pleasure in it once you had it." Anyone who has ever been hooked on cigarettes or watched *Nancy Grace* knows this intuitively.

Wanting things we don't like. If true, it pretty much demolishes the entire field of economics. Economists base their studies on the premise that rational human beings pursue things that will increase their "utility," economist-speak for happiness. Joe works overtime, hardly seeing his family, so he can save money to buy a new BMW. Therefore, the new BMW must increase Joe's utility, his happiness. What economists fail to take into account is that Joe is a moron. No, that's not entirely fair. Joe is not a moron; but Joe's brain clearly is. It's been wired in a way that compels Joe to chase after things that don't make him happy.

So much of human misery can be explained by this crazy way we're wired. We assume that our intense feelings of wanting something—a new car, winning the lottery—means that, once obtained, these things will make us happy. But that is a connection that, neurologically speaking, does not exist. We are disappointed but don't learn from our disappointment because our software is flawed. It's not faulty data but faulty programming that is holding us back, and that is much harder to rectify.

Addicted to sadness. Lisa's words are still rattling around my head when my saag paneer arrives. The waiter insists on ladling it onto my plate and, I suspect, would cut it up and feed me if I asked. By doing so, he is increasing my comfort, yes, but also denying me the tactile pleasure of heaping the spinach and cheese onto my plate. But he is just doing his job, so I decide not to point this out to him.

Addicted to sadness. I still don't buy it. Sadness is not pleasurable. I neither want nor like it. No, Lisa is wrong this time. Or is she? Feeling sad is still feeling, in the same way that believing in drivel is still believing. Both mind-sets are preferable to the alternative: nothingness. Human beings will go to great lengths to avoid nothingness. We will conquer foreign lands, fly to the moon, watch cable TV alone in hotel rooms, shoot thirty-two people dead, compose beautiful music.

Addicted to sadness. As I tear off a piece of naan, it's starting to make sense. Certainly, I am sad. No disagreement there. And I do have my share of addictions. There's one in particular that springs to mind. My wife thinks I should seek professional help. Once she found me, late at night, furtively hunched over my laptop.

"What are you looking at?" she asked accusingly, as I quickly minimized the browser window.

"Nothing."

"It's not nothing. I saw you looking at a picture."

I was found out. Game over. I clicked the mouse and the picture filled the screen. There she was, in all her glory. A real beaut, too, zippers undone.

"Oh, God," my wife sighed in disgust, then grew silent.

I just sat there, my head hung in shame, waiting for her to say something else. Finally, she spoke.

"Why can't you look at porn like a normal guy?"

On the screen was a Billingham 335, a beautifully handcrafted British camera bag with double stitching and padded shoulder strap. Yes, my name is Eric, and I am addicted to bags. There, I said it. I feel better already.

Like all addictions, this one snuck up on me, unbidden. I'm not sure when I turned that corner from a merely enthusiastic interest in bags to a full-blown addiction. The signs were there. Like the time I opened a closet door and a pile of bags fell on my head, smothering me, cartoonlike. Or the time, in Tokyo, when I bought a five-hundred-dollar Gurkha briefcase and so feared the wrath of my annoyingly sane wife that I hid the bag in a coin locker at our local subway station for a good week or two before I could safely sneak it into our apartment, into the closet with the other bags.

Currently, my collection of bags ("collection" is my preferred term; it sounds normal) numbers sixty-four. Does that seem excessive to you? My wife thinks so. But she doesn't understand. She doesn't understand the tactile pleasure I derive from the feel of quality canvas against my naked skin. Doesn't understand the joys of thoughtful ergonomics, of a pocket located in exactly the right location, or a zippered compartment that holds my Filofax (another collectible) just perfectly. A well-designed bag is like a well-designed appendage, and just as necessary.

If I could be addicted to something as quotidian as bags, I realized as the waiter brought the masala chai, then certainly I could be addicted to something much weightier. Like sadness.

It's Wednesday at 3:00 p.m. I decide to do what any self-respecting Qatari would do at this time. I go to Starbucks. Qatari men are sipping lattes and smoking directly under the no-smoking sign, secure in the knowledge that no Filipino barista would dare ask them to obey the rules. In Qatar, the question isn't: What is the rule? But rather: Who's enforcing it?

Music is playing. *We will, we will rock you.* But no one will be rocked here. There will be no revolution. People are too comfortable, and comfort is the revolutionaries' worst enemy. Qatar, like all countries flush with natural resources, suffers from the Curse of Oil. As *New York Times* columnist Thomas Friedman has shown, there's an inverse relationship between the price of oil and democracy. As the price of oil rises, moves toward democracy decline. The leaders of these oil-rich nations feel no compunction to relax their grip on power. Why should they? Everybody is comfortable, and therefore happy.

Or are they? Maybe they are slowly dying of psychic wounds, self-inflicted with a gold-plated knife that makes incisions so painlessly you don't notice them until it's too late. A comfortable, air-conditioned death.

In the nineteenth century, one hundred years before a country called Qatar existed, Emile Durkheim, the French sociologist, wrote of "anomic suicide." It's what happens when a society's moral underpinnings are shaken. And they can be shaken, Durkheim believed, both by great disaster and by great fortune.

The first part we understand. We expect those who suffer financial hardship to spiral into despair. But we don't expect despondency from lottery winners or citizens of oil-rich nations. Yet it happens. Most of us have, at one time or another, felt a strange and wholly unexpected flash of unease accompany good news: a promotion, say, or a sudden windfall. People are congratulating you, you know you should be happy, but you're not, and you can't explain why.

I struggle to find a table. Starbucks is crowded. A little too crowded for a Wednesday at 3:00 p.m. Don't these men have jobs? In fact, I later learned, they did have jobs, and they were, at that very moment, midlatte, earning full salaries. They are what's known here as ghost workers. People who don't show up for work but, owing to their tribal clout, collect a paycheck nonetheless.

Paid to hang out at Starbucks. It sounds like a great gig, a wonderful, caffeinated path to bliss. A traditional economist would agree. The ghost workers have eliminated a negative externality, work, while maximizing a desired commodity: leisure time. They still receive a salary, so therefore they should experience a net gain in utility—that is, happiness.

Except they don't. Several studies have found that unemployed people in Europe are significantly less happy than people with jobs, even though the laid-off workers still receive the equivalent of a full salary, thanks to the generous welfare system. This inconvenient fact pokes holes at notions that the good life is a languid one. In fact, researchers have found that people who are too busy are happier than those who are not busy enough. In other words, the playwright Noël Coward got it right when he observed that interesting work is "more fun than fun."

I sense a gnawing distance between myself and Qatar. I'm here, but am I really here? I need to think like a Qatari, to get inside their *dishdasha,* figuratively speaking, if only for a few minutes. But how? I'm not about to convert to Islam or take up smoking or drive like a maniac. Walking past the hotel gift shop, it dawns on me. I will buy a pen. Yes, a Ridiculously Expensive Pen. I've never owned a Ridiculously Expensive Pen, never felt the need. I'm certainly capable of mindless materialism, as my bag collection attests, just not when it comes to pens. It's treacherous territory, this materialism. Studies have found that materialistic people are less happy than people who are not. It's their attitude toward money, not their bank balance, that matters. And yet the allure of a nice pen or car or whatever is irresistible. They represent potential happiness. Despite ourselves, we believe they will change us.

Choosing a Ridiculously Expensive Pen is an exercise in intuition. There is no rationally correct choice. Unlike buying a car, safety is not an issue. As long as the pen doesn't explode in your pocket or emit noxious gas like in a James Bond movie, it is a safe pen.

I test-drive several models, balancing each one between my thumb and forefinger to gauge its heft. Heft is very important when choosing a Ridiculously Expensive Pen. Too little isn't good. The pen feels cheap, which defeats the purpose. Too much heft, though, can result in strained hand muscles. Not good, either. The next criteria is appearance. I was going for understated absurdity. Last and, surprisingly, least, a Ridiculously Expensive Pen should be able to write. You'd be surprised how many don't do this very well. They leave splotches or fade in midstroke.

Finally, after much hemming and hawing, I find just the right Ridiculously Expensive Pen for me. A sleek Lavin with clean lines and a black matte finish. I use it immediately, to sign the credit-card slip. It performs admirably.

Moza al-Malki is a rarity in the Arab world—a firebrand and shameless self-promoter who also happens to be a woman. I had met her once before. I was doing a story on women in the Arab world. She was one of the first women to run for office. She was defeated soundly but still considers the experience a success. Moza possesses what, in a different cultural context, would be called chutzpah.

When I call, she remembers me, or at least pretends to; it's hard to tell with self-promoters like Moza. She agrees to meet with me.

I wait for thirty minutes, but she doesn't show up. Finally, I call her. She sounds agitated.

"Where were you?" she says.

"I was waiting for you at the Starbucks, like you said."

"Which one?"

It never occurred to me that there would be two Starbucks in the same shopping mall in a country that a few years ago barely existed. But indeed there are, and I was waiting at the wrong one.

Moza has already left this particular mall and has returned to her natural state: perpetual motion. She won't backtrack to the old mall, for Moza never backtracks. Instead, she suggests we meet at another mall, across town. This time she tells me to meet her at the Häagen-Dazs café, assuring me that there is only one.

When I arrive, Moza is waiting. Her face is uncovered, with wisps of jet-black hair poking out of her flimsy head scarf. She's pushing the limits of acceptable *hijab,* the Islamic dress code for women, and indeed is engaged in what many Qatari women would consider scandalous behavior: meeting a man who is not a relative in a public setting.

But Moza is not most Qatari women. She's been driving a car since 1983. Not a mind-boggling fact unless you consider that Qatari women were not allowed to drive until 1997.

"So many times the police caught me on the street. They would say, 'You're a woman. You're not supposed to drive.' And I said, 'What are you going to do? Take my license? I don't have a license.' They would say they were going to take my car, and I said, 'Fine, I have another car.' Then they would say, 'We're going to put you in jail' and I said, 'Wow! Jail. That's great. I can write three or four research papers while I'm in jail.'" It was at this point that the police officers usually let Moza go with a warning.

I order the raspberry sorbet. She gets a fudge waffle with low-fat vanilla ice cream on top. We chat about the dearth of bookstores, Qatari politics, her unsuccessful bid for local office, and, of course, whether she's happy.

"Oh, yes," she says, all bubbly. "On a scale of one to ten, I'm a ten. I travel around the world. Last month, I went to three conferences. They paid for all of my expenses, flew me first class, and put me in top hotels."

"So can money buy happiness?"

She pauses, staring into the pool of melted low-fat ice cream on her plate.

"No, not exactly. But luxury facilitates your happiness. It helps. You need money to travel first class, to go all around the world to stay in luxury hotels. For me, this is part of my happiness. My great-grandmother was happy in a tent, but I couldn't be happy in a tent."

Then she tells me a story, a true story. A few days ago, a wealthy Qatari man purchased a lucky phone number for his cellphone. I was surprised to hear what the number was, 66666 (a lucky number in the Arab world), and even more surprised to hear the price: $2.5 million. This caused a bit of a stir. This materialism, this dollar worship, has gone too far, some Qataris said. Moza, though, went on television defending the man. Everyone has their own idea of happiness, she said, and if this man was happy to spend $2.5 million for a phone number, then who are we to argue?

"But there are worthwhile ways to spend money and silly ways," I say.

"It's up to them," counters Moza. "For them it is not silly. One of my friends just spent eight thousand dollars for a purse. It's a beautiful purse, from Saks Fifth Avenue, and it made her very happy."

I don't doubt that it did. But the latest social-science research, not to mention ancient Stoic philosophy, predicts that purse won't make Moza's friend happy for very long. Chances are she'll soon want a $10,000 purse, then a $15,000 purse to derive the same amount of satisfaction.

Moza and I say goodbye. She's so westernized in her outlook I almost slip up and give her a peck on the cheek. That would have made many people unhappy. She promises to fax me her résumé and latest articles. By the time I return to my hotel, they are waiting for me. A big, thick pile.

"Ahh, Eric," the voice on the other end of the line says, warmly, as if we're old friends. "I've been expecting your call."

Usually, I hate when people I've just met use my name like we're old high school buddies. But Abdulaziz does it naturally, endearingly. I like him already.

I've been told that he's someone I must meet. An introspective Qatari. He agrees to meet me later that day at a French pastry shop called Eli France, located in one of Doha's modern *souks*. When my taxi pulls up a few hours later, the *souk* looks an awful lot like what we in America call a strip mall. But I guess "souk" sounds more exotic than "strip mall."

I'm a few minutes early. I ask the hostess for a table for two. She freezes, speechless. After a moment, I realize the problem. I have not given her enough information. She needs to know who my dining companion will be: male or female. If it's a woman, she'll seat us in the "family section"—discreetly cordoned off from the rest of the restaurant where husbands, wives and their children can dine unmolested by the eyes of strange men. If my guest is a man, then she'll seat us in the singles section, reserved for men unaccompanied by their families. I revise my request and ask for a table for two men. She looks relieved and leads me to a small, marble-topped table. I order a lime juice and wait for Abdulaziz.

He arrives a few minutes later. His eyes are crinkly and bright and twinkle just a little when he talks. He orders Earl Grey tea. I notice that he treats the waitress respectfully, like a human being, not a servant.

Abdulaziz's father was a schoolteacher, a job that no Qatari today would consider worthy. His father owned a car, but not much of one. Maybe it would start in the morning, maybe not. Doha at that time consisted of one road and a few houses. Qataris cleaned their own homes, raised their own children. Life was harsher than today but sweeter.

Then came the boom in the 1980s, and everything changed. First, a Sheraton hotel, shaped like an Egyptian pyramid and just as revered. Then, other hotels, condos, office buildings, all built by a growing army of foreign workers, wearing identical blue jumpsuits and happy to be earning three or four times what they could back home. Then came the maids, the cooks, the nannies, and others whose sole purpose was making life for Qataris more comfortable.

"Now we search for happiness in the wrong way. People equate happiness with money." Money, he has concluded, not only is the root of all evil but is the root of all unhappiness as well.

"Qataris complain a lot. They think the government should make their lives easier. If the government asks people to pay for electricity—even a tiny amount—they complain. If they try to tax them, just a little bit, they complain. And the government is to blame, too. This government thinks the only way to make people happy is by giving them money—and that is stupid. I would gladly give up half my salary for a better system."

Abdulaziz relays a joke making the rounds in Doha.

One man says to his friend, "Did you hear about the criminals who kidnapped the rich man's eight-year-old son? They couldn't collect ransom because the rich man didn't notice the son was missing."

"Big mistake," says the other man. "They should have kidnapped the maid. That way, the rich guy would have noticed that someone is missing."

A generation of Qatari children is being raised by nannies who don't speak their language and have no authority to discipline them. Boys are cherished and spoiled. "Once they reach thirteen or fourteen years old, the family doesn't try to discipline them anymore. They won't monitor their behavior in public. It's a living hell for the teachers, who often are foreigners with no real authority. These young men don't listen to anyone. Not even the police," says Abdulaziz.

It doesn't sound like a recipe for happiness, I concede. But the diversity in modern Qatar, the people living here from all over the world, surely that is a good thing. Surely that adds some spice to desert life.

"Not really," says Abdulaziz, sipping his tea. "Look at it from the point of view of a Qatari. You are only 20 percent of the population in your own country, so every day you are confronted by a sea of foreign faces. You need these foreigners to make your country run, otherwise all this wealth is useless. But you resent them, exactly as much as you depend on them. This multiculturalism, it looks beautiful from far away. But not from close up."

"What would happen if Qatar simply asked all the foreigners to leave?"

"The country would collapse. We need these people. For God's sake, even our judges are foreigners. Imagine that. Our judges are foreigners!"

I ask Abdulaziz about the tribal nature of a country like Qatar. We know that families are important to our happiness. And, again, what is a tribe but an extended family? So, therefore, you'd think a tribal society like Qatar would be very happy, especially when you factor in the free-flowing money that makes life so easy, so comfortable.

Tribal life is nurturing, agrees Abdulaziz. It's a safety net, but the net is wrapped around their necks and strangling them.

"Here, you are constantly on guard, afraid to do or say anything wrong because you are always being watched."

"By the secret police?"

"No," says Abdulaziz, laughing softly at my ignorance, "by your own family."

He continues, "Let's say you want to marry a foreigner or even someone from another tribe. You will find life very difficult. It can be done, but you have to launch a kind of political campaign. A feast must be held, minds must be changed."

In Qatar, your position within the tribe trumps money or education. Despite all of the changes to Doha's skyline, all of the fast-food joints, the country is socially stagnant. You will die with exactly the same status with which you were born. Nothing you do matters. What matters is your name.

With that information, Abdulaziz can determine someone's standing, their place within the tribe, their income level. He grabs a napkin and, plucking a pen (a nice pen, I notice, but not a Mont Blanc) out of his breast pocket, draws a series of concentric circles.

"This is Qatari society," he says, pointing to the napkin. "And these are families, or tribes," indicating the circles. "In the middle, of course, are the al-Thanis, the ruling family."

"And where do you fit in?"

He draws an X, close to the center. I'm surprised how close. Judging from his discontent, I would have pegged him for an outsider. I decide not to mention this and move on to another subject.

"All this wealth. Does it make people happy?"

"No, not really. You need enough money to have your dignity. Beyond that, it won't make you happy."

I note his use of the word "dignity." Not enough money to buy your comfort or your security but your dignity or, to extrapolate slightly, your honor: the driving force in the Arab world. We liberated males in the west are not beyond its pull, either. The Wall Street executive working an eighty-hour week in hopes of boosting his million-dollar salary is motivated by an insatiable need for honor, for the respect of his herd.

We finish our drinks and head next door to Jarir's, Qatar's only bookstore of any size. Abdulaziz, a man of obviously great intellectual curiosity, is embarrassed by the paucity of selection here. A few American self-help books, which make me feel right at home, and a bestseller from Saudi Arabia called *Riyadh Girls,* Arab chick lit. There is nothing, though, that could remotely be called Qatari literature. "Money can't buy culture," says Abdulaziz, contradicting the philosophy of his government and sounding an awful lot like Lisa.

"But it can buy a lot of artwork," I say, referring to the sheikh who scooped up all of those masterpieces.

Abdulaziz lowers his voice. We are now talking about a member of the royal family; discretion is required. "The problem is that he confused the buying he was doing for the national museum with the buying he was doing for his own personal collection." Hundreds of millions of dollars were squandered, all at the expense of the Qatari taxpayer. That is, if Qataris paid tax.

"No rules," continues Abdulaziz. "This guy was given a billion dollars to spend and no rules."

No rules and yet, within one's tribe, too many rules. What a horrible way to live. Not for the first time, I feel sorry for Abdulaziz, living here in this gilded sandbox. He senses this, I think, and tells me how he had once planned to immigrate to Canada, but not now. Not after the attacks of September 11. Not with a name like Abdulaziz.

It's time to leave. He offers to drop me off at my hotel. A few minutes into the drive, Abdulaziz's cellphone rings. My Arabic barely exists, but my ears perk up when I hear the word "*mushkala*": problem. "*Mushkala*" is a very popular word in the Middle East. Usually, it's used during, say, a tense moment at a checkpoint. "*Ayn mushkala*," no problem, your driver will assure you. Translation: big problem. Very big problem.

"Eric," says Abdulaziz, after hanging up. "What do you do when a problem weighs so heavily on you, so heavily you don't know if you can keep on living? What do you do?"

The question throws me, makes me squirm in my seat. I am touched that Abdulaziz has confided in me, given that I'm not exactly a member of the tribe, not his tribe anyway. But my other tribal affiliation is interfering with my humanity. The tribe known as journalist. Like all tribes, this one has strict, though unspoken, rules. Rule number one: Take freely from the people you interview, consume their stories and their pain, but never, ever give anything in return. Don't give money (that makes sense) and don't give friendship or advice either. Yet that is exactly what Abdulaziz is asking of me now.

So I wing it. I decide to tell Abdulaziz a story. (My tribe approves of stories.) As stories go, it is rather lame, and I'm not even sure it relates to Abdulaziz's question. But it's a start.

I was home listening to NPR when I heard a familiar voice, a colleague who also works as a reporter for the network. She had woven a small masterpiece. A story that was pitch-perfect. My old nemesis, professional envy, kicked in. God, I thought, her life is perfect. So together. Everything is going swimmingly for her, while I am drowning in a sea of irrelevance. I sent my friend an e-mail, telling her how much I liked her story and adding, breezily, without a trace of envy, that I hoped life was good.

Thanks, she wrote back, but no, life was not good. Just yesterday, her three-year-old son had been diagnosed with a rare, debilitating disease.

I felt like a fool. I had misread reality, once again failing to realize that, as the Hindus say, all is *maya*, illusion. Things are not as they seem. We humans do not know a damn thing. About anything. A scary thought but also, in a way, a liberating one. Our highs, our accomplishments, are not real. But neither are our setbacks, our *mushkala*. They are not real either.

Abdulaziz absorbs my story in silence. I'm not sure what he's thinking, and I doubt if my story has helped. He never tells me what his *mushkala* is, and it doesn't feel right to ask. Finally, he says, "I see what you mean. Thank you." I can't tell if he's just being polite.

Abdulaziz drops me off at my hotel. By now, I have downgraded to something approaching a fleabag. I've learned my lesson. Comfort is best when interspersed with moments of great discomfort. Here, there is no cloying bevy of attendants, just a Pakistani guy with hair growing out of one ear who mans the front desk and, if I ask nicely, can procure a cold beer. Tonight, I need two.

I keep thinking about something Abdulaziz said. When he's feeling down, he said, he talks to his God. Not prays but talks, that's the word he used. I liked how that sounded. Talking comes naturally to me. Praying does not. Of course, Abdulaziz's God is Allah. Not exactly my God. I wonder: Who is my God? No obvious answer springs to mind. Over the years, I have been spiritually promiscuous, dabbling in Hinduism, Buddhism, Zoroastrianism, and even occasionally Judaism. None, however, could qualify as my full-time faith, my God. Then, suddenly, His name pops into my mind and His is not a name I expected. Ambition. Yes, that is my God.

When Ambition is your God, the office is your temple, the

employee handbook your holy book. The sacred drink, coffee, is imbibed five times a day. When you worship Ambition, there is no Sabbath, no day of rest. Every day, you rise early and kneel before the God Ambition, facing in the direction of your PC. You pray alone, always alone, even though others may be present. Ambition is a vengeful God. He will smite those who fail to worship faithfully, but that is nothing compared to what He has in store for the faithful. They suffer the worst fate of all. For it is only when they are old and tired, entombed in the corner office, that the realization hits like a Biblical thunderclap. The God Ambition is a false God and always has been.

I leave Qatar the next evening. It's dark when I arrive at the airport, but I swear I can still feel the sun, a phantom heat that would shadow me for weeks afterward.

I've tucked Abdulaziz's business card into my breast pocket, alongside my Ridiculously Expensive Pen. The intense pleasure I derive from the pen—the way it rests in my palm perfectly, the way it glides across the page as if riding a cushion of air—will, according to Ruut Veenhoven and the other happiness experts, diminish over time. I will crave a better, more expensive pen, as I fall prey to the hedonic treadmill.

The experts were dead wrong. I enjoyed the pen for as long as I owned it. Which was exactly nine days. That's when I lost it, in a taxi in New York. Or maybe transiting at Heathrow Airport. That's not the point. The point is: It's gone. My first and only Ridiculously Expensive Pen, gone forever. And while at times I pine for my lost Lavin, I know in my heart that its joys were illusory, a mirage in the desert.

I'm back to a ninety-nine-cent Bic. It has no heft or style. It doesn't say anything about me. It's just a pen. I don't ask anything more of it, and that, I suspect, is why we get along so well.

# Chapter 5

# ICELAND

# Happiness Is Failure

Of all the substances known to man, the least stable is something called francium. It's never lasted longer than twenty-two minutes. At any given time there is only one ounce of francium in the earth's crust. "Vanishingly rare" is how it's often described. There are places like that, too.

I arrive to blowing snow and an inky black sky as dark and vast as outer space. It is 10:00 a.m.

"When does the sun rise?" I ask the nice man at reception.

He looks at me like I'm daft. When he replies, he speaks slowly and deliberately.

"The sun? Oh, I don't think you'll be seeing the sun today."

He says this like it's an obvious fact, as in, "Oh, it's Sunday, so of course the shops are closed today."

Not see the sun? I don't like the way this sounds. In the past, the sun has always been there for me, the one celestial body I could count on. Unlike Pluto, which for decades led me to believe it was an actual planet when the whole time it was really only a dwarf planet.

I had plenty of time to ponder celestial bodies on the long flight from Miami. Flying from Florida to Iceland in the dead of winter is at best counterintuitive and at worst sheer lunacy. My body sensed this before the rest of me. It knew something was wrong, that some violation of nature was taking place, and expressed its displeasure by twitching and flatulating more than usual.

I have my reasons, though. According to Ruut Veenhoven's database of happiness, Iceland consistently ranks as one of the happiest countries in the world. In some surveys, it ranks number one.

When I first saw the data, I had the same reaction you're probably having now. Iceland? As in land of ice? As in cold and dark and teetering on the edge of the map as if it might fall off at any moment? Yes, that Iceland.

As for the winter part, I figured anyone could be happy during the Icelandic summers, when the sun shines at midnight and the weather turns "pleasantly not cold," as one Icelander put it. But the winter, yes, the cold, dark winter, that was the real test of Icelandic happiness.

I plop down on my hotel bed and drift off to sleep for a few hours. This is easy to do in the middle of the day since it looks an awful lot like the middle of the night. When I awake, the sky has lightened a bit, achieving a state of pleasantly not dark, but pleasantly not dark isn't the same as light any more than pleasantly not cold is the same as warm.

I find myself pondering darkness, something I admit I haven't pondered much in the past. For me, as I suspect for most people, dark has always been dark. What is there to ponder? In fact, there are as many varieties of darkness as there are types of landscapes or clouds. Some darkness is hard and unforgiving. Other darkness is softened by the glow of the moon or distant city lights. Then there is the expectant darkness of 5:00 a.m., when we sense though can't yet see the coming dawn.

Icelandic darkness is in a category of its own, a stingy darkness that reveals nothing and, if it could talk, would probably do so with a thick New York accent: "Yo, ya gotta problem wit Mista Darkness, bub?" It is a darkness that for several months each year engulfs Iceland, smothers it, encases it, like one of those head-to-toe burkas worn by some Muslim women. Just as black and just as confining.

How, I wonder, staring out my hotel window into black nothingness, can Icelanders possibly be happy living under this veil of darkness? I've always associated happy places with palm trees and beaches and blue drinks and, of course, swim-up bars. That's paradise, right? The global travel industry certainly wants us to think so. Bliss, the ads tell us, lies someplace else, and that someplace else is sunny and eighty degrees. Always. Our language, too, reflects the palm-tree bias. Happy people have a sunny disposition and always look on the bright side of life. Unhappy people possess dark souls and black bile.

But the number crunchers at the World Database of Happiness say that, once again, we've got it wrong. Climate matters, but not the way we think. All things considered, colder is happier. The implications of this are tremendous. Maybe we should all be vacationing in Iceland, not the Caribbean. And global warming takes on added significance. Not only does it threaten to ravage ecosystems, flood coastal cities, and possibly end life on earth, it's also likely to seriously bum us out. This might be the most inconvenient truth of all.

Theories abound as to why cold or temperate climes produce happier people than warm, tropical ones. My favorite theory is one I call the Get-Along-or-Die Theory. In warm places, this theory states, life is too easy; your next meal simply falls from a coconut tree. Cooperation with others is optional. In colder places, though, cooperation is mandatory. Everyone must work together to ensure a good harvest or a hearty haul of cod. Or everyone dies. Together.

Necessity may be the mother of invention, but interdependence is the mother of affection. We humans need one another, so we cooperate—for purely selfish reasons at first. At some point, though, the needing fades and all that remains is the cooperation. We help other people because we can, or because it makes us feel good, not because we're counting on some future payback. There is a word for this: love.

I desperately need a stiff drink. For research purposes, of course. Before my trip, people who know Iceland told me that to really get at the heart of the Icelandic soul, to understand what makes these quirky sons and daughters of the Vikings tick, I needed to observe them in their natural state: pickled.

Luckily, I've arrived on a Saturday, in the midst of the decadent Icelandic weekend, which is not to be confused with the sober Icelandic week. Icelanders practice bracketed indulgence. Everything in moderation, they believe, including moderation. It's perfectly acceptable to drink yourself comatose on the weekend, but so much as sip a glass of Chardonnay on a Tuesday night and you're branded a lush. Icelanders attribute this oddity, like all of their peccadilloes, to their Viking past. The theory goes like this: During the harsh days of yore, people never knew when the next catch of fish or crop of vegetables might arrive, so when it did, they devoured it greedily. Of course, nowadays there isn't a shortage of anything in Iceland, except sunlight, but the old binge mentality remains, like an appendix or tailbone. Only more fun.

Actually, the best explanation I heard for the weekend binge drinking came from a sunburned penguin. Okay, not a real penguin, but an Icelander named Magnus who lives in Miami Beach. When we met for lunch one day, I was instantly reminded of a sunburned penguin—an image I tried but failed to dislodge from my mind for the two hours that we ate and drank at a bookstore café. Magnus believes that Icelanders drink so much because the population is so small. They see the same familiar faces, day in and day out. By the end of the week, they need a break, but getting off the island isn't easy. So they drink—heavily—and suddenly all those familiar faces look a little less familiar. "It's sort of like putting on a new pair of glasses, with a different prescription," the sunburned penguin told me. "The world looks a bit different, a bit less familiar."

Here in Reykjavík, Iceland's capital, there's a bar right next to my hotel. It's called Sirkus. The fronting is painted bright reds and greens. It looks like it belongs on a Caribbean island, not in cold, dark Reykjavík. I ask the nice man at reception whether he can recommend it. He quickly looks me up and down before declaring, "I don't think it's for you."

"Are you suggesting," I say, doing my best to sound hurt, "that I'm not hip enough for that bar?"

"Not exactly. I'm suggesting you don't listen to punk music and buy your clothes at secondhand stores."

He has a point. I back down and head instead to the more grown-up establishment he recommends.

The bar is indeed grown-up, if you were a grown-up living in, oh, 1982. There's a worrisome abundance of wood paneling and track lighting. The piped-in music sounds suspiciously disco. I notice a group of young Icelandic men sitting at a table, eyes trained on the centerpiece: two large bottles of Tanqueray nestled in buckets of ice. Clearly, they are settling in for a serious evening of bracketed indulgence.

I order a beer, which costs as much as a college education in some countries. The high cost of alcohol (and pretty much everything else) in Iceland is another explanation for their take-no-prisoners style of drinking. Since booze is so expensive, Icelanders figure if you're not getting drunk you're wasting your money. It is difficult to argue with such sturdy, Nordic logic.

Iceland has a long and twisted history with alcohol. The country briefly experimented with prohibition, at roughly the same time as the United States did and with roughly the same success. Prohibition was lifted in the 1930s, and Icelanders have been drinking heartily ever since. Oddly, the government continued to ban beer for many more decades—apparently concerned that people would remain lightly buzzed all week rather than bookending their drunkenness with a few days of sobriety. Finally, in 1989, the ban on beer was lifted, and Icelanders put down their shot glasses and picked up their beer steins. One Icelandic psychologist told me, "Icelanders used to get drunk on hard liquor, like vodka; now they get drunk on wine and beer." He said this like it represented progress.

I'm sipping my extravagant beer, amusing myself by calculating how much each sip costs—gulp, there goes $1.25; gulp, that one was small, only seventy-five cents—when I hear a female voice. She is speaking English, and she is speaking to me.

"Can you tie me up?" I spin around to find a heavyset woman with a tattoo of something—it's hard to say what—on her left forearm. I just sit there, staring blankly for a beat too long.

"Can you tie me?" she repeats, this time dropping the preposition that has lent a lascivious air to her request. She points to the bow on the back of her dress that has come undone. I tie it and introduce myself.

Her name is Eva, and she is drunk. Within a few minutes, I learn that it's her birthday today, that she's a single mother, that her ex-husband beat her, that she's lived outside of Iceland for the past seven years, and that she's now holding down three jobs. She is clearly not shy, nor is she particularly happy. A six on a scale of one to ten, she says. She introduces me to her friend Harpa, who is both drunker and happier—a solid nine, she says, putting an arm around me like we are old friends. I quickly do the math. Harpa and Eva, when averaged, are a 7.5, making them only slightly less happy than your typical Icelander. No wonder they're friends.

Harpa and Eva didn't get drunk at this bar. They arrived drunk. Typically, they tell me, Icelanders start drinking at home, where the booze is cheaper and then, once sufficiently prelubricated, head to the bars. Some people, those on an especially tight budget, will park a bottle of booze on the sidewalk near the bar and then step outside for a nip every few minutes. It is this kind of resourcefulness, I think, that explains how this hardy band of Vikings managed to survive more than one thousand years on an island that is about as hospitable to human habitation as the planet Pluto—if Pluto were a planet, that is, which it's not.

The music is loud. Eva and Harpa are sloshed. I am jet-lagged. These three facts conspire against coherent conversation. "I'm a writer," I tell Eva, trying to break through the fog.

She looks confused. "A rider? What do you ride, horses?"

"No, a WRITER," I shout.

This scores me points. In Iceland, being a writer is pretty much the best thing you can be. Successful, struggling, published in books or only in your mind, it matters not. Icelanders adore their writers. Partly, this represents a kind of narcissism, since just about everyone in Iceland is a writer or poet. Taxi drivers, college professors, hotel clerks, fishermen. Everyone. Icelanders joke that one day they will erect a statue in the center of Reykjavík to honor the one Icelander who never wrote a poem. They're still waiting for that person to be born.

"Better to go barefoot than without a book," the Icelandic saying goes. The government supports writers with generous grants—salaries, really—that might last for three years. Iceland's most famous writer, the Nobel Prize winner Halldór Laxness, once remarked, "I don't understand this myth of the starving artist. I never missed a meal."

I figure now is a good time to dive in with the question that has brought me to this overpriced, wood-paneled bar.

"So, why do Icelanders drink so much?"

"It's because of the darkness," declares Harpa confidently. "We drink because it is so dark."

"So you don't drink in the summer?"

"Oh, no, we drink in the summer, too. Because of the light. We drink because we're so happy that it's light."

Harpa just stands there for a moment, swaying back and forth, mug in hand, her beer-soaked brain contemplating the unavoidable conclusion: Icelanders drink all year long.

I can't afford another beer, and Harpa and Eva have grown virtually incomprehensible. It is time to leave.

"Wait," says Harpa, mustering a final burst of lucidity, "you need to know something. About the darkness."

"Yes, what about it?"

"Don't fight it. Embrace it."

And with that, she and Eva disappear into a cloud of cigarette smoke and the pleasant hum of Icelandic chatter. Funny, I think, as I bundle up, it sounds exactly like seals barking.

* * *

The next morning, I try, as Harpa suggested, to embrace the darkness. It's not working. If anything, the darkness is embracing me, suffocating me. My alarm clock says 8:00 a.m., but outside says midnight. I slam the snooze button again and again and again until, finally, at 9:30 a.m., I muster the resolve to get out of bed. I peer out of my hotel window. Still dark. Not even a hint of dawn. The sun is like most things in life. You don't miss it until it's gone.

Wait, I do see some sort of light. Not sunlight but a bluish glow. Is it the aurora borealis, the northern lights? It's coming from the building across the street. Perhaps some exotic Viking ritual? I put on my glasses. The light, I now realize, is that of computer terminals. The Icelandic workday has begun. How do they do it? How do they begin and end the day in darkness?

My alarm clock says 9:55. Oh, no. The free breakfast buffet ends in five minutes, and in Iceland free food is precious indeed. I scramble downstairs, pile my plate high with herring and gouda, until it's nearly overflowing, and fill my coffee mug to the brim. In Iceland, coffee is a staple, as necessary as oxygen.

You'd think all of this darkness would lead to an epidemic of Seasonal Affective Disorder (SAD). Caused by a lack of sunlight, SAD leads to symptoms such as despair, listlessness, and a craving for carbohydrates. It strikes me as a particularly cruel affliction. Not only are you depressed, but you're likely to gain weight from all of those carbs, thus making you more depressed and therefore turning once again to carbs, which make you more depressed.

Yet the ailment is virtually nonexistent in Iceland. There is a higher prevalence of the disorder in the northeastern United States than in Iceland. Perplexed by the results, psychologists theorize that over the centuries Icelanders developed a genetic immunity to the disease. Those who got SAD died out, taking their gene pool with them. Survival of the felicitous.

I've finished my third cup of coffee and am eager to get going. There's no point in waiting for the sun—that would take months—

so I bundle up and head outside. Icelanders, for obvious reasons, have several words for ice. The particular kind underneath my feet at the moment is called *"hálka"*: flying ice. The ice doesn't fly, you do. I slip and slide, almost falling on several occasions, before getting a handle on the flying ice.

I immediately like Reykjavík. Iceland's capital is not so much a small city as a cosmopolitan village. The best of both worlds. Small-town neighborliness but with sushi, too. Anywhere you can't reach in Reykjavík within a ten-minute walk probably isn't worth reaching. I like this—not only because it limits the amount of time I am exposed to flying ice but also because it feels right. Most cities are bigger than necessary. Beyond a certain point, the liabilities of urban life start to outweigh the benefits.

Reykjavík is in no danger of crossing that Rubicon. The entire population of Iceland is only three hundred thousand, roughly the same as that of Louisville, Kentucky, or your average bus stop in China. Iceland is about as small as a country can be and still be a country.

Thirty years ago, the maverick economist E. F. Schumacher argued that when it comes to economics, smaller is better. But is smaller also happier? Are microstates like Iceland more likely to achieve national bliss than bigger countries like the United States or China?

On a practical level, Iceland's smallness means that parents needn't bother with that old bromide about not talking to strangers. There are no strangers in Iceland. People are constantly running into friends and acquaintances. It's not unusual for people to show up thirty minutes late for work because en route they encountered a parade of friends. This is a perfectly valid excuse, by the way, for being late. The Icelandic equivalent of traffic was hell. On the downside, Iceland is the worst place in the world to have an affair, though that doesn't stop people from trying.

Former French president Jacques Chirac, in his farewell speech, declared: "A nation is a family." Chirac was speaking figuratively, but Iceland really is a family. Geneticists have found that everyone in the country is related to everyone else, going back seven or eight generations. Icelanders can go to a website and find out how closely they are related to a colleague, a friend—or that cutie they slept with last night.

One woman told me how unnerving this can be. "You've slept with this guy you've just met and then the next day you're at a family reunion, and there he is in the corner eating smoked fish. You're like—'Oh, my God, I just slept with my second cousin.' "

All of this closeness, this familiarity, has a direct effect on how government works. Take unemployment. Politicians are more likely to care if Hans is unemployed if Hans is their brother's best friend. In the United States, there is an unspoken understanding that an unemployment rate of 5 or 6 percent is acceptable, yet inflation must stay very low—no more than 1 or 2 percent.

In Iceland, the reverse is true. If the unemployment rate reaches 5 percent, it's considered a national scandal. Presidents are booted from office. Yet Icelanders will tolerate a relatively high inflation rate. Why the different approaches?

The answer lies in how countries feel about pain, economic pain. High inflation is shared pain; everyone feels the pinch of higher prices when they go to the grocery store or the gas station. Everyone suffers a little; no one suffers a lot. Unemployment is selective pain. A relatively few people suffer greatly, yet most of us don't suffer at all.

Or do we? High unemployment, research has found, reduces overall happiness much more than high inflation. The specter of losing one's job spreads through a nation like a ripple across a pond.


An older man shuffles by. He is disheveled, has a scruffy beard, and is wearing a leather bomber jacket. I wonder if it's Bobby Fischer. I'd heard that the former chess champion was living here. Icelanders love Bobby Fischer. He took part in one of the most famous chess matches ever, right here in Reykjavík. Fischer was brilliant, beating his Russian counterpart, Boris Spassky, in a match watched around the world. For Americans, Fischer became an instant hero, a Cold Warrior who had defeated the Evil Empire, albeit only on the chessboard. For Icelanders, Fischer was also a hero but for a different reason. He had put Iceland on the map, and that is the best thing anyone can do for this tiny nation.

Fischer has not aged well. He's grown ornery and, at times, incoherent. He spewed anti-Semitic comments and, after the attacks of September 11, anti-American ones as well. When, in 2004, Fischer was detained in Tokyo and faced deportation to the United States on charges he violated a travel ban to the former Yugoslavia, the Icelandic parliament came to his rescue. They granted him citizenship, and he's been living here ever since, shuffling around Reykjavík, muttering to himself. A Cold War ghost.

The strange and sad case of Bobby Fischer says more about Iceland than it does about Bobby Fischer. Icelanders possess a deep love for the game of chess, an abiding loyalty to their friends, an obsession with getting on the map, and a high tolerance for idiosyncrasy—not only when it comes to people but, as I discovered, in food as well.

The connection between food and happiness is well documented. The good people at McDonald's know this. That's why they call their burger-and-fries combo the Happy Meal, not the Worthwhile Meal or the Existential Meal. People may like to chew on misery, but they want to swallow happiness.

"He who tastes, knows," goes the old Sufi saying. France's most famous epicure, Jean Anthelme Brillat-Savarin, believed that food is the mirror to our souls: "Tell me what you eat, and I'll tell you what you are."

So what does this say about the Icelanders? Quite a lot, it turns out, for these people have some funny ideas about food. Traditionally, Icelanders won't eat anything ugly. Until the 1950s, Icelandic fishermen threw lobsters back into the sea. Too ugly. And to this day most Icelanders avoid eating cod for the same reason, even though the fish is so plentiful in the North Atlantic waters it practically swims up to your dinner plate, fillets itself, and jumps into a nice lemon meunière sauce. Instead, Icelanders export cod to America, where people apparently have no compunction about eating ugly things.

The Icelanders' fussiness about how food looks does not extend to how it tastes. How else to explain such favorites as *súrsaðir hrútspungar*, ram's testicles, or *harkarl*, rotten shark? The latter supposedly promotes virility and intestinal health.

The poet W. H. Auden sampled *harkarl* when he visited Iceland in the 1930s. He was blunt in his appraisal. "It tastes more like boot polish than anything else I can think of," Auden wrote, adding that, "owing to the smell, it had to be eaten out of doors."

Not exactly a stellar Zagat recommendation. But I was curious. Can it really be that bad? Besides, I felt a certain reportorial responsibility. If food is indeed the mirror of a nation's soul, then I had an obligation to stare into that mirror, no matter how foul.

The best place for *harkarl*, I'm told, is the weekend flea market. Held in a cavernous warehouse near the harbor, it's where Icelanders go for bargains, such as they are in this land of ten-dollar cups of coffee. It's crammed with used books and clothing and all manner of bric-a-brac. I find it refreshingly unsophisticated, an island of squareness in a vast sea of hipness.

After some meandering, I stumble on the *harkarl*. It looks harmless enough. Cubes of gray meat, the size of dice. The woman behind the counter is grim and muscular, and I wonder if she killed the shark with her bare hands. I approach meekly and ask for a piece, please. In one smooth motion, she spears a gray cube with a toothpick and hands it to me, unsmiling.

I take a deep breath, then swallow. Instantly, my mind is flooded with one thought: Auden was right. I've never actually eaten boot polish, but this, I imagine, is what it tastes like. The *harkarl* has an acidic, unnatural flavor. Worst of all is the persistent aftertaste. It lodges on the roof of my mouth and resists eviction, despite my attempts to flush it out with many glasses of water, a bag of honey-roasted cashews, an entire wheel of gouda cheese, and two bottles of beer. By the time I return to my hotel, an hour later, the taste has, ominously, migrated to my throat, and shows no signs of leaving soon. I feel sick.

"Tried the *harkarl,* did you?" says the nice man at reception, sensing my discomfort.

"Yes, how did you know?"

He doesn't answer, just makes a quiet tsk-tsking sound and then suggests I try a drink called *svarti dauoi,* or black death. It is the Icelandic national drink, and it is, I can report, the only substance known to man that is strong enough to dislodge the taste of rotten shark from your throat. True, it inflicts an especially nasty hangover, but that is a small price to pay for liberation.


I'm sliding around Reykjavík, and something seems…off. Not right. The city, I realize, doesn't feel solid. Not exactly gaseous, like Qatar, but temporary, fleeting, as if it were erected yesterday and could just as easily disappear tomorrow. I half expect to hear someone shout, "Cut, that's a wrap" and see stagehands cart away the city en masse. The architecture, such as it is, partly explains this feeling. Many of the buildings are made from corrugated steel and look flimsy. Then there are the cliffs, mountains, and sea, which loom around every corner, threatening to erase the city. One minute I'm immersed in urbanity—cafés, designer shops— then I turn down a street and suddenly the view has transfigured to a wild, natural one.

Unlike New York or Shanghai, Reykjavík has no delusions of grandeur. It's a city that knows its place in the cosmos, knows it's an insignificant place, and is comfortable with that. Icelanders thrive on this provisional nature of life. It keeps them on their toes, fires their imaginations. Most of all, it reminds them of the fragility of life. Big cities feign immortality, deluded that somehow their sheer size, their conquest over nature, will forestall death. In Iceland, a land where nature always gets the last word, immortality is so obviously a joke that no one takes it seriously.

In fact, Icelanders seem to thrive on nature's sense of impending doom. Kristin, a television producer, told me about a recent walk she took, just ten minutes from her house in a suburb of Reykjavík, which abuts a lava field: "Not another human being in sight. If I fell and broke an ankle, I'd die of exposure in a matter of hours." It sounded frightening to me, but she found it exhilarating. Is this the same thrill that motivates the skydiver or the motorcycle stuntman? I don't think so. She's not talking about an adrenaline rush but rather a deep, timeless connection to nature—a connection that includes the prospect of death but is not defined by it.

Sliding around Reykjavík, it doesn't take long to realize that this is an exceptionally creative place. Every other building, it seems, is an art gallery or a music store or a café filled with writers penning the Great Icelandic Novel. Maybe, I speculate, this is the secret to Icelandic happiness.

Clearly, happiness is not a function of cold, hard logic—or all accountants would be ecstatic. The great thinkers have long pointed to a connection between creativity and happiness. "Happiness," Kant once said, "is an ideal not of reason but of imagination." In other words, we create our happiness, and the first step in creating anything is to imagine it.

The British academic Richard Schoch, in his book *The Secrets of Happiness,* put it this way: "Your imagination must, to some extent, be found in a realm beyond reason because it begins with imagining a future reality: the self that you might become."

We tend to think of culture as something old and fragile. Culture is what we inherit from our ancestors and either preserve or, more likely, squander. True, but that tells only part of the story. Culture is also invented. Of course it is. Someone had to invent it so we could fuck it up.

Iceland—and this is the part that is truly mind-blowing—is inventing its culture now. As you read these words, some Icelandic musician is composing the quintessential Icelandic song. So far, no such thing exists. There is no tradition of instrumental music in Iceland. It was too cold and dark back then to bother, or maybe the ancient Icelanders were too drunk at the time. So young Icelanders are deciding for themselves what is quintessentially Icelandic. It is a wonderful thing to watch. To be present at the moment of creation.

If it is possible for language, mere words, to nurture happiness, to tickle the creative soul of an entire people, then surely that language is Icelandic. Icelanders love their language. Love it even more than they love their country, which is saying something. For Icelanders, language is the tabernacle of the culture. That's what one person here told me. In any other country, I'd dismiss such a statement as nationalistic hyperbole. I might even laugh. Not in Iceland.

As any Icelander will tell you (and tell you and tell you), they speak the pure language of the Vikings, while other Scandinavian countries speak a bastardized, diluted version. Like the French, Icelanders are fiercely protective of their native tongue. Unlike the French, Icelanders aren't sanctimonious about it. Everyone here speaks English as well as Icelandic. "Bilingualism" is not a dirty word.

With every new invention—the computer or, say, low-fat blueberry muffins—countries around the world need to invent new words, in their own languages, for these things. Most take the easy way out and simply borrow the English word, bending it to fit their language. Thus, in Japan a personal computer becomes a *persu-con*. But Icelanders insist on inventing purely Icelandic words for these modern devices.

Icelandic linguists do this by drawing upon the language of the Vikings. Of course, the Vikings didn't have a word for lightbulb, let alone broadband, so the linguists have to get creative. The Icelandic word for television—*sjónvarp*—for instance, means, literally, "sight caster." The intercontinental ballistic missile presented a real challenge. Ultimately, the linguists came up with a word that means "long distance fiery flying thing." Not bad. My favorite, though, is the word for computer: *tolva,* or "prophet of numbers." I like the way it makes my PC sound like something magical and vaguely ominous. Which, actually, it is.

The highest compliment any foreigner ever paid Iceland came when, in the nineteenth century, a Dane named Rasmus Christian Rask claimed he had learned Icelandic "in order to be able to think." When I heard that, it made *me* think—about the connection between language and happiness. Can language make us happy? Do words alone have the power not only to describe our moods but to create them?

Clearly, some words can elicit instant joy. Words like "I love you" and "you may already be a winner." Yet other words—"audit" and "prostate exam" come to mind—have the opposite effect.

All languages share one trait, and it is not a happy one. As I discovered in Switzerland, every culture has many more words to describe negative emotional states than positive ones. This partly explains why I've found it so difficult to get people to talk to me about happiness. They literally don't have the words to express it. It also makes me wonder: Are we hardwired for misery? Are we a species of whiners? Perhaps. Or maybe happiness is so sublime, so self-evident, that it doesn't require many words to describe it.

An optimist might point to some hopeful evidence from the field of neuroscience. Researchers at the University of Wisconsin have discovered that the part of the brain that controls language is, like the part that controls happiness, relatively new, in evolutionary terms. So is there a connection between these two recent upgrades to our brains? If so, is language merely along for the ride—or is it in the driver's seat, in ways we don't yet understand?

That's hard to say, but there is no denying that, for Icelanders at least, language is an immense source of joy. Everything wise and wonderful about this quirky little nation flows from its language. The formal Icelandic greeting is *"komdu sæll,"* which translates literally as "come happy." When Icelanders part, they say *"vertu sæll*," "go happy." I like that one a lot. It's so much better than "take care" or "catch you later."

The Icelandic language, like the people who speak it, is egalitarian and utterly free of pretense. Bill Holm captured the casual elegance of the Icelandic language in—what else?—a poem.

> In an air-conditioned room you cannot understand the
> Grammar of this language,
> The whirring machine drowns out the soft vowels,
> But you can hear these vowels in the mountain wind
> And in heavy seas breaking over the hull of a small boat.
> Old ladies can wind their long hair in this language
> And can hum, and knit, and make pancakes.
> But you cannot have a cocktail party in this language
> And say witty things standing up with a drink in your
>     hand.
> You must sit down to speak this language,
> It is so heavy you can't be polite or chatter in it.
> For once you have begun a sentence, the whole course of
>     your life is laid out before you

I love that last line in particular. It speaks to how words can possess a momentum of their own, beyond the literal meaning they convey.

The greatest Icelandic poet of all was a Viking named Egill Skallagrímsson, who lived about one thousand years ago and is widely known, as one Icelandic artist told me, "as that mean motherfucker who wrote beautiful poetry." Egill was not a poet to be trifled with. "He wrote some of our most beautiful poems but would also throw up on his host and take out their eyes if he felt in any way offended." I imagine that the literary critics of the time reviewed Egill's works very...carefully. So embedded is the link between verse and violence in Iceland that the ancient Norse god Odin is the god of both poetry and war.

Does this fierce literary streak explain Icelandic happiness?

I'm not sure. A love of language may not guarantee happiness, but it allows you to express your despair eloquently, and that is worth something. As any poet (or blogger) knows, misery expressed is misery reduced.

But it still didn't make sense. Why is Reykjavík, this cosmopolitan village at the end of the world, such a bastion of creativity? Other Nordic countries, Sweden and Denmark, have much larger populations but don't produce the same caliber of art. What is so special about Iceland?

The answer, I suspect, lies in the name. Ice Land. First, the ice part. Imagine what life was like a few hundred years ago during those long, cold winters. People lived in a sort of sensory deprivation. The mind abhors a vacuum, as the popularity of cable TV attests, so the ancient Icelanders invented dwarves, elves, and other creatures that supposedly populated the rough countryside. Fantastical? Insane?

Alda, a popular blogger, told me about an experience she had recently. She and a friend were visiting a remote part of the country, a breeding ground for Arctic terns. They were walking along the shore, when all of a sudden they heard the sounds of a party, laughter and clinking glasses. Who would be having a party out here, in the middle of nowhere? they wondered. Alda and her friend spent the next ten minutes trying to find this party, but with no success.

It was then that they realized: There was no party. It was an acoustic illusion caused by the echoes of the waves crashing against the cliffs and the birds chirping. Alda, a child of the Enlightenment, not to mention the Information Age, was tricked by the dark magic of Iceland. Her ancestors of one thousand years ago didn't stand a chance.

Then there is the land part of the Iceland equation. Most land just sits there. It may be beautiful land, stunning even, but ultimately that's all it does: sit there. Not Icelandic land. It hisses. It spits. It belches and, on occasion, farts. There are, I'm told, sound geologic reasons for this. None of which interests me. What interests me is how all of this hissing and spitting and belching (and occasional farting) affects Icelandic happiness.

For one thing, Icelanders tell me, the land itself is a source of creative inspiration and, indirectly, happiness. The ground is, quite literally, shifting beneath their feet. There are, on average, twenty earthquakes a day in Iceland. Not cataclysmic ones, of course, but all of that seismic activity must shake things up.

In Iceland, geologic time is speeded up. Volcanoes are born not over the course of centuries but in a single lifetime. And if you are inclined to believe in energy vortexes and other such things, then Iceland is the country for you. People talk about energy here more than anywhere else I've been. One Icelander, a graphic designer, told me he squirrels away energy, in the form of sunlight, during the bright summers so that he can make it through the dark winters. Another person, a music producer, told me the "weird energy" explains why most albums are released during the autumn, when everything is dying.

Over the centuries, the world has witnessed a handful of Golden Ages. Places and times of immense creativity and human flourishing. Fifth-century Athens. Elizabethan London. Renaissance Florence. Late-twentieth-century Seattle. Golden Ages never last long. They are fleeting, francium places.

"History shows that golden urban ages are rare and special windows of light, that briefly illuminate the world, both within them and outside them, and then again are shuttered," writes British historian Peter Hall in his marvelous book *Cities in Civilization*.

Is tiny, quirky Reykjavík one of these rare and special windows of light? I wouldn't say it's another Renaissance-era Florence—that would be a stretch—but the two cities have a few things in common. The same population, roughly 95,000. And in Reykjavík, as in fourteenth-century Florence, there is no creative elite. Art is produced and enjoyed by everyone.

Do history and seismic energy alone explain the creative buzz in Reykjavík? Or is there something else, something I'm missing?

One thing is certain. Icelanders possess a natural sense of style, which, as far as I'm concerned, is the most annoying kind. Fake style can be faked; natural style cannot. I know. I've tried. I own an inordinate amount of black clothing, two pairs of funky glasses I wear all the time, several Kangol hats, some of which I've been known to wear backward. My facial hair is sculpted. My collars are peasant. To the casual observer, I look like a middle-aged man with a decent sense of style. But people with real style, and pretty much anyone under the age of twenty-five, can see me for what I am. A counterfeit fashionista. The walking, talking equivalent of a Louis Vuitton knockoff.

My low point, the moment when I know all is lost, fashion-wise, comes in of all places a thrift store. Its name, like all Icelandic words, is impossible for foreigners to pronounce lest they risk total and irreversible facial paralysis, so for safety reasons I will not divulge it here. The store sells secondhand goods at firsthand prices, which in Iceland makes it a bargain hunters' paradise.

I find a particularly stylish scarf and go to pay for it. The young guy working the register is busy digging around for something; he bends over, exposing a good swath of underwear. I am shocked. Not by the unexpected display of undergarment—I've seen that before—but by the fact that it is cool underwear. Hip underwear. Fashionable underwear. A series of horizontal stripes—red, blue, and green, with a tasteful splash of purple—all nicely arranged on a brief. Good god, even their underwear is hip! Hipper than most of my outerwear. I stand there, staring at this Icelandic clerk's underwear for a while and then, I know, just know. I don't stand a chance in this country.

Iceland's hipness is endemic, afflicting not only the young but also the middle-aged. People like Larus Johannesson. He owns a small music store and a recording label. Everyone knows Larus. If I wanted to understand Iceland's rampant creativity, people told me, I must meet Larus.

We meet at his record store, a cozy hodgepodge of couches and CDs. Larus is wearing a plaid sports coat and black-rimmed

glasses, which he presses against his nose when making an important point. He has natural style. I like him anyway. Outside, a soft
darkness has settled over the city.

Larus tells me that he used to be a professional chess player.
Yes, I think, that makes sense. It explains the mind, clearly churning behind those hip glasses, and the endearing shyness, which I
suspect he has worked hard to overcome. Icelanders are renowned
chess players. Why? Once again, I'm told, it's because of those
long winters. What else is there to do in the dark?

To say Larus has an eclectic background is like saying Roger
Federer dabbles in tennis. In his forty-odd years, Larus has earned
a living not only as a chess player but also as a journalist, a
construction-company executive, a theologian, and, now, a music
producer. "I know," he says, sensing my disbelief. "But that kind
of résumé is completely normal in Iceland."

Having multiple identities (though not multiple personalities)
is, he believes, conducive to happiness. This runs counter to the
prevailing belief in the United States and other western nations,
where specialization is considered the highest good. Academics,
doctors, and other professionals spend lifetimes learning more
and more about less and less. In Iceland, people learn more and
more about more and more.

I ask Larus about the creative buzz in the Reykjavík air. Where
does it come from—and how can I get some?

He presses his glasses against his nose.

"Envy."

"What about it?"

"There's not much in Iceland."

The lack of envy he's talking about is a bit different from what
I saw in Switzerland. The Swiss suppress envy by hiding things.
Icelanders suppress envy by sharing them. Icelandic musicians
help one another out, Larus explains. If one band needs an amp
or a lead guitarist, another band will help them out, no questions
asked. Ideas, too, flow freely, unencumbered by envy, that most

toxic of the seven deadly sins. Once unleashed, writes Joseph Epstein in his treatise on the subject, "envy tends to diminish all in whom it takes possession."

This relative lack of envy is one sure sign of a Golden Age, says Peter Hall. Here he is describing turn-of-the-century Paris but could just as easily be describing twenty-first-century Reykjavík: "They lived and worked in each other's pockets. Any innovation, any new trend, was immediately known, and could be freely incorporated into the work of any of the others." In other words, the Parisian artists of 1900 believed in open-source software. So, too, do Icelanders. Sure, they compete, but in the way the word was originally intended. The roots of the word "compete" are the Latin *competere,* which means to "seek with."

Okay, I had found another piece of the puzzle. Minimum envy. But I still sensed I was missing something. How can it be that this flyspeck of a nation produces more artists and writers per capita than any other?

"It's because of failure," says Larus, pushing his glasses hard against the bridge of his nose.

"Failure?"

"Yes, failure doesn't carry a stigma in Iceland. In fact, in a way, we admire failures."

"Admire failures? That sounds...crazy. Nobody admires failure."

"Let me put it this way. We like people who fail if they fail with the best intentions. Maybe they failed because they weren't ruthless enough, for instance."

The more I thought about this, the more sense it made. For if you are free to fail, you are free to try. We Americans like to think that we, too, embrace failure, and it's true, up to a point. We love a good failure story as long as it ends with success. The entrepreneur who failed half a dozen times before hitting the jackpot with a brilliant idea. The bestselling author whose manuscript was rejected a dozen times. In these stories, failure serves merely to sweeten the taste of success. It's the appetizer. For Icelanders, though, failure is the main course.

Larus tells me how it's perfectly normal for Icelandic teenagers to start a garage band and have the full support of their parents. These kids don't expect success. It's the trying that counts. Besides, if they fail, they can always start over, thanks to the European social-welfare net. This is a nation of born-agains, though not in the religious sense.

The psychologist Mihály Csíkszentmihalyi wrote in his book *Flow,* "It is not the skills we actually have that determine how we feel but *the ones we think we have*" (emphasis added). When I first encountered that sentence, I reread it four or five times, convinced that it must be a misprint, or perhaps Csíkszentmihalyi was strung out on consonants. He seems to be advocating a delusional outlook on life. If I think I'm a violin virtuoso but in fact I'm tone-deaf, aren't I fooling myself? Yes, but it doesn't matter, Csíkszentmihalyi argues. Either way, we experience flow, a state of mind where we are so engaged in an activity that our worries evaporate and we lose track of time. Likewise, Martin Seligman, founder of the positive-psychology movement, discovered that happy people remembered more good events in their lives than actually occurred. Depressed people remembered the past accurately. "Know thyself" may not be the best advice after all. A pinch of self-delusion, it turns out, is an important ingredient in the happiness recipe.

It works for the Icelanders. There's no one on the island telling them they're not good enough, so they just go ahead and sing and paint and write. One result of this freewheeling attitude is that Icelandic artists produce a lot of crap. They're the first to admit it. But crap plays an important role in the art world. In fact, it plays exactly the same role as it does in the farming world. It's fertilizer. The crap allows the good stuff to grow. You can't have one without the other. Now, to be sure, you don't want to see crap framed at an art gallery, any more than you want to see a pound of fertilizer sitting in the produce section of your local grocery store. But still, crap is important.

There is almost a willful ignorance among Icelanders when it comes to the difficulties that lie ahead. Larus says this is by design. "Icelanders are ignorant, and that is our greatest strength. It's like walking through a minefield, but you don't know the mines are there, so you just plow ahead. I can't believe how naïve some of these young musicians and writers are. It's an amazing thing to watch."

I smile, though Larus can't possibly know why, can't possibly know how pleased I am to hear the word "naïve" used as something other than a pejorative.

Nearly twenty years ago, I had a run-in with the "n" word. I was twenty-six years old, a young man in a hurry. I desperately wanted to work at a big-time news organization, and, of course, nothing was bigger-time than *The New York Times*. To presume I had a shot at the paper of record was, at the very least, unrealistic and quite possibly delusional. I did not have the requisite pedigree—no Ivy League education nor fluency in foreign languages. No impressive oeuvre. No idea what the word "oeuvre" meant. Indeed, I had never worked at a newspaper before, any newspaper, let alone the august *New York Times*.

But I had a plan. I knew aviation—I had a private pilot's license and had written about small planes—so I tried to convince the *Times* they needed someone to write authoritatively about air travel. My timing was lucky. The paper's aviation reporter was about to retire.

I was summoned for an interview. Actually, a series of interviews, held at increasingly stuffy and intimidating venues, starting at the Harvard Club in New York and culminating at the sanctum sanctorum: the *Times* executive dining room.

As I sat stiffly in my padded leather chair, I tried to conceal my awe and nervousness. My interrogator was a courtly man named John Lee. His southern charms camouflaged a determined ruthlessness, and he did little to put me at ease. Lee didn't resort to stress positions or waterboarding but instead relied on a more old-fashioned interrogation technique: brute intimidation.

Aiding Mr. Lee in this endeavor was a roster of dead white men. Former Pulitzer Prize winners, they stared down at me reproachfully from the wood paneling of a nearby wall. "So, do you really think you are *New York Times* material?" I imagined them asking snidely. No, wait, that wasn't my imagination. That was John Lee.

"So, do you really think you are *New York Times* material?"

"Yes, sir, I do," I said, recovering nicely, I thought.

Lee wasn't the kind of man to take people's word for anything, and he certainly wasn't going to start with some twenty-six-year-old punk who had the audacity—the chutzpah!—to think he was a *Times*man.

He asked me how I would go about investigating the big news story at the time, the bombing of Pan Am Flight 103 over Lockerbie, Scotland. I had absolutely no idea and bluffed my way through an answer. To be honest, I don't even recall what I said, but it must have been *Times*ian enough, for I made it to the next round: a trial assignment. I dutifully submitted the story and then...nothing. Three weeks went by and not a word.

I had all but given up on my future as a *Times*man when I was walking down Second Avenue one morning and, as usual, picked up a copy of the paper at a newsstand.

"Jesus Christ," I shouted. Passersby gave me a wide berth, worried I might be some sort of religious nut. There was my story. On the front page. Granted, it was tucked way down in the lower right-hand corner, and my name was missing (bylines were reserved for staff members) but still. My story. On the front page of *The New York Times*!

Thus began my short but exceptionally eventful career at the newspaper of record. I was hired on a contractual basis, a sort of double-secret probation, owing to my young age and suspect pedigree. The implicit promise was that if I did well, I would make it on staff. I worked furiously, digging up the kind of stories that would land me on the front page. I stretched the boundaries of the aviation beat to its limits. I convinced my editors to let me write about Latin American drug smugglers, since they used airplanes to ferry their illicit cargo. I wrote about terrorists, since they blew up airplanes. My suggestion that I write about the president of the United States, since he flew on an airplane, was quickly torpedoed, though my gumption was duly noted.

I shared a cubicle—a pod, we called it—with two other reporters. Floyd was a large man, in the horizontal sense, who wrote about the financial markets with real authority. Floyd had a habit of leaning back in his chair when talking on the phone, forcing me to retreat to the far side of the pod. There, I encountered my other podmate: Kurt. Kurt was an investigative reporter who operated in a world of shadowy intrigue. I'd hear Kurt on the phone saying things like "Snow White is in the castle," and he wasn't covering the Walt Disney Company. I didn't mind Kurt's code talk—it lent an air of mystery to the pod—but I did mind the way he paced constantly when he was on the phone, which was pretty much all the time, and the way his phone cord would occasionally wrap around my neck, cutting off the oxygen that my brain has always cherished.

Every six months, John Lee would summon me into his office, where he would look down his glasses, tug at his black dress socks, and tell me that I was doing fine, fine work. A solid B, perhaps even a B-plus, but not an A, and an A is what is expected of a *Times*man. Another six months' probation. I redoubled my efforts, convinced I would eventually make the cut. Until one day my world came crashing down.

Kurt came up to me, looking ashen.

"What happened?" I asked.

"Sneezy is in the forest."

"Kurt, just tell me in English. What happened?"

It turned out to be worse than any fairy tale. My name was mentioned in the daily editorial meeting, the one where the editors decide which stories to put on the front page of tomorrow's newspaper. The executive editor, Max Frankel, didn't like my story, a ditty about air-traffic controllers. My work, he declared, was "naïve and unsophisticated."

If you're a journalist, especially a *New York Times* journalist, "naïve and unsophisticated" is the absolute worst thing anyone can say about you. Better if Frankel had called me a wife beater or devil worshipper. Anything but naïve and unsophisticated.

I was radioactive, and like all things radioactive I needed to be disposed of quickly and decisively. Sure enough, a few weeks later, I was let go. No, I wasn't let go. I was fired.

I now had plenty of time on my hands to ponder those fateful words: naïve and unsophisticated. The unsophisticated part didn't sting too badly; to be honest, there's probably some truth to it. But naïve? That hurt.

I never really got over the insult. Until now. Sitting here with Larus, in this pitch-dark speck of a nation, I could feel the wound cauterizing. Here was an entire nation of naïve people, and they seemed to be doing just fine.

Besides, what's wrong with being naïve? Wasn't Christopher Columbus naïve? Wasn't Gandhi naïve? Weren't the 1969 New York Jets naïve? The world, I now conclude, would be a far better place with a bit more naïveté.

In Iceland, Larus tells me, being naïve is okay because you can always start over. He has. Four times. We Americans also pride ourselves on being a can-do nation, where anything is possible. That's true, but the system is set up to discourage people from taking such leaps of faith. Leaving your job in America means giving up health insurance, working without a net. In Iceland, though, one person told me, "You never have to worry about falling into a black hole, because there is no black hole to fall into."

Larus is turning out to be as insightful as advertised, and I have more questions for him. I want to know about the elves and dwarves, the "hidden people" who supposedly live in boulders. I had heard that a majority of Icelanders today, in the twenty-first century, still believe in such craziness.

There was the story—a true story, people swore to me—about a road-construction crew working in southern Iceland. Things kept going wrong. Bulldozers broke down. Trucks wouldn't start. It's the hidden people, living in that boulder over there, someone suggested. We must be disturbing them. At first, the crew ignored these warnings, but things continued to go awry. Finally, they decided to arc the road around the boulder and, sure enough, the problems ceased.

Then there was the levelheaded Icelandic woman I met who one moment dismissed the notion of elves but the next moment told me how a ghost—"a very real presence"—once sent her fleeing her house into the cold outdoors. Stark naked.

I ask Larus, diplomatically, if he believes in these things. Larus pauses and gives me a wry smile that emanates from the corner of one eye, before pressing his glasses against his nose. Twice. This is going to be good.

"I don't know if I believe in them, but other people do, and my life is richer for it."

What the heck does that mean? Larus was playing the Sphinx. He wasn't going to reveal more. Indeed, it took me weeks of digging and asking and thinking before I figured out what he was talking about. Icelanders, not an especially religious people, occupy the space that exists between not believing and *not* not believing. It is valuable real estate. A place where the door to the unexplained is always left slightly ajar. Just in case.

I once visited this place. It was the early 1990s, when I was living in New Delhi, working as a correspondent for NPR. I awoke one morning to an unusual sound. Actually, it was the complete absence of sound—a deep and troubling silence that I couldn't explain. India is many things; quiet is not one of them. But quiet it was. No singsong calls of the *subzi wallah*, pushing his wooden cart of vegetables. No clatter in the kitchen as my cook prepared breakfast. I stepped onto my balcony and saw a man carrying a tin milk pail and moving at a pace considerably faster than the requisite Indian dawdle. "Where are you going? Where is everybody?" I called to him.

"At the temple, sahib. Everyone is at the temple. It's a miracle."

"What's a miracle?"

But the man had already turned a corner and was out of earshot.

My journalist's instincts kicked in. India has more than its share of alleged miracles, but this seemed to be of a different magnitude altogether. I grabbed my tape recorder and rushed to the temple. From one hundred yards away, I could see a crowd gathering outside, swarming. Cars had stopped in front of the temple, causing a massive traffic jam in both directions. The crowd, seeing my microphone and white face, cleared a path for me. "What's happening?" I asked no one in particular.

"It's a miracle," said one man.

"Yes, I know it's a miracle. What kind of miracle?"

"The gods. They are drinking milk."

This was a new one. In my two years living in India, I had heard of holy water from the Ganges appearing from nowhere, of amazing healings of the infirmed. But gods drinking milk? I wondered if this was some clever new marketing campaign from the Dairy Farmers Association. I inched forward. Once inside the temple, I could see several people crouched over a statue of Ganesh, the elephant-headed god, pouring spoonfuls of milk onto it. Sure enough, the milk evaporated as soon as it touched the statue. I didn't know what to think but dutifully recorded it all and, later, broadcast a report on it.

That evening, with life slowly returning to normal, I switched on the TV. The newscaster, a pretty woman wearing a sari, was recounting the day's events. The "milk miracle," as it was now dubbed, had begun that morning at a temple in the Punjab. Word had quickly spread to all parts of India—and eventually to Hindu temples in Britain and Hong Kong. Life in India had ground to a halt, as government workers abandoned their posts to witness the miracle. The TV now filled with images of ecstatic believers like those I had seen earlier in the day.

The program then cut to an interview with a physicist who explained that the "miracle" was actually the result of capillary action, which made it appear as if the statues were drinking milk. It was not a miracle at all but simple high-school physics. Later, I sat down for an interview with Kushwant Singh, a founding member of the Indian Rationalists Association. "Once again," Singh told me, "we Indians have made complete asses of ourselves."

Indian officials were less blunt, but I suspect they, too, were concerned what the "milk miracle" said about a country that was on the verge of becoming a major economic power, not to mention a nuclear one. What did I think? I honestly don't know, but now, years later, I know what Larus would say: I don't believe in such miracles, but others do, and my life is richer as a result. This twilight of half belief is, I think, not a bad space to inhabit.

Larus has to get going, something about a new band with a great sound. He writes down a phone number and hands it to me. "This is my friend Hilmar. You must, absolutely must, meet him. He's a Heathen."

"He's a what?"

"A Heathen."

Silly me. I thought Heathens had gone the way of dinosaurs and warm meals on airplanes.

As Larus gets up to leave, I can think of only one question, my default question. "Is he happy, this Heathen?"

"Oh, yes, very much so."

And so it came to pass that a few days later I found myself sitting down for an afternoon coffee with Hilmar the Happy Heathen.


I had never met a Heathen before. I didn't know what to expect, so I decided to do what journalists call reporting, academics call research, and normal people call reading. Paganism, it turns out, was the original Icelandic religion before a mass conversion in the year 1000. That was largely seen as a business decision, and Icelanders have never been particularly good Christians. They attend church if someone is born or wed or dies, but otherwise they are, as one Icelander put it, "atheists with good intentions."

The more I learn about Hilmar, the more I am intrigued. Hilmar—whose last name I will not even attempt to write, let alone pronounce—is the head of the Heathen faith in Iceland. Sort of the Chief Druid. He officiates at Heathen weddings and funerals. Hilmar is no ordinary Heathen, though. He is a musically talented one. He's composed dozens of scores for films and was an early mentor of the pop star Björk.

My first contact with Hilmar the Happy Heathen is by e-mail, a small irony that makes me smile. He says he's busy—possibly with human sacrifices, I suspect—and can't meet for a few days.

Finally, the day arrives and we meet at my hotel lobby. Hilmar walks in and introduces himself with a hardy, Heathen handshake. He has a fuzzy, unruly beard and kind eyes. Around his neck is a small silver pendant: the hammer of Thor, the Norse god. We sit down at a nearby café and order drinks. Me green tea. Him cappuccino. Funny, I think. I didn't know that Heathens drank cappuccino.

Hilmar is shy, almost painfully so. He looks down when speaking, which he does in a barely audible murmur. I keep leaning closer to make out the words. He's wearing a heavy green coat, which he leaves on during our entire conversation.

Hilmar seems like a man from another time. I've met people like this before. People whom I can easily picture walking down the streets of Elizabethan London or turn-of-the-century New York. It's not only their appearance—a walrus mustache, for instance—but their body language and verbal tics that make them seem chronologically out of place. I place Hilmar in the early 1800s. I can picture him composing his music by lamps fueled by whale blubber.

As I said, Hilmar's life revolves around his two loves: paganism and music. I'm unsure how to broach the former, so I start by asking about the music.

When Hilmar was eight years old, he'd listen to a relative, a professional musician, play the violin. He practiced ten hours a day. This struck young Hilmar as too much work. How could he be a musician and not work so hard? he asked his relative. Become a composer, was the reply. And so Hilmar did. He's dabbled in other fields over the years but keeps coming back to his music. Haunting, beautiful music.

Hilmar operates at the level of the sublime. The quotidian—parking his car, paying his bills—doesn't interest Hilmar at all. So invariably he parks poorly and forgets to pay his bills.

I ask Hilmar how he feels when he's composing music.

"I lose track of time when composing. It is a blissful activity. You are doing something you couldn't imagine doing. It is bigger than yourself. You are enlarging yourself."

These are the classic signs of flow, as defined by Mihály Csík-szentmihalyi. The line between the actor and the act blurs and, in some cases, disappears entirely. There is no dancer. There is only dancing. Flow is not the same as happiness. In fact, when we interrupt flow to take stock of our happiness, we lose both.

Hilmar also says that when he's composing music, the mathematical centers of his brain are fired. At some point in the creative process, the musical score becomes a puzzle to be solved, a mathematical puzzle. Personally, I've never associated math and happiness, but they seem linked in Hilmar's mind.

Hilmar is a successful Heathen but not an ambitious one. His goals today remain what they've always been: to compose his music. To own a good sofa. To read good books. Hilmar owns many books, even by Icelandic standards. The other day, when he came home with a wheelbarrowful, his five-year-old daughter looked him in the eye and implored, "Please, Daddy, please, no more books!" Hilmar has a stock answer to those who criticize his excessive book buying. "It is never a waste of time to study how other people wasted time."

Hilmar has an opinion about Icelandic love of verse ("There is nothing that an Icelander can't turn into poetry"), and he has an opinion about the heroic failure that Larus and I had discussed. It's true, Icelanders do love a good failure, and, even more, he says, they indulge in "enjoyment of misery." I think I know what he means. Misery is like a gamy piece of meat: not particularly nourishing, certainly not tasty, but still it's something to chew on, and that's better than nothing. I've been chewing on my misery for about forty years now.

Finally, I screw up the courage to ask Hilmar about his Heathenism. Was he born a Heathen or did he convert?

It turns out that Hilmar didn't so much convert to Heathenism as Heathenism converted to Hilmar. It was the early 1970s, and young Hilmar was searching for meaning. By chance, he met Joseph Campbell, the great scholar of myths. Campbell convinced Hilmar that his future lay in his past. Iceland had a rich tradition of mythology, embodied in a book known as the Eddas. Hilmar was smitten. He liked the idea of connecting to his past, of a religion with no revealed truths, no shalls and shallnots. He read and reread the Eddas, joining the small band of other Icelanders who went on to revive a religion that had been dead for the past thousand years.

Hilmar wants to make a few things clear. The ancient Vikings didn't rape and pillage, at least no more than anyone else of their day. Those were stories drummed up by Irish settlers who wanted to discredit the newly arrived Vikings. Heathenism is a peaceful religion, based on a love of the earth, the spirit of the place, he tells me. There are many gods, and the Eddas contain fantastical tales of one-eyed giants performing miracles.

"Hilmar," I say, "you seem like a levelheaded, rational guy. Do you really believe these stories?"

Hilmar pauses for a moment before answering, and it's not the answer I expect.

"Well, I suppose it could be a muddle of thought, but everyone needs a belief system, in order to have these transcendental moments."

This is incredible. Here is the head of the Heathen faith of Iceland telling me that the entire religion might be a "muddle of thought." That's like the pope saying, "Well, the Bible might be a bunch of hogwash, but hey, it's something to believe in." Yet that is exactly what Hilmar is saying. It's not what we believe that makes us happy but the act of believing. In anything.

"So has anything bad ever happened to you, any setbacks?" I ask.

Hilmar thinks for a moment, scratching his fuzzy beard. "Yes, I was once fucked over by my manager who left me broke, starving in a flat in London. But I was young enough to enjoy it. I guess you could say I am fatalistic, but in a happy sense."

Hilmar has some time on his hands, so we brave the flying ice and walk to a bookstore. It's called, simply, The Book, and it is a temple of random erudition. Subjects and languages are arranged in no discernible order. A book, in Icelandic, about chess strategy sits next to a book, in English, about gardening.

Hilmar is a regular here. He starts expertly searching among the disarray for a copy of the Eddas for me. And not just any copy. "There are a lot of bad translations out there," he warns. He keeps looking until he finds a good one.

Back in my hotel room, I open the book, the muddle of thought, and begin to read. First, the introduction, by one Jesse Byock, a professor of Icelandic and Old Norse studies at UCLA: "Unlike the gods of Greek and Roman mythology the [Norse gods] rarely quarrel among themselves over the control of human or semi-divine heroes, nor do they enjoy the complacency of immortality. Their universe is constantly in danger, and their actions frequently have unanticipated consequences."

Wow. In ancient Iceland, even a god's life was tough. Why bother being a god, if you can't enjoy the complacency of immorality? Isn't that the whole point of divinity?

I read on. A lot of the tales are hard to follow even in this, a good translation. I find a section called "Sayings of the Wise One." This appeals to me. Fortune-cookie Heathenism. There is advice for travelers:

*Who travels widely needs his wits about him.*
*The stupid should stay at home.*

And for drinkers:

> *A man knows less the more he drinks,*
> *Becomes a muddled fool.*

But my favorite is this gem:

> *It is best for man to be middle-wise,*
> *Not over cunning and clever*
> *The learned man whose lore is deep*
> *Is seldom happy at heart.*

Middle-wise. It had never occurred to me that we could be too wise, too learned. Leave it to some Heathens to teach me this life lesson.


I'm sitting at a café called Cultura. It is one of Reykjavík's few international hangouts, an eclectically decorated place where the hummus is served by Spanish waiters. Completing the international tableaux is the young man sitting across from me: an American named Jared Bibler. He's lived in Iceland for the past two years.

Jared is beaming—there is no other word for it—and his lips are curled into a chronic grin. He looks happy, annoyingly so.

"So, Jared," I say, opting for the direct approach, "what the hell are you doing in Iceland?"

Jared chuckles, his grin blossoming into a full-fledged Cheshire smile. "Sometimes life takes you somewhere," he says enigmatically.

To fully understand the riddle that is Jared Bibler, you need to know something about international aviation. Iceland happens to lie directly on the North Atlantic air corridor. That means people jetting between New York and, say, London, fly directly over Iceland, just as people jetting between New York and Los Angeles fly directly over Kansas. Iceland, in other words, is a flyover country.

Icelanders, like Kansans, I imagine, are not especially fond of those looking down at them from thirty-five-thousand feet. But a few years back an executive at Icelandair, the national airline, came up with a brilliant idea. Stopovers. Say you're flying between New York and London. Icelandair will let you stop in Reykjavík for a few days at no extra charge. The plan worked, attracting mostly budget travelers who have a few days to spare.

In the spring of 2002, Jared, a recent college graduate living in Boston, bought one of the Icelandair stopover tickets and, on his way back to Boston, spent three days in Reykjavík. Back home, Jared's friends asked about his trip to Europe. All he could talk about, though, was his few days in Iceland. Jared was in love with Iceland—deeply, madly, irretrievably in love. And like most people in love, Jared was insufferable. He couldn't shut up about Iceland and how great it was. Soon his friends stopped asking about his trip to Europe.

Jared was determined to return to Iceland, not as a tourist but as a resident. He made some phone calls, friends of friends of friends. Did anyone know anyone in Iceland? Nothing. Then, finally, a nibble. The Iceland Chamber of Commerce put him in touch with a two-person software company that was looking to expand into a three-person company. Jared flew to Iceland for the interview. They took Jared out to lunch, at a trendy restaurant called Vegamot. It was a Saturday afternoon and, right there and then, with the noon sky chocolate-black, they offered Jared a job.

And so it was that Jared Bibler, a young man who never thought he would live outside the United States, who until recently couldn't find Iceland on a map, packed his belongings and moved to Reykjavík. "I just had a feeling," he tells me, dipping a pita wedge into his hummus, "that life was better here."

Jared senses my skepticism and, unprompted, elaborates. "Look, we're living in an unprecedented age of mobility. You can determine how your life plays out by deciding where you live. You really can get away from yourself, or at least away from your past.

But Americans, when they think of moving somewhere, they think of North Carolina or North Dakota. They don't think of Canada. Or Iceland."

Okay, I concede, we've all had that urge to pack it up and move to some faraway place. Usually, though, that faraway place involves a white sandy beach or, at the very least, sunlight. Why Iceland?

"I just love it here."

"Yes, but what do you love about it here?"

Jared takes a deep breath and then, with measured passion, tells me what he loves about Iceland. I am writing it all down, barely able to keep up.

He loves the way hot water spouts from the ground like geo-thermal gold. He loves the way people invite you over for coffee for no particular reason and talk for hours about nothing in particular. He loves the way Icelanders call their country, affectionately, "The Ice Cube." He loves the fact that, without even trying, he already knows three members of Parliament. He loves the way on a brisk winter day the snow crunches under his feet like heavenly Styrofoam. He loves the choirs that line the main shopping street in December, their voices strong and radiant, turning back the night. He loves the fact that five-year-olds can safely walk to school alone in the predawn darkness. He loves the magical, otherworldly feeling of swimming laps in the middle of a snowstorm. He loves the way, when your car gets stuck in the snow, someone always, always stops to help. He loves the way Icelanders applaud when the plane lands at the international airport in Keflavík just because they're happy to be home. He loves the way Icelanders manage to be tremendously proud people yet not the least bit arrogant. And, yes, he loves—not tolerates but actively loves—the darkness.

Most of all, Jared loves living in a culture that doesn't put people in boxes—or at least allows them to move freely from one box to another. A year after joining the software firm, he switched to banking—a move that would have been unthinkable in the United States. "They would have said, 'You're a software guy, what do you know about banking?' But here people just figure it will work out." Which is another thing Jared loves about Iceland: the attitude that no matter what, no matter how bleak life seems, things will always work out. And they usually do.

Jared doesn't love everything about Iceland. The smallness of the place renders it claustrophobic and prone to cronyism; women are so independent minded they won't allow him to open a door for them. That drives him nuts. But these are quibbles. Jared Bibler is happy in Iceland, happier than he's ever been.

It's not as if Jared just sat back and let Icelandic bliss wash over him like a geothermal mud bath. He's worked at it. He learned to speak Icelandic, learned to enjoy Icelandic food (except for rotten shark; no one learns to like that). I notice that Jared uses "we" and not "they" when referring to Icelanders.

Jared, in other words, displays all of the symptoms of someone who has "gone native"—the term used to describe foreign correspondents, diplomats, and other expatriates who fall in love with a place so fully they cross the line between what anthropologists call a "participant-observer" and simply a participant. Those who have gone native are easy to identify. They speak the local language, get the local humor. They wear the local dress. In some cases, they develop immunities to local microbes. I remember meeting an Englishman who had lived in India for so long he could actually drink the tap water and not die.

The term "gone native" is almost always used disparagingly by those who have not. Yes, we diplomats and journalists are supposed to learn the local language, eat the local food, know the lay of the land. But only up to a point. We're expected to maintain a certain professional distance. The gone-natives are seen as weak souls, traitors of a sort, who should have known better. Going native is like marrying the girl you had a fling with during a drunken Mardi Gras party. Likewise, our time abroad is supposed to be a fling. Nothing more.

And yet, over the years I've met so many people like Jared who seem to be more at home, happier, living in a country not of their birth. People like Linda in Bhutan. She and Jared are refugees. Not political refugees, escaping a repressive regime, nor economic refugees, crossing a border in search of a better-paying job. They are hedonic refugees, moving to a new land, a new culture, because they are happier there. Usually, hedonic refugees have an epiphany, a moment of great clarity when they realize, beyond a doubt, that they were born in the wrong country.

For my friend Rob, that moment came late at night, at a truck stop in Billings, Montana. Rob, who is British, was young and backpacking around the world. By the time he made it to Billings, he was flat broke. His plan was to spend the night at the truck-stop diner and figure things out in the morning.

Rob ordered a cup of coffee; he had only enough money for one. A few minutes later, the waitress came around, carafe in hand, and was about to pour another cup when Rob put up his hand and said, "Sorry, I don't have any more money." The waitress smiled gently at Rob and said two words, two words that would change Rob's life: "Free refills."

Free refills. Unlimited. Gratis. For Rob, those two words spoke volumes about the incredible bounty, the generous soul, that is America. And suddenly, sitting there in a grimy truck stop in Billings, flat broke and jittery from excess caffeine, Rob realized, beyond a doubt, that he had found his place, what Tennessee Williams called "the home of the heart."

A few years later, Rob moved to Boston. Soon, he joined NPR and we became colleagues. Rob still has his British accent, of course, but I don't hear it. I hear an American.

Social scientists have been investigating this phenomenon. They call it "cultural fit," and it explains a lot about happiness. Like people, each culture has its own personality. Some cultures, for instance, are collectivist; others are individualistic. Collectivist cultures, like Japan and other Confucian nations, value social harmony more than any one person's happiness. Individualistic cultures, like the United States, value personal satisfaction more than communal harmony. That's why the Japanese have a well-known expression: "The nail that sticks out gets hammered down." In America, the nail that sticks out gets a promotion or a shot at *American Idol*. We are a nation of protruding nails.

One research project examined the personalities of Japanese and American college students. First, they determined if each student was more individualistic or collectivist in demeanor. Did they value words like "personal achievement" or words like "group harmony"? Then they measured the students' happiness, their subjective well-being. The Japanese students who had individualistic leanings (American leanings, that is) were less happy than the students with more collectivist personalities. In other words, those with a good cultural fit were happier than those without.

What to do with this information? Should we administer cultural-compatibility tests to high school students, the way we used to test for career compatibility? I can imagine the phone call from the school guidance counselor. "Hi, Mrs. Williams, we've tested little Johnnie and determined that he would fit in perfectly in Albania. He'd really be much happier there. A flight leaves at 7:00 p.m. Should I go ahead and make that booking for you?"

Of course not. Just because the culture fits doesn't mean we should wear it, and, besides, every society needs its cultural misfits. It is these people—those who are partially though not completely alienated from their own culture—who produce great art and science. Einstein, a German Jew, was a cultural misfit. We all benefit from Einstein's work, whether he was happy or not.

The last time I saw Jared was at another café. It was 4:00 on a Friday afternoon. I ordered beer; Jared a cappuccino. He needed to stay awake and sober. He was driving north, to the edge of the Arctic Circle, for a ski trip with his colleagues. He was in no real hurry, though, and our conversation unspooled, easy and relaxed. Outside, the sky had turned a deep charcoal-black. "I don't know," said Jared, staring into his cappuccino as if the swirls of foam and espresso held the answer to all of life's riddles. "I just had a feeling I'd be happy here."

I'm beginning to get into this darkness thing. I'm not yet embracing it, but we're edging closer, darkness and me. Cold has its virtues. Without cold, there would be no coziness. I learned this living in Miami, where coziness is in short supply, along with sane driving. Also, the darkness makes it easy to feel like you've got a jump on the day. How cool is that? You get that ahead-of-the-sun feeling, a feeling normally reserved for stockbrokers and doughnut makers, simply by getting out of bed before noon.

Maybe I have started to turn Icelandic. Well, not really Icelandic. I can still pronounce only two Icelandic words safely, but I have started to appreciate the deep coziness. I feel like I've fallen off the map yet am, oddly, in the center of the universe at the same time. I'm running into people I know, just like a local.

I'm at Kaffitar, my favorite café. I like the way the walls are painted blues, reds, and other soft primary colors. I like the way the baristas yell out, in a singsong voice, when a latte or cappuccino is ready.

I can hear Ragnar, an Icelandic artist I met earlier, laughing, cackling at another table. Ragnar has a brightly colored scarf flung around his neck. He is snapping his fingers with one hand and gesturing with the other. But there is something wrong with the scene, something not right. I can't put my finger on it. Then suddenly it dawns on me. Ragnar is happy. Ragnar is an artist. These two facts do not normally go together. Artists, real artists, are supposed to suffer, and suffering is generally not a happy state of mind.

The Myth of the Unhappy Artist has persisted for a long time. Nineteenth-century English poets like Byron and Shelley died young. More recently, singers like Jimi Hendrix and Kurt Cobain did their bit to promulgate this myth.

Iceland puts this silly myth out of its misery once and for all. I met dozens of artists and all of them were, for the most part, happy. I remember what Hilmar had said when I asked him if he was happy. "Yes, but I cherish my melancholia."

Magnus, the sunburned penguin, said something very similar.

"You nurture your little melancholia, and it's like a buzz that makes you feel alive. You snap yourself a little bit, and you feel this relief of how fragile life is and how tremendously fragile you are."

"So you can have this melancholia and still be happy?"

"Absolutely!"

Modern social science confirms what the sunburned penguin says. The psychologist Norman Bradburn, in his book *The Structure of Psychological Well Being,* describes how happiness and unhappiness are not opposites, as we often think. They are not two sides of the same coin. They are different coins. It is possible, in other words, for a happy person to also suffer from bouts of unhappiness, and for unhappy people to experience great moments of joy. And here in Iceland, it seems, it is even possible to be happy and sad at the same time.


Profundity is a funny thing. Sometimes it is absent in the expected places—Ivy League universities, for instance—but smacks us upside the head in the most unexpected of venues.

It is my last night in Iceland, and I am determined to stay up late enough to experience the weekend debauchery in all its drunken splendor. I head to a bar that Jared had recommended. It's 9:00 p.m., and only a handful of people have shown up, yet already the bar is smoky. It is, I think, the smokiest room I've ever been in, as smoky as a room can be without the room actually being on fire.

I order a shot of Blue Opal, a popular drink based on an even more popular candy. It tastes like a Halls cough drop that has been marinating overnight in vodka.

Something about the smoke-filled bar, or perhaps the vodka-infused cough drop, gets me thinking about Nietzsche. Usually, Nietzsche gives me a headache. But one thing he said keeps bubbling up to my consciousness, like a geothermal spring. The measure of a society, he said, is how well it transforms pain and suffering into something worthwhile. Not how a society avoids pain and suffering—for Nietzsche, a deeply troubled man himself (he went insane in his latter years), knew that was impossible—but how it transforms it. The Icelanders have done a good job of not only surviving on this odd moonscape but also transforming their suffering into something worthwhile. Happy, even.

I meet a woman named Sara. At least I think she is a woman. The first thing she says to me is, "People are always mistaking me for a man or a lesbian." I can see what she means. Sara's hair is cropped short, her face is square and mannish.

Sara says she is "not a sunlight person." One of her favorite things to do is go swimming at 6:00 on an especially cold morning and do laps with the steam rising above the water. "It's even better if it's snowing," she says. Sara does a mean imitation of both American tourists ("Hey, Harvey, is that my coofeee or yows?") and mental patients. The former she encountered regularly at the national park where she worked during summers, the latter at the psychiatric ward where she currently works. I like Sara.

The conversation, naturally, turns to happiness. When I tell people about my project, everyone asks the same two questions: How can you measure happiness? How can you even define it?

"I'm not sure," I reply. "How do *you* define it?"

Sara thinks for a moment then says, "Happiness is your state of mind and the way you pursue that state of mind."

Aristotle said more or less the same thing, though he didn't say it in a smoky Icelandic bar frequented by androgynous women. How we pursue the goal of happiness matters at least as much, perhaps more, than the goal itself. They are, in fact, one and the same, means and ends. A virtuous life necessarily leads to a happy life.

I walk out of the bar, pushing past a crowd of people entering.

It's 4:30 a.m., and the morning is still young. I stumble home and collapse onto my bed. For once, I am grateful for the darkness.

I recently came across a great ad for Dos Equis, the Mexican beer. There's a photo of a man in his late fifties, cigar in hand and looking vaguely like Hemingway. On either side of him are two younger women, gazing admiringly. (And, oh, yeah, some beer, too.) The man has this look in his eye, this I-know-things-about-life look. The text reads: "Being boring is a choice. Those mild salsas and pleated khakis don't buy themselves."

And so it is with happiness. When the talk of genetics and communal bonds and relative income is stripped away, happiness is a choice. Not an easy choice, not always a desirable one, but a choice nonetheless.

Faced with a brutal climate and utter isolation, Icelanders could have easily chosen despair and drunkenness. The Russian option. But instead these hardy sons and daughters of Vikings peered into the unyielding blackness of the noon sky and chose another option: happiness and drunkenness. It is, I think, the wiser option. Besides, what else is there to do in the dark?

# Chapter 6

# MOLDOVA

## Happiness Is Somewhere Else

All of this happiness is starting to bum me out. As the German philosopher and fellow malcontent Schopenhauer once said, "Because they feel unhappy, men cannot bear the sight of someone they think is happy."

Exactly. What I need, what will cheer me up, is a trip to an unhappy place. According to the Law of Relative Happiness, such a place will boost my mood since I'll realize there are depths of misery to which I have not yet sunk.

Such a place, too, could lend valuable insights into the nature of happiness. We know a thing by its opposite. Hot means nothing without cold. Mozart is enhanced by the existence of Barry Manilow. And happy places owe their station, at least in part, to the unhappy ones.

Yes, I need to travel to the dark side of the planet, some place not merely a bit blue, a bit down in the dumps, but truly and deeply miserable. But where?

Iraq immediately jumps to mind. Now, there is an unhappy place, as the daily carnage on my TV screen attests. But Iraq's unhappiness says more about the nature of war than it does about the nature of happiness. I dig up my notes from the World Database of Happiness. Let's see. A few African countries certainly qualify as miserable, and I briefly consider hopping the next flight to Zimbabwe. But African misery, too, is easily diagnosed, though the remedies may prove elusive.

Then it occurs to me: Moldova. Of course. The former Soviet republic is, according to Ruut Veenhoven's data, the least happy nation on the planet. Even the name sounds melancholy. Mol-doooova. Try it. Notice how your jaw droops reflexively and your shoulders slouch, Eeyore-like. (Unlike "Jamaica," which is impossible to say without smiling.) I can even imagine the word "Moldova" doubling as a synonym for generic disquiet.

"How are you doing today, Joe?"

"Not so well. A bit Moldoooova."

"Sorry to hear it. Cheer up."

Yes, Moldova is just the tonic I need.

How to pack for a trip to the world's least happy place? Maybe I should bring some dark Russian literature—is there any other kind?—some Dostoevsky, perhaps, just to show that, you know, I am one of them.

First, though, I need two visa-sized photos. I'm sitting on the little stool at one of those quickie photo shops. "Smile," says the clerk. I freeze. What should I do? Would a smiley photo score me points, like arriving in a famine-stricken nation with bags of wheat? Or might it be seen as subversive? I imagine a dour immigration official—is there any other kind?—taking one look at my beaming mug and shouting to his colleague, "Hey, Boris, come here. We've got a troublemaker." I opt for the middle path: a neutral half grin that could be interpreted as either mirth or snideness.

The next order of business: finding Moldova on the map. This proves trickier than expected. I scan my atlas several times before finally locating it, sandwiched between Romania and the Ukraine, two significantly unhappy countries in their own right. Misery loves company.

Getting to Moldova turns out to be nearly as tricky as finding it on a map. It's almost as if the Moldovans are off sulking in their corner of the globe. "Leave us alone. We're not happy, and we like it that way. We said go away!"

I know it's just a cry for help, though, and am not about to give up. Let's see, there's a flight from Frankfurt on Air Moldova. But

I dismiss this option out of hand; I'm not about to trust my fate to some seriously bummed out Moldovan pilot. There's an Austrian Airways flight from Vienna. Good. The Austrians may be a bit humorless, in a Teutonic way, but they score a respectable 6.5 on the happiness scale. I book my ticket.

The small jet touches down in Chisinau, Moldova's capital, and before long I'm standing in line at immigration control. The airport is small; it feels more like a Greyhound bus terminal than an international gateway. I find myself checking for overt signs of unhappiness. Is it in the air? Is it the emotional equivalent of landing at a very high altitude airport—La Paz, Bolivia, say—and immediately feeling light-headed? No, I detect no immediate drop in my mood.

A sour-looking woman is sitting behind a counter marked "Visa upon arrival." I hand her my visa photo, with its neutral half grin, and three crisp twenty-dollar bills. As a rule of thumb, the more fucked-up a country, the more said country insists on crisp bills. The Swiss, for instance, don't mind rumpled, torn, or otherwise imperfect bills. But I remember standing at an airline ticket office in Kabul, as the clerk examined each hundred-dollar bill I handed him like it was a genuine Matisse, or possibly a good forgery. He rejected at least half. One had the slightest of tears, another was deemed too old; a third just didn't feel right.

The woman looks at my photo, then up at me, then at the photo again. Oh, no, I've been found out. I knew I shouldn't have showed any teeth. But then she suddenly stamps my passport, asks me to sign something, and says, "Enjoy your stay." She doesn't sound like she means it, though.

I've officially entered Moldova, the world's least happy country. There's something oddly exhilarating about this, as if I were Sir Edmund Hillary climbing Mount Everest or, a more accurate analogy, Jacques Cousteau diving to the ocean floor.

I'm scanning the crowd for Natasha. She's supposed to meet me and take me to her grandmother's apartment. That's where I'll be staying. Hotels are wonderful inventions, but they are not the ideal window to the soul of a nation. In fact, as my stay in

Qatar demonstrated, they are designed to do exactly the opposite, to keep you and the country you're visiting at a comfortable distance. No, if I was going to plumb the depths of Moldovan misery, I needed to plumb up close and personal. I needed to stay with a real, live Moldovan. I had found a woman named Marisha, of Marisha.net, who provides just such a service. She puts travelers like me in touch with Moldovans like Natasha who are strapped for cash (which is pretty much every Moldovan) and who will gladly rent out an extra room for a few crisp American dollars. Marisha and I had exchanged a few e-mails—I was circumspect about my happiness research, lest I arouse undue suspicion. In a few days, Marisha e-mailed back. She had found an apartment for me. Centrally located. Genuinely Moldovan. Perfect.

Except where was Natasha? She was supposed to be here, holding a sign with my name on it. I scan the crowd. Nothing. Finally, a young woman, not more than nineteen, runs up to me, with a crumpled cardboard sign in one hand.

"Mr. Eric?"

"Natasha?"

"Yes, sorry for late."

"That's okay."

Natasha and I walk to the taxi she has waiting outside. For the first time, I get a good look at her. She's wearing an alleged skirt, spiked heels, and so much eye makeup she looks like a raccoon. A sexy raccoon. I begin to wonder what I've got myself into. Is Marisha, of Marisha.net, renting out rooms or something else?

We climb into an old Mercedes taxi with worn seats and a pungent, unidentifiable odor. Natasha sits in the front seat, her knees resting so close to the stick shift I'm worried the driver might shift her into third.

The radio is blaring Russian pop music. Russian pop is—how do I put this diplomatically?—bad. Very bad. So bad that it may have contributed to the collapse of the Soviet Union. I ask the driver to turn it down. He complies, begrudgingly. As we approach the city, the streets grow increasingly crowded with pedestrians, and I see other Natashas, many others, all wearing the same microskirts, with the same raccoon makeup. My god, I think, is every woman in Moldova a prostitute? This is worse than I imagined. Then it dawns on me. They are not prostitutes. They just dress that way. It's the national uniform.

Otherwise, the city looks pleasant enough. The streets are tree lined, and while the cars—and the people—look like they could use a good scrubbing, I see no overt signs of misery. In this, the Visual Age, our minds are trained to look for obvious signs of distress: bombed-out buildings, gun-toting teenagers, smog, so we assume some place is reasonably happy if it lacks any of these prominent signposts of despair. Yet misery, like still waters, runs deep.

"Is it true," I ask Natasha, "that people here are unhappy?"

"Yes, it is true," Natasha says, in passable English.

"Why?"

"We have no money for the life," she says, as if that settles the issue and I could go home now. Funny, I think, I was recently in a country where they have too much money for the life. Maybe you and Qatar could work something out.

"How long you stay in Moldova?" asks Natasha, as the driver shifts her into overdrive.

"Nearly two weeks," I say. She nods, impressed, as if most visitors don't last that long.

We arrive at my accommodation, inside a series of low-rise apartment buildings designed in typical Soviet fashion. The Soviets did for architecture what Burger King did for gourmet food. The apartment fronts a park of sorts, which features a few stray pieces of decrepit playground equipment, far outnumbered by the empty beer bottles strewn about. There's more trash inside the stairwell, plus some examples of Moldovan youth at their most expressive, graffiti that says, "White Power" and "Fuck the System."

Natasha introduces me to her grandmother and my host for the next two weeks: Luba. She is a babushka. Stocky, with a crown of reddish hair and a fierce expression that, frankly, scares me. This is offset, slightly, by the housecoat she is wearing, an unfortunate collage of bright colors and floral prints.

Russian by birth, Luba came to Moldova decades ago, one of the millions of Russians who fanned out throughout the Soviet Union, determined to spread Russian good cheer. Life was sweet. Until the Berlin Wall came down, the Soviet Union collapsed, and so did Luba's life. Now she is reduced to scrimping for food and renting out her spare bedroom to a neurotic American on some crazy search for happiness. The wheels of history can be cruel.

Luba's English consists entirely of the words "no" and "feevty-feevty," the latter of which she invariably accompanies with a see-sawing of her palm. For Luba, everything is feevty-feevty, from the fish sold at the local market to the president of Moldova. Except for Mikhail Gorbachev. The former Soviet leader, the man who hastened the collapse of the Soviet Union, scores much lower than feevty-feevty in Luba's estimation.

My Russian is more extensive than Luba's English, but just barely. In addition to "no," I can also say "yes" and "I don't understand" and "one more vodka, please." So you can imagine my horror when Natasha explains that she's leaving, and I will be spending the next two weeks alone with her grandmother. God help me.

Luba's apartment looks like it hasn't changed much since Khrushchev's day. The centerpiece is the TV, which Luba spends hours in front of, watching Russian soap operas and occasionally making a pssst sound, like air seeping from a leaky tire, when something on the TV displeases her, which is often. The apartment makes sounds too. Creaking sounds and construction sounds, which I find alarming since there is no construction anywhere nearby. Must be the plumbing, I tell myself.

I ask Luba if I can use her phone, a request I convey by holding an invisible phone to my ear, and she points to a black thing on a table in the corner. It's a rotary phone. I can't remember the last time I used one. It feels so heavy and slow, like dialing upwind. Yet there's something unexpectedly satisfying about the heft of the dial, the feel of my finger snuggled in the casing, the whirring sound as each number spins. By the time I've dialed the last number, a half hour later, I feel like I've earned my phone call.

At the other end of the line is Vitalie, a blogger, one of the few in Moldova. He seemed like someone who could shed some light on Moldovan misery. We agree to meet the next day. Vitalie asks me if I know any good restaurants. This strikes me as odd, since he's lived here all of his life and I've been in Moldova for about one hour. I take this as a discouraging sign about the culinary prospects in Moldova. Later, someone explained that in Moldova the relationship between host and guest is reversed. It is the guest's obligation to make the host feel at ease. Reverse hospitality. One of the many peculiar customs in this country.

I pantomime to Luba that I am going for a walk, and she hands me a key and shows me how to unlock the many latches on her double door. The streets are pleasant enough, in a gray, Soviet sort of way. At least there are trees. I hop on a bus to go downtown. It is packed. Every face is frozen in an expression that is simultaneously vacant and vaguely pissed off, an expression I came to identify as the Moldovan Scowl. (A close relation of the Moldovan Shuffle, which is the preferred walking style.)

The Moldovans got the short end of the Soviet stick, and, truth be told, it wasn't a very long stick to begin with. When the Russian empire collapsed, the Moldovans, unlike the Baltic states, had no fervent nationalism to fall back on. And unlike the Muslim nations of Central Asia, the Moldovans had no abiding faith or culture on which to rely. They had only themselves, and clearly that was not enough.

All around me, I see misery. A blind man with sunglasses and cane, like some caricature of a blind man, hobbling down the street. An old woman hunched over so far that her torso is nearly parallel to the ground. I hear someone sobbing behind me, and turn to see a middle-aged woman with dark hair, her eyes red from crying. I wonder, though: Is this place really so miserable, or have I fallen prey to what social scientists call confirmation bias? I expect Moldova to be miserable, so I see misery everywhere.

I pass a building labeled the Special Institute for Infectious Diseases. It is ramshackle and dirty, the kind of place where you might catch an infectious disease as opposed to cure one. Maybe, I wonder, that's what makes it special. I decide to stop at a small outdoor café. A group of Moldovans are drinking beer. It's 11:00 a.m.—a bit early for beer, I think—but they look happier than anyone I've seen so far, except for the smiling faces on billboards selling cellphones. The air is thick with smoke. Moldovans smoke like there is no tomorrow, which in their case might be true.

Moldova is nation building gone horribly awry, and, like plastic surgery gone horribly awry, the results are not pretty. You want to look away. The Russians tried to create a nation out of Moldova, when historically one never really existed, at least not the kind of nation the Soviets had in mind. Moldovans are basically Romanians. They share the same historical roots; the Moldovan language isn't a distinct language any more than American English is distinct from British English. Someone once published a Romanian-Moldovan dictionary; it was more of a pamphlet.

That old saw about the glass being half full or half empty is dead wrong. What really matters is whether water is flowing into or out of the glass. In Moldova, the water is gushing out. During Soviet times, Moldova was wealthier than neighboring Romania. Now Romanians poke fun at their impoverished neighbors to the east. During Soviet times, Moldovans could travel freely to any of the fourteen other republics. Now they need a visa to go just about anywhere except the Ukraine, and how much fun can that be? The most popular song in Moldova is the Beatles' *Yesterday,* and no wonder.

It wasn't supposed to be this way. In the early 1990s, hundreds of millions of dollars in foreign aid poured in. There was talk of Moldova being the next Luxembourg. Today, the only thing Moldova has in common with Luxembourg is that no one can find it on a map.

I pass a couple of Moldovan cops. The cops, like all Moldovan men, have a thuggish quality and look like they could use a bath.

Unlike most Moldovan men, they are markedly pudgy. It's never a good sign when a country's people are thin and its police fat.

I spot a bookstore and decide to check it out. It's dark inside, another power outage, but in the dim light I can make out lots of Pushkin. Moldovans are proud of the Russian writer, who lived here for several years in the nineteenth century. Alexander Pushkin does not return the affection. "Accursed town of Chisinau," he wrote of the Moldovan capital. "To abuse you the tongue will grow tired." Part of Pushkin's animus, I suspect, owes to the fact that he was not here by choice. He was exiled to Moldova, and rarely can we muster affection for our places of exile, even if they are lovely places, which Moldova is not.

I pass a guy, thick-necked and thuggish. He looks like he could be in the mafia. As he walks by, I turn and see that on the back of his T-shirt is printed the word "mafia."

On my way back to Luba's apartment, the bus suddenly stops. The driver makes an announcement—apparently there's a mechanical problem—and everyone starts to get off. What strikes me is the resignation. No grumbling, no sighing, not a word or a sound. It's tempting to conclude that the Moldovans are accepting of their lot in life and have achieved a Buddha-like acceptance. I don't think that's the case, though. I suspect something more is going on here.

In the late 1960s, a young Martin Seligman, now the poohbah of the positive-psychology movement, conducted experiments with dogs. He would place a dog in a cage and give it a (supposedly harmless) electric shock. The dog, though, could escape to another side of the cage and avoid the shock, the onset of which was signaled by a loud noise and a flashing light. Then Seligman put the dog in a no-win situation. No matter what he did, he couldn't avoid getting shocked. Then, and this is the part that surprised Seligman, when he returned the same dog to a cage where he could easily avoid the shock (by jumping over a low fence), the dog did nothing. He just sat there and endured the shocks. He had been taught to believe that the situation was hopeless. He had learned to be helpless.

As I stepped off the broken-down bus, I wondered: Are Moldovans like Seligman's dogs? Have they been beaten down—shocked—so many times that they've simply stopped trying? Is this a nation of the learned helpless?

No, Moldovans tell me, the source of their despair is much simpler than that. In a word, money. They don't have enough. Per-capita income is only $880 per year. They need to travel abroad to make money. Some Moldovan women are tricked into working as prostitutes. A few Moldovans even sell one of their kidneys for cash.

None of this is good, of course, and I don't mean to belittle the economic difficulties Moldovans face. But if I've learned anything in my travels, it's that things are rarely as simple as they seem. Many countries are poorer than Moldova yet happier. Nigeria, for instance, or Bangladesh. The problem is that Moldovans don't compare themselves to Nigerians or Bangladeshis. They compare themselves to Italians and Germans. Moldova is the poor man in a rich neighborhood, never a happy position to be in.

When I return to the apartment, Luba greets me at the door—after spending a few minutes unlatching the various latches. Palms opened, shoulders shrugged, I "ask" her how she is. "Feevty-feevty," she says, pointing to her left shoulder, which is sore, I presume, and fanning herself to indicate that the heat is getting to her. It's amazing, I think, how much two people can communicate with a shared vocabulary of only six words, one of which is "vodka."

A few minutes later, Luba cocks her head to one side and rests it on her hands. She's going to bed. I take the opportunity to look at the photos, framed and sitting on the mantel. Luba's past. There's a picture of a man, Luba's now-deceased husband, I figure. It's taken from a distance—too much distance, I think, squinting to make out his face. He has a shock of salt-and-pepper hair and

strong masculine features. He's standing in front of some gray Soviet monument. He's not smiling, but neither would I describe his
expression as a frown. I squint some more, and then I see it: the
trace of an aborted smile, barely perceptible but definitely there.
Later, Luba would explain through an interpreter that the picture
was taken in Kazakhstan, where they had lived years ago. I wonder if that faint smile survived Moldova.

My days fall into a comfortable routine. In the morning, Luba
makes me breakfast: a sharp Moldovan cheese, instant coffee, and
a biscuit filled with something mushy. Then I shower and head
onto the streets of Chisinau, probing Moldovan unhappiness.
Within a few days, I forget that the world beyond Moldova exists.
How amazing, I think, that in this age of broadband and satellite
TV, places can still engulf us so thoroughly that they make their
world our world.

I buy a bottle of Moldovan wine and bring it back to the apartment. Moldovans are proud of their wine, one of the few products
they export. There are tours of Moldovan vineyards and exhibi-
tions of Moldovan wine. People make wine in their homes and
proudly serve it to guests. I pour a glass for Luba, and she takes a
swig, then closes her eyes for a second or two, before pronouncing
it feevty-feevty. She is being generous. Moldovan wine doesn't rise
to the level of feevty-feevty. The sad truth is that nobody has the
heart to tell the Moldovans that their wine, their national treasure, stinks.

The next day, I meet Vitalie, the blogger, at a nearby restaurant—one that serves authentic Moldovan cuisine. I'm eager to try
it, mindful that food is the mirror of a nation's soul. Vitalie is in
his twenties, with a shiny face and perfect English, which he says
he learned by throwing away his textbook. A surly waiter leads
us downstairs to a dark and musty basement. It's noon. We're the
only customers.

So why are Moldovans so unhappy? I ask, diving right in. Vitalie gives me a how-much-time-do-you-have look. "Well, there is
the problem of Transnistria," he says.

"Can't antibiotics take care of that?" I ask.

It turns out that Transnistria is not a disease but a breakaway republic, a thin strip of Moldova controlled by pro-Russian forces. They make Cognac and textiles in Transnistria. Every once in a while, a bomb goes off, and mediators from Brussels fly in, wearing double-breasted suits and drinking Evian water. Conferences are held, and resolutions resolved. Then the men from Brussels fly home. Until the next bomb.

Vitalie declares the whole Transnistria situation "definitely dumb," and I'm inclined to agree. Later, I'd detect a strange pride that some Moldovans take in Transnistria, as if they're thinking, "Yes, we are a backward, profoundly unhappy nation, but at least we have our very own breakaway republic, just like a real country."

Vitalie is a freelance financial advisor. Most of his clients are foreign, so he earns a good living by Moldovan standards: $230 a month. His wife earns about the same, putting them solidly in the Moldovan upper-middle class. They live in a Khrushchev-ka, an apartment style named after the former Soviet leader best remembered for banging his shoe on a table at the United Nations, and about as charming. Mass-produced five-story apartment blocks, each the length of a football field. Each unit is tiny. "They were built for sleeping. You were working during the day, so what do you need space for?" explains Vitalie.

The surly waiter arrives to take our order. Vitalie recommends something called *mamaliga,* the national dish. I like the way it sounds. Like a *Sesame Street* character. Hey, boys and girls, say a big hello to the *mamaliga.*

Vitalie regales me with interesting Moldovan facts. Like the fact that the president of Moldova is a former baker and the prime minister a former confectioner. They'd make a great catering team but apparently not such a great political team. Moldovans despise their government—if they think of it at all, that is. They have other concerns.

Vitalie's biggest gripe—and he has many—is the lousy service in Moldova. A holdover from the Soviet era, he says, when sales clerks viewed the customer as a necessary interruption that, if ignored long enough and with enough animus, would eventually go away. That attitude persists, and it drives Vitalie nuts. Unlike most Moldovans, Vitalie doesn't just take it. He fights back. Just the other day, he yelled at a supermarket manager, telling her to train her staff to be more courteous. She didn't take the suggestion kindly. "This is the staff we have," she said. Typical, says Vitalie. The Moldovan default mode is defensiveness.

The food is taking a long time. Where is my *mamaliga*?

Trust—or, to be more precise, a lack of trust—is why Moldova is such an unhappy land, Vitalie tells me, echoing the findings of researchers about the relationship between happiness and trust. Moldovans don't trust the products they buy at the supermarket. (They might be mislabeled.) They don't trust their neighbors. (They might be corrupt.) They don't even trust their family members. (They might be conniving.)

Another reason for Moldovan misery? "People in Moldova are neither Russian nor Moldovan. We have been abused and abandoned by everyone. We have no pride in anything. Not even our language. There are ministers in the Moldovan government who don't speak Moldovan. They speak only Russian. I hate to say it, but it's true: There is no Moldovan culture."

I'm instantly reminded of Qatar, which has no culture either. Qatar, however, is a fabulously wealthy country with no culture. Moldova is a dirt-poor nation with no culture. All things considered, the Qataris have the better deal. At least they can afford to rent other people's culture for a while.

I ask Vitalie about democracy, reflexively gesturing toward my Sprite, as if a carbonated artificially flavored lemon-lime beverage somehow symbolized humanity's eternal quest for freedom. Moldovan democracy may be far from perfect, but certainly it is better than the totalitarian regime under the Soviets. Isn't that a source of happiness?

No, says Vitalie, without the slightest hesitation. "In Soviet times, nobody thought about freedom. Communism was all they knew. They didn't wake up every day and say, 'Gee, I wish I had more freedom.' Freedom to do what? At least back then, people had jobs and a place to live. That was a kind of freedom, and they don't have that now."

For years, political scientists assumed that people living under democracies were happier than those living under any other form of government. It made sense, intuitively, and there was some data to back it up. But the collapse of the Soviet Union changed all that. Most (though certainly not all) of these newly independent nations emerged as quasi-democracies. Yet happiness levels did not rise. In some countries they declined, and today the former Soviet republics are, overall, the least happy places on the planet. What is going on? That old causality bugaboo, political scientist Ron Inglehart concluded: It's not that democracy makes people happy but rather that happy people are much more likely to establish a democracy.

The soil must be rich, culturally speaking, before democracy can take root. The institutions are less important than the culture. And what are the cultural ingredients needed for democracy to take root? Trust and tolerance. Not only trust of those inside your group—family, for instance—but external trust. Trust of strangers. Trust of your opponents, your enemies, even. That way you feel you can gamble on other people—and what is democracy but one giant crapshoot?

Thus, democracy makes the Swiss happier but not the Moldovans. For the Swiss, democracy is the icing on their prosperous cake. Moldovans can't enjoy the icing because they have no cake.

"Okay," I say to Vitalie, grasping at straws, "but you have a McDonald's now. That must mean something, yes?"

No, says Vitalie. It means nothing. McDonald's is prohibitively expensive for ordinary Moldovans. Only a few wealthy oligarchs and the Russian mafia can afford to eat there. And schoolkids on field trips. He tells me that his ten-year-old sister's class recently visited McDonald's. Vitalie wondered what the educational benefit was. He asked his sister if she and her classmates got to go behind the counter to see how the burgers are made. No, she said. They just ate and left. Vitalie suspects nepotism—maybe someone at the school had a relative who worked at McDonald's? In Moldova, nepotism is the default explanation for everything. It's usually the correct explanation. Corruption is rampant, unbelievable, says Vitalie. He tells me of patients bribing hospital staff so they can jump the queue. "It's very difficult to remain clean here," he says.

Finally, my *mamaliga* arrives. I dig in. If food is a window to a nation's soul, then Moldova's soul is bland and mushy. And has something to do with corn, I think.

"How is it?" asks Vitalie.

"Not bad," I lie.

We talk a bit more while I nibble at my *mamaliga,* just enough not to appear rude. I pay the check, and we get up to leave.

We're standing on a busy street corner surrounded by brooding pedestrians, about to say goodbye, when it dawns on me that I have forgotten an obvious question.

"Vitalie, is there anything you like about life in Moldova?"

Vitalie pauses for a moment before answering. "We haven't become too soft, like people in the west. We're a little less expecting, and I think that's a good thing. Also, the fruits and vegetables."

"What about them?"

"They are very fresh."

As if on cue, a woman carrying plastic buckets brimming with raspberries and cherries walks by. Yes, I think, they do look fresh.

In the former Soviet republics, there are three staples of life: vodka, chocolate, and corruption. I know someone who once survived in Uzbekistan for two weeks solely on these three items. I pick up two of them at a local grocery store and head home; that's how I think of Luba's apartment now, as home. And so I eat my chocolate and drink my vodka, a brand deceptively called Perfect Vodka, while

Luba sits in front of the TV, making psst noises, and laughing occasionally. All things considered, I think, not a bad way to pass an evening in Moldova.

The next day, I sit down for lunch with Marisha, of Marisha. net. She is the happiest Moldovan I've met, possibly because she just married a British guy and can leave the country any time she wants. Her husband was one of her clients. Marisha makes a living helping the few foreign tourists who brave Moldova. For a while, she also helped men who came to Moldova looking for brides. But no more. Too many of the women, she explains, were looking for something other than love. "Scammers," that's the word she uses, who would write to their boyfriends in America or Britain, saying they needed money for a visa to visit or claiming to have won a new car in a lottery and just needed a few thousand dollars to pay the tax. Could you please send the money? It is such a beautiful car.

"Do the men fall for it?" I ask Marisha.

"Some do," she says.

I picture some poor slob, sitting in front of a computer screen in Cleveland, wondering why he hasn't heard from Olga since he mailed that check a while ago. Maybe he sends a follow-up e-mail or two, figuring the Moldovan server is down again. How long does it take him to realize he's been scammed? A week? A month?

That might explain the guy in Cleveland's unhappiness, but what about Moldovans themselves? I ask. Why are they so unhappy? Money, she answers, but she doesn't mean a lack of it. "We are substituting real values with money values."

A few minutes later, though, Marisha is gushing about the new megamall, Moldova's first, that is being built on the outskirts of town. Marisha sees this as a sign of progress. I want to shout NO! Don't do it! Before you know it, you'll be drowning in malls. But I hold my tongue.

After lunch, we walk a few blocks, down pleasant tree-lined streets, to the Museum of Nature and Ethnography. The museum looks like it hasn't changed one iota since Soviet times; neither do the women who work there. They seem annoyed by our presence. The exhibits are rudimentary yet oddly endearing. My favorite is the one about Moldovan dirt. Different shades and colors of soil are displayed in large Plexiglas cylinders. "We don't have minerals—no gas or oil—the treasure of Moldova is our soil," explains Marisha. It's true. As Vitalie said, Moldovan soil produces some very fresh fruits and vegetables. You'd think the wine would be better.

In another room, there is a giant mural, a Soviet ideal of the cosmos and humanity's place in it. The Soviets denied God's existence yet tried to improvize a spirituality. The mural is a raucous, dizzying hodgepodge of images that covers the entire ceiling and parts of the walls. My eyes don't know where to focus first. There are spaceships and skyscrapers—all drawn with hard angles and dark colors. On one wall, a young couple, completely naked, is holding their infant skyward, toward the godless heavens. No wonder the Moldovans are spiritually adrift. This is what they had to endure for more than fifty years.

I learn more at the museum. I learn that over the centuries, the Moldovans have been invaded by the Turks, Mongols, Tartars, Kazakhs, and, of course, the Russians. Yet Marisha claims that Moldovan unhappiness is a recent development. "We've always been happy people," she says, unconvincingly.

Marisha and I are about to say goodbye. But there is something I want to know.

"Marisha, I'm not sure how to ask this, but have you noticed how Moldovan women dress. It's very . . ."

"Sexy."

"Yes. Why is that?"

"They think it's normal."

Marisha offers an explanation, one rooted firmly in the principle of supply and demand. So many Moldovan men have left the country in search of work abroad that Moldovan women must compete fiercely for what has become a scarce resource: the Moldovan man. This imbalance also explains why Moldovan men care so little about their appearance. "It is not their job to look good," Marisha tells me. "It's their job to make money."

I take the bus back to Luba's apartment. It's hot. The driver has completely unbuttoned his shirt, revealing a hairy, flabby chest and, unknowingly, underscoring Marisha's point.

The Moldovans have amassed a repertoire of expressions to blunt their despair or at least explain it away. One of the more popular is "*ca la Moldova*": "This is Moldova." It's usually said plaintively, palms open. That and its companion "*ce sa fac*"— "What can I do?"—are employed when the bus breaks down, again, or the landlord demands an extra forty dollars a month in rent, just because.

My favorite, though, the expression that sums up this country, ties it into a neat little package and sticks a bow on it, is: "*No este problema mea*." Not my problem. A country with so many problems yet nobody's problem. Nobody takes ownership. Luba's apartment building, for instance, desperately needs a new water pump. (That explains the strange noises.) She tried to get people to pitch in—it would benefit everyone—but nobody would. No one is willing to contribute money to something that will benefit others as well as themselves.

What the Moldovans fail to recognize is the power of selfish altruism. It may sound a bit Sunday school–ish, but helping others makes us feel good. Psychologists at Kobe College in Japan proved this. They divided a group of college students into two groups. One group did nothing differently for a week. The other group was asked to count the number of kind acts they performed during that week. They weren't asked to perform any kind acts, merely to take note of them. After a week, this second group reported a marked jump in happiness levels compared to the control group. "Simply by counting the acts of kindness for one week, people become happier and more grateful," concluded the researchers.

Neuroscientists, meanwhile, believe they have located the part of the brain linked with altruism. To their surprise, it turns out to be a more primitive part of the brain than initially suspected—the same part associated with our cravings for food and sex. That suggests that we are hardwired for altruism and not just faking it.

"Nothing is funnier than unhappiness," says Nell, the legless trash-can dweller in Samuel Beckett's one-act play *Endgame*. Beckett never visited Moldova, I bet. I see no humor here, not even the unintentional variety. The Moldovans, though, do have at least one joke. It explains a lot about Moldova.

A visiting dignitary is being given a tour of hell. "Over here," says the tour guide, "is our room reserved for Americans." Flames shoot up from a boiling-hot cauldron, while scores of armed guards keep a careful eye on their captives. "And over here is the room for the Russians." More flames and another cauldron, though fewer guards. "And over here is the room for the Moldovans." Another cauldron, more flames. But this time there are no guards at all.

"I don't understand," says the visitor. "Why are there no guards watching the Moldovans?"

"Oh, that's not necessary," replies the tour guide. "If one gets out of the cauldron the others will drag him back in."

Envy, that enemy of happiness, is rife in Moldova. It's an especially virulent strain, one devoid of the driving ambition that usually accompanies envy. So the Moldovans get all of the downsides of envy without any of its benefits—namely, the thriving businesses and towering buildings erected by ambitious men and women out to prove they are better than everyone else. Moldovans derive more pleasure from their neighbor's failure than their own success. I can't imagine anything less happy.

I begin to wonder if perhaps not all Moldovans are unhappy. Maybe it's just the inhabitants of its capital city who are so miserable. I need to get out of Chisinau.

I call Marisha and explain my plans. She translates for Luba, telling her I'll be away for a few days. My destination, a town called Cahul, in the far south, is reachable by a series of shared taxis, called *rutieras*. Luba offers to show me where to catch the first one. We walk out of her apartment and step into the elevator. I gesture toward the graffiti—a riot of colors, as if a tie-dye factory exploded inside here, mingled with some foul language. Luba throws up her arms and says, "*Perestroika*." It is her one-word explanation for all that is wrong with Moldova, for why her life is such crap. Potholes? *Perestroika*. Crime? *Perestroika*. Lousy vodka? *Perestroika*.

We walk to a bus stop. We both stand there, waiting in silence, until finally a *rutiera* arrives. Luba says something in Russian to the driver, and I wave goodbye. The *rutiera* is packed. They always are. Standing-room only. Not more than six inches in front of my face is a woman's breast. It is a nice breast. I know this because a good two thirds of its surface area is exposed. After a few minutes, beads of sweat begin to collect on the breast. Soon, they form rivulets. I am fascinated, not in an erotic way but more in a fluid-dynamics way. After about fifteen minutes, I notice that the rivers of sweat have formed tributaries and are branching out to the other breast.

The *rutiera* stops every few minutes, and more people board. I can't believe how many people they manage to cram into this small van. No one complains. Not a word. The ceiling is low. I have to crouch. I notice that the driver is barefoot. This disturbs me, though I'm not sure why. Some guy's sweaty armpit is in my face. This disturbs me, and I know exactly why. We, the passengers on this overcrowded van, are like a living organism, expanding and contracting at each stop, as a few people disembark and many more board. Finally, a seat opens up, and I experience a jolt of joy, of good fortune. Benjamin Franklin, America's first self-help author, once wrote that happiness "is produced not so much by great pieces of good fortune that seldom happen as by little advantages that occur every day." He was right.

We pass a billboard, an ad for a plasma-screen TV. "LG: Life is good," it says. They've squeezed a lot of irony into those few words. For one thing, life is not good in Moldova. Also, nobody in the van can remotely afford the plasma-screen TV—except for me, and I prefer my plasma in my veins, not my living room. The billboard, indeed, all consumer culture, is mocking the Moldovans, most of whom will never be able to afford the products advertised—unless they sell a kidney. Joseph Epstein, in his book on envy, described the entire advertising industry as "a vast and intricate envy-producing machine." In Moldova, all of that envy has nowhere to dissipate; it just accumulates, like so much toxic waste.

I switch vans. This one is less crowded, but one seat is occupied by a farmer with about two dozen chirping chicks. At first, I find this endearing local color, but after a few minutes it starts to drive me nuts, and I want to strangle those little chirping birds. But I don't. *Ca la Moldova.* This is Moldova. One must remain passive at all costs.

It's hot, so I crack open the window next to me and drift off to sleep. When I wake up, maybe a half hour later, I notice that someone has closed the window. I open it again and doze off once more. When I wake up, it's closed again. What's going on? Later, I learned that it's considered bad luck to open a window in a moving vehicle, even if the moving vehicle in question is not air-conditioned and it's one hundred degrees outside. The Moldovans, it turns out, are a superstitious people. A few of their superstitions are optimistic, like the one that says, "If you sneeze it means someone is thinking of you." But most involve the terrible things that will befall you should you be careless enough to wash your clothes on Sunday, or give money on Monday, or toast with a glass of water (your children will be stupid), or go back for something you've forgotten, or sit on the bare pavement, or put your bag on the ground, or, of course, open the window of a moving vehicle. I realize that many people around the world are superstitious, but usually this is yoked to some larger belief system, religious or spiritual. Moldovan superstition is free-floating, anchored to nothing but the cloud of pessimism that hovers over this sad land.

A few hours later, I arrive in Cahul. It's supposedly Moldova's third-largest city, but it feels more like an overgrown village. I find my hotel, and, in a combination of broken English and broken Russian, the woman at reception explains that I have a choice of three types of rooms: Simple, Semi-Luxe, and Luxe. Keeping in mind the ancient Greek advice about "all things in moderation," I choose Semi-Luxe.

The room has a certain decrepit charm. Cracked wood furniture, towels like sandpaper, and a TV that gets sixty-seven channels, not one in English. I watch it anyway. I find it a pleasant diversion, and I play a guessing game. There's a woman in a headscarf shouting angrily. What is that story about? Click. There is President Bush dubbed into Russian. What's he saying? Click. A soccer match. What's the score? I'm not sure exactly how long I do this, but I'm pretty sure it's longer than most people would consider normal.

The official mission of the U.S. Peace Corps is "helping the people of interested countries in meeting their need for trained men and women" and "helping promote a better understanding of Americans on the part of the peoples served." Really, though, the mission is to spread a bit of American happiness around the world. We can't very well call it the U.S. Bliss Corps, but that's what it is: an attempt to remake the world in our own happy image.

I feel sorry for the Peace Corps volunteers in Moldova. They have their work cut out for them. I've arranged to meet with a group of volunteers. My arrival is eagerly awaited. I'm fresh blood, a new set of ears upon which to vent. I find the café, which is pleasant enough, sort of half indoors and half outdoors. We sit and eat salads and drink beer. It doesn't take long for the whining to begin.

Abby, a cheerleader blonde, gets things going. She went to the bank the other day to withdraw money from her account. But the bank teller wouldn't let her. "He kept saying, 'Why do you need to take out the money? You just took out some yesterday.' I couldn't believe it. It's my money."

"They don't know how to treat customers," says another volunteer.

Everyone here has a different gripe, large or small. The bad fish, for instance, which I'm told is caught in polluted rivers and can be deadly. The biggest complaint, though, is the lack of queuing. "It's not first-come, first-served, it's most-obnoxious, first-served," says Abby. The lack of trust is another popular gripe. "Friends don't even trust friends. If bad things happen to their friends, people think, 'Good, maybe it won't happen to me,' " says one volunteer.

Corruption is another theme. Paying professors for passing grades is widespread, so much so that Moldovans won't go to doctors under thirty-five years old. They suspect—with good reason—that they bought their degrees. Thus, the radius of mistrust is widened.

Mark is a thirty-two-year-old from Denver. I like him. He speaks Spanish and wanted to go to South America, so the Peace Corps sent him to Moldova. He complains that everything in his apartment has something wrong with it: drippy pipes, squeaky doors. He works at a center for the victims of domestic violence. He sees only one woman a week, which, Mark is convinced, says more about how scared women are to seek help than it does about the extent of domestic violence in Moldova.

Mark is concerned that Moldova is beginning to affect him. The other day, a woman came up to him on the street. "She said, 'Mark, what's wrong with you? You used to smile. I never see you smile anymore,' and I thought, She's right. I don't smile anymore. What's happened to me?" This is not the way the Peace Corps is supposed to work. The young, cheerful, and generally gung-ho Americans are supposed to instill a sense of hope in the hopeless. In this case, Moldovans seem to be getting the last laugh. That is, if they laughed.

These once-cheery Americans can't wait to leave Moldova.

Until that time, they cope as best they can by drinking lots of beer. Abby likes to pretend she's in Greece. It's warm, and the country-side is nice, and they have feta cheese here, sometimes, though it's really not very good.

I mostly listen, absorbing their grievances like a sponge. I can't believe things are so bleak here. "Come on, surely there must be something nice about life in Moldova. This place must have some redeeming traits."

The loquacious group suddenly grows silent. Everyone is staring down at their salads. Finally, someone, Mark, I think, says, "The fruit and vegetables. They're very fresh."

"Yeah," others chime in, enthusiastically, "very fresh fruits and vegetables."

I return to the hotel. My Semi-Luxe room is hot, very hot. I call down to the front desk.

"Where is the air-conditioning?"

"Oh, no, sir, there is no air-conditioning in the Semi-Luxe room. Only in the Luxe room."

"Well, can I upgrade to a Luxe room?"

"No, sir, that is not possible."

"Can I get a fan?"

"No, sir. That is not possible. But you are free to bring your own."

I turn on the TV. The national channels are trying to promote Moldovan culture. From what I can tell, this consists of women in Heidi outfits, dancing in a circle, arms at hips, while a man wearing a peacock hat sings. I fall asleep but do not sleep well.

The next morning, I trundle downstairs to meet Joanna for breakfast. She's another Peace Corps volunteer. She's been here nearly two years, making her the dean of the bunch. Everyone said I should meet Joanna.

She's waiting for me at the hotel's coffee shop, a dingy place with a waitress who is widely known as The Bitch, a moniker that is not used ironically. She is quite possibly the surliest waitress I've ever had in my life. Anywhere. Yesterday, there was much discussion about whether The Bitch ever smiled. Someone said yes, they had seen her smile once, but the others had quickly dismissed this as a grimace; the lighting conditions had created the illusion of a smile.

Joanna and I take a seat and place our orders, cowering behind the little cardboard menus. The Bitch's expression cannot be construed as a smile, under any lighting conditions.

Joanna asks me to pass the salt and proceeds to empty a shakerful into her coffee. "I'm a salt person," she declares, in response to my look of disbelief. Joanna, it turns out, puts salt in pretty much everything and does other "weird food things," a habit she gets from her mother.

I ask Joanna why she decided to join the Peace Corps in the first place. "I'm a doer. I do things," she says. But that's not the real reason, she adds. The real reason is airplanes. She used to be terrified to fly. She'd cry every time she flew, afraid the plane would crash. Then one day she stopped crying. She hadn't gotten over her fear of flying. She just didn't care anymore if the plane crashed. "That's when I realized I needed something to make me care again, care if the plane went down." So she quit her job at American Express in New York and joined the Peace Corps.

Joanna had asked to be sent to a "rice-based, not a bread-based society." Asia, maybe. But there was a mix-up with her paperwork, and by the time it was sorted out all of the rice countries were spoken for and Joanna ended up in Moldova. "This was about the last place I wanted to go," she says. It strikes me, not for the first time, that nobody wants to be in Moldova, including the Moldovans.

Joanna volunteers, unprompted, that she is a recovering alcoholic. Moldova is either a great place to be an alcoholic or a terrible one, depending on whether you're in recovery or not. Moldovans drink heavily. Unlike Icelanders, though, they do so joylessly. I see well-dressed Moldovan women slip into one of the tiny bars that dot the city, down a shot of vodka, and then be on their way to work. Alcohol as anesthetic.

Joanna's on a roll, pouring more salt into her coffee and talking at a breakneck pace. (At one point, she tells me she meditates every morning for forty-five minutes. This surprises me, and I shudder to think how fast she would vibrate if she didn't meditate.) She tells me how she tried to organize AA meetings in her Moldovan village, but it didn't work out as planned. Most people showed up drunk. They heard the word "alcohol" and thought it was some sort of drinking club, she concludes. "If I were Moldovan, I would drink, too," she says.

Joanna lives in a nearby village with her Moldovan host family and a small bird named Bu-Bu. They are nice enough people, but they give her no privacy. They just walk into her room at any time and force her to eat. And they won't let her open the window in her room, even when it's ninety degrees inside and there's no air-conditioning. That might bring bad luck. (In Moldova, how could you tell?) And she's only allowed to flush her toilet twice a day, which she reserves for "special moments." Plus, they think she's old.

"In New York, I was this thirtysomething *Sex and the City* chick. Here, I'm a babushka. That came as a real shock to me."

"Why are Moldovans so unhappy?" I ask.

Joanna doesn't hesitate. "Powerlessness. As a Moldovan, you are helpless, powerless, and there is nothing you can frickin' do about it. That's the way things are here. Every day, every step of the way. Then there's the nepotism, which seems designed to prevent people from trying. It takes a year to start a frickin' business here. And they buy college degrees, and they think there's nothing wrong with it. It just frickin' freaks me out." At this point, Joanna bangs her hand on the table to underscore her point. Out of the corner of my eye, I spot The Bitch glowering at us.

Joanna isn't finished, though. "When students register for college and pay their tuition, they are guaranteed a degree, no matter what they do in school. If a child fails, then it's the teacher's fault. I could just throw things when I hear about this."

I truly hope she is speaking figuratively. The Bitch would not be happy if things were thrown. Joanna is out of breath and takes a moment to sip her salty coffee.

The happiness research backs her up. People are not likely to be happy if they don't have control over their lives—not in some abstract geopolitical sense, but in a real, everyday sense. Moldovans are caught in a misery loop. Their unhappiness breeds mistrust, which breeds more unhappiness, which leads to more mistrust. I feel obliged to ask Joanna if she is happy here, though it seems like a formality.

"Actually, yes, I am," she says. "Happier than I was in New York. I feel more useful here."

I can hardly believe it. Yet it makes sense. Being useful, helpful, is one of the unsung contributors to happiness. Researchers at the University of Chicago recently surveyed some fifty thousand people in widely varying professions. The results were surprising. The high-prestige jobs—lawyers, doctors, bankers—scored low. Who were those who reported the highest levels of happiness? Clergy, physical therapists, nurses, and firefighters. In other words, helping professions. Those engaged in selfish altruism.

Besides, says Joanna, life in Moldova isn't all bad. There are some nice traditions here, she says, like the respect for elders and the dead. Once a year, there's a holiday, a sort of "Easter for the Dead"—that's what she calls it—where everyone brings flowers to the grave sites and pays homage to their deceased families. Moldovans, it seems, treat the dead better than the living.

"And of course, there are the fruits and vegetables," she says.

"Very fresh, right?"

"Exactly."

I pay The Bitch, who takes my money without a word or a smile, and head up to my room to pack. I've seen enough of the Moldovan countryside.

On the ride back to the capital, the van is hot, but I don't bother opening the window. I worry that I'm turning Moldovan, and I

scan my mind for other signs of this ailment. Yes, I'm not as polite as I was. I no longer say "thank you" or "please," since these
niceties are never reciprocated. Moldovans just walk into a shop
and say, "Give me this, give me that." Marisha had told me, in so
many words, that Moldovans can't afford the luxury of politeness.
A few weeks ago, I might have agreed with her. I spent four years
living in probably the politest country in the world, Japan, and it
drove me nuts. All of that please and thank-you and *gomen nasai,*
I'm sorry.

I was wrong about the Japanese. They understand intuitively
that politeness is the lubrication that makes the gears of society
turn smoothly. Without it, the parts start grinding against one
another, wearing one another down. Yes, I will take Japan's ersatz
politeness over Moldova's genuine rudeness any time. Thank you
very much.

Luba greets me at the door, wearing that lurid housecoat.
Funny, I think, in my short time here we've become like an old
married couple. She cooks for me. I do odd jobs around the apartment like changing lightbulbs and opening pickle jars. Sometimes
we bicker, which is quite an accomplishment, given our language
limitations.

"How was your trip?" she pantomimes.

"Feevty-feevty," I say, and she smiles.

She offers me dinner. A nice-looking fish, which I devour. A
few minutes later, panic sets in. Oh, no, I ate the fish! I'm going to
die, just like the Peace Corps people warned.

Luba pantomimes that she has to leave for a while to get her
hair cut. I peer out the window and catch a glimpse of her as she
walks past the pathetic park and heads toward the, no doubt, pathetic beauty salon. I am suddenly filled with a deep affection for
this babushka, a feeling that catches me unawares.

I realize, though, that I know very little about Luba, about her
past. I call Marisha and arrange for her to come later that week to
translate. I need to hear Luba's story.

Meanwhile, I pick up the rotary phone and call a cellphone, a technological leapfrog of sorts. On the other end is Alexandru, or Sandru as he calls himself, a dyed-in-the-wool Moldovan nationalist. I hadn't known there was such a thing. I'm hoping to meet him.

"So you don't have a mobile phone?" Sandru asks, incredulously.

"No, I don't believe in them." This is my new thing. I've decided to stop using cellphones. Having had fleeting moments of bliss interrupted by them in Switzerland and Bhutan, I've decided that cellphones are antithetical to happiness. They take you out of the moment and, even more important, out of the place.

"Yes, but you're calling a cellphone now."

"That is different," I counter. "I don't believe in using them, but other people are free to do so."

He grudgingly accepts this explanation, and we agree to meet.

I hop on a bus, and, for the first time since I arrived in Moldova, witness an act of kindness. An old woman, with gold teeth and tufts of gray hair protruding from her chin, is trying to get on the bus, but she's too weak. A man grabs her arm and pulls her on board. I can't believe my eyes. Maybe there is hope for this place after all. Or not. It turns out that the woman is on the wrong bus. Everybody is yelling at her angrily, including the man who helped her get on board. At the next stop, her fellow passengers practically push her off.

Sandru is thin and young and twirling a pair of sunglasses. I apologize for being late, but in Moldova ten minutes late is not really late. We walk to his favorite hangout, a pleasant place with outdoor tables and umbrellas. Sandru is only twenty-six but has enough hatred and bitterness in his heart for a seventy-year-old.

Sandru hates the Russians for what they did to Moldova. "We lost our identity. We Moldovans don't fit in anywhere. In Russia, they say you're Romanian. In Romania, they say you're Russian. Moldova is an injured body. It needs to heal." Moldovans are unhappy because they don't know who they are. How can you feel good about yourself if you don't know who you are?

When the waitress comes to take our order, Sandru speaks to her in Moldovan. The waitress replies in Russian. Two people having a conversation in two completely different languages, neither willing to back down.

"Do you speak Russian?" I ask Sandru, after the waitress has gone.

"Yes, fluently."

"So why don't you talk to her in Russian?"

"Why should I? This is my country, not hers. She should speak Moldovan. I can't take this, being humiliated all the time. Do you know what they say to me? They say, 'Why don't you speak Russian? Why don't you speak a human language?'"

In Moldova, language is not a source of joy, as in Iceland, but a source of divisiveness. Language as weapon.

"You know," I say, "the Russians claim they liberated Moldova."

"Yes, they liberated it from the people."

I try another tack and tell him about Luba. She is Russian, ethnically at least, and she is the nicest woman. She is suffering, too. She lost everything.

"I'm glad she lost everything," he says, refusing to back down. "The truth will come out. It always does."

My meeting with Sandru has put me in a funk. On the bus ride home, I wonder if I've misread this place. Misread Luba. Was this kindhearted babushka really complicit in the decimation of Moldova? Was I, once again, naïve and unsophisticated?

I am ninety minutes late for dinner. Luba is angry. She gestures toward her watch—or the part of her wrist, rather, where a watch would be if she had one.

After dinner, Marisha arrives at Luba's apartment. She is smiley and bubbly, as usual—proof that not everyone in a hopeless situation slips into learned helplessness.

We all sit down at the kitchen table and, over a snack of tea and cheese, the story of Luba's life unfurls.

These are the facts: one of thirteen children born in the Russian countryside. Meets her husband at construction college. They marry and move to Kazakhstan. Mine uranium. (Yes, for nuclear bombs.) Have a beautiful daughter, Larissa, and a son, too. Daughter falls ill from the radiation, so they move to Moldova.

Luba takes out a yellowing staff directory and shows me her picture. She looks important. She had risen high in the construction ministry; she had a car and a dacha. She lived well, not extravagantly but well. Then a man entered her life. His name was Mikhail Gorbachev, and he was a fool, she says, with a roll of her eyes. He moved too quickly in dismantling the Soviet Union. She lost everything. With this, she begins to sob. I hand her a tissue. Her husband had a stroke and lapsed into a coma for a year, then died. Now she survives on a forty-dollar-a-month pension. Her daughter is in Turkey working as a "hairstylist for dogs." (At least that's how Marisha translates it.) Her son is in Russia's Far East, working construction. She hasn't seen him in ten years. He'd have to work six months to pay for the airfare.

"Is there anything better about life now?" I ask.

"Yes, the stores are bigger, and there is more selection, but only 10 percent of the people can afford these goods."

"And the freedom?"

"Freedom to do what? Freedom to consume? I don't need this freedom. Today, the free ones are the ones who have money. My daughter knows the value of work, but my granddaughter, Natasha, only knows the value of freedom." And, it's implied, that is not very valuable at all.

Luba is not happy. That much is clear. But I ask anyway: What makes for a happy life? I expect her to mention money, at least enough money to survive, but she doesn't.

"I have a different attitude toward money. Everything comes with hard work. So you must be hardworking. And be good to people. All people are good and deserve love."

We all just sit there for a moment, then the spell is broken. It's back to business. I need to settle my account. I hand Luba a crisp hundred-dollar bill. She takes it and then presses it against her lips in an exaggerated kiss.

I go back to my room to pack and contemplate Luba's sadness. Journalistically, it's an old story. I've written many of these sad tales over the years. The geopolitical landscape shifted, tectonic forces beyond Luba's control, and so she lost everything. The privileged position, the nice car, the country home. Thus, she is unhappy. Case closed. Plausible, I suppose, but what does the science of happiness tell us about Luba's unhappiness? It would point to other reasons for her misery besides the obvious monetary ones: the loss of camaraderie at work, for instance, or the fact that she hardly sees her children. It is these relationships that account for a large chunk of our happiness, and they have little to do with money. Something wasn't right though. That golden rule of positive psychology, hedonic adaptation, states that no matter what tragedy or good fortune befalls us, we adapt. We return to our "set point" or close enough anyway. It's been fifteen years since the collapse of the Soviet Union. Why hasn't Luba adapted?

I think it comes back to culture. That sea we swim in. Drain it, as happened in Moldova, and we can't breathe. We lose our bearings, and hedonic adaptation is short-circuited. Luba lives in a sort of Russian shadow land. It is Russia, but it's not. The ethnic Moldovans live in their own shadow land. Romanians, but not.

Charles King, author of one of the few books about Moldova, calls this place a "stipulated nation." I would go a step further. Moldova is a fabricated nation. It does not exist. Oh, yes, you can go there, as I did, and walk its streets, eat its *mamaliga,* drink its bad wine, talk to its miserable people. Later, safely home, you can flip open your passport and admire, if that's the word, the stamp that says "The Republic of Moldova." None of this matters. Moldova does not exist, and existence is, in my book, a prerequisite for happiness. We need a solid identity—ethnic, national, linguistic, culinary, whatever—in order to feel good about ourselves. We may not use these identities every day, but they're always there, like money in the bank, something to fall back on during hard times, and times don't get much harder than they are now in Moldova. That is, if such a place existed.

Yes, it's time to leave this nonexistent place and return to the real world, which, while troubled in many ways, does at least exist. First, though, I decide to do something. It is impulsive and, really, silly. I hesitate to tell you about it. When Luba is not looking, I slip an extra hundred-dollar bill into the English-Russian dictionary she has on a bookshelf and is always using to look up words. I put the bill next to *"schaste,"* the Russian word for happiness. It's a melodramatic gesture, maybe even a selfish one—in the altruistic sense, that is. Certainly, it is ineffectual. Who am I kidding? All of the research, not to mention my time in Qatar, concludes that one hundred dollars will not make Luba happier in the long run. But it just might in the short run, and sometimes the short run is good enough.

We're standing outside her apartment building, Luba and I, waiting for the taxi that will take me to the airport and the outside world. "Come back to Moldova," Luba says, surprising me with her sudden burst of English. I tell her I will, but I'm lying, and she knows that. The truth is, I've never wanted to leave a place as much as I want to leave Moldova. Charles Dickens once said, "One always begins to forget a place as soon as it's left behind." God, I hope he's right.

I arrive at the airport early—I'm not taking any chances—and so I find myself with plenty of time on my hands. I order a glass of bad Moldovan wine and assess my journey to this wretched place. First of all, I can pretty much discard the Law of Relative Happiness, which claimed that a miserable place like Moldova would make me feel better about myself, since I am, comparatively speaking, less miserable than your average Moldovan. It didn't turn out that way. The Moldovans just dragged me down a rung on the hedonic ladder, and I didn't have many rungs to go.

Are there bigger lessons, though, to be gleaned from Moldova's unhappiness, other than the obvious point that one should at all costs and under all circumstances avoid being Moldovan? Yes, I think there are. Lesson number one: "Not my problem" is not a philosophy. It's a mental illness. Right up there with pessimism. Other people's problems *are* our problems. If your neighbor is laid off, you may feel as if you've dodged the bullet, but you haven't. The bullet hit you as well. You just don't feel the pain yet. Or as Ruut Veenhoven told me: "The quality of a society is more important than your place in that society." In other words, better to be a small fish in a clean pond than a big fish in a polluted lake.

Lesson number two: Poverty, relative poverty, is often an excuse for unhappiness. Yes, Moldovans are poor compared to other Europeans, but clearly it is their reaction to their economic problems, and not the problems alone, that explains their unhappiness.

The seeds of Moldovan unhappiness are planted in their culture. A culture that belittles the value of trust and friendship. A culture that rewards mean-spiritedness and deceit. A culture that carves out no space for unrequited kindness, no space for what St. Augustine called (long before Bill Clinton came along) "the happiness of hope." Or as the ancient Indian text the *Mahabharata* says: "Hope is the sheet anchor of every man. When hope is destroyed, great grief follows, which is almost equal to death itself."

No, there is nothing I will miss about Moldova. Nothing. Well, that's not entirely true. I will miss Luba and her floral housecoat. She's a good soul. And, of course, the fruits and vegetables. They are very fresh.

# Chapter 7

# THAILAND
## Happiness Is Not Thinking

Sometimes, despite our best intentions, we fall face-first into a cliché. And so I find myself at 1:00 a.m. at a bar called Suzie Wong's, watching naked Thai women painted in Day-Glo colors grinding and shimmying and doing things with Ping-Pong balls that, frankly, never occurred to me before.

I told myself I wouldn't let this happen, but one thing led to another, and here I am. I'd like to think my friend Scott is to blame. He lives in Bangkok and should know better. But the truth is that even on the flight over I had an inkling of the trouble that lay ahead.

Sitting next to me was Nick, an entrepreneur who jets between New York and Bangkok, where he has his hand in all sorts of businesses. He's wearing shorts and sandals and has a wild, unruly beard. Nick knows many things about Thailand, and he's eager to share all of them with me during the seventeen-hour flight. I will spare you the unabridged version and cut to the highlights.

Nick on *muay Thai*, or kickboxing: "Don't sit in the front rows. That's for tourists. Besides, you'll get blood splattered all over you. Sit in the back."

Nick on proper Thai business attire: "This is what I wear to business meetings. Shorts. But no tank tops. I made that mistake once. The Thais don't like hairy armpits in their face. It's bad for business."

Nick on Thai dating customs: "Not all Thai girls are easy.

Most, but not all. A proper girl, from an upper-class family, you might have to take her out thirty times before you can bang her."

The girls at Suzie Wong's go on break. Scott takes advantage of the respite to share with me his theory about sex. In order for it to happen, three elements must align perfectly: method, motive, and opportunity. For a middle-aged, overweight male, the odds of such an alignment are about as great as the earth, moon, and sun aligning for a total solar eclipse. Ah, but not in Bangkok, where that elusive third element—opportunity—clicks into place, thanks to the alchemy of international exchange rates and Thai permissiveness.

I nod in agreement and scan the crowd. The customers at Suzie Wong's consist almost entirely of out-of-shape, middle-aged men, hands clutching beers, faces frozen in permanent ogles. I am instantly reminded of those Canadian rats. As you recall, in the 1950s Canadian psychologists implanted electrodes deep within the brains of rats and connected the electrodes to levers that the rats could press to stimulate the pleasure center of their brains. Left to their own devices, the rats would repeatedly press the lever—up to two thousand times per hour. They ceased almost all other normal behavior, even eating.

That pretty much describes the life of a foreign man living in Bangkok. Except instead of pressing a lever, he's digging into his wallet for a few more baht. The same principle is at work, though. The same mindless obedience to their pleasure centers. Yet if pleasure were the path to happiness then the *farang*, the foreigner, in Thailand would achieve bliss, and so would the Canadian rats. Yet neither has. Happiness is more than animal pleasure.

At first glance, Thai permissiveness looks a lot like Dutch permissiveness. But they are different. Dutch permissiveness is a system, one the Dutch are proud of and even promote in videos they show to prospective immigrants. Take a look, the Dutch say. This is what we are about. Can you handle it? The Thais do not say anything like that. They merely acknowledge human urges, erotic and monetary, and get on with it. Canadian author Mont Redmond put it best when he wrote that, in Thailand, "Anything too big to be swept under the carpet is automatically counted as furniture." The Thais might not like the furniture, might constantly be bumping into it, but they don't deny its existence.

In Bangkok, apocryphal stories abound. Cautionary tales. Like one I heard about a young reporter for an august British newspaper who fell so deeply into Bangkok's world of vice that he could no longer perform his duties and had to be recalled to London. It was a sort of medical evacuation, though not in the usual sense; the evacuee was suffering from an excess of pleasure, not pain.

They're called "sexpats," Scott tells me. A conflation, of course, of "sex" and "expat." The sexpat is easily identified by his sunburned face, huge beer belly, and generally unkempt appearance. The sexpat knows that as long as his wallet is in reasonably good shape, the rest of him can fall to pieces. "It's really quite pathetic," says Scott. What I don't have the heart to tell Scott is that he's starting to develop a paunch himself, and he has the slightest trace of a sunburn, and his shirts are always untucked.

Back at Scott's apartment, we watch a pirated DVD, but the sound is so bad and the image so shaky, we give up after ten minutes. Scott hands me a chunky book titled *The Teachings of the Buddha*. It looks like one of the books you see in hotel rooms across Asia, the Buddhist version of the Gideon Bible. Scott explains that's because he lifted it from a hotel room in Asia. He briefly ponders what this means for his karmic account, which is already seriously overdrawn, but decides not to pursue this line of thought, figuring it can't lead anywhere good.

Scott is a devout atheist, but since he moved to Thailand three years ago he's acquired some distinctly Buddhist tendencies, though of course he would deny this. For one thing, he's mellowed, and Buddhists are nothing if not mellow. He's stopped amassing material possessions, even his beloved books. After he's read one, he passes it on. "Once I realized that books weren't trophies, it was easy," he says, and proves his point by giving me a worn copy of Somerset Maugham's *The Moon and Sixpence*. Scott is a big Somerset Maugham fan. He lives his life the way Maugham advised: "Follow your inclinations with due regard to the policeman round the corner." Of course, in Thailand that policeman round the corner is most likely on the take or simply doesn't care what you are up to. I choose not to point this out to Scott.

In Bangkok, the bizarre is as inevitable as the tropical heat, and Scott has done things here that he would never imagine doing back home. Like the time he ate a strawberry pizza. But some things are too bizarre, even for Scott. The "no-hands" restaurant, for instance. That's where Thai waitresses feed their male customers dinner the way a mother feeds an infant. No hands. Freud would have had much to say about this place, I'm sure. Scott declares it "just too weird for me."

Scott's girlfriend is a bouncy young Thai woman named Noi. She used to be a "dancer." (I don't ask too many questions.) Now she does Scott's laundry and cooks for him. Mostly, though, she sits in front of the TV, watching Thai soap operas. She can do this for fifteen hours continuously. It's really quite amazing. She can also haggle like a demon with taxi drivers and whip up a pad thai that tastes better than anything I've had in the finest Thai restaurants. It has a real kick. Thais firmly believe that spice is the spice of life. Oh, and she eats insects. That might seem shocking, but really it's no big deal. Most people from Noi's part of Thailand eat insects—large black crickets and water bugs that are deep-fried in oil and served whole. I hear they make quite a crunching sound when you bite into them, but I feel no compunction to investigate further. My culinary bravado stops cold at rotten Icelandic shark.

Noi has a dazzling smile, even by Thai standards. It arrives fully formed, in a flash. Hers was voted "best smile" by colleagues at the beach resort where she once worked. In Thailand, the Land of Smiles, that is high praise indeed.

A number of years ago, Thai Airways ran a clever advertisement. The ad showed two photos of flight attendants smiling: one from Thai Airways, the other from the competition. The photos seemed identical. The copy read: "Can you spot the genuine smile?"

Indeed, there was a difference, one that any Thai person could spot instantly but not most foreigners. What the Thais know instinctively is that a smile, a *real* smile, is not located in the lips or any other part of the mouth. A real smile is in the eyes. To be precise, the *orbicularis oculi* muscles that surround each eye. We cannot fool these tiny muscles. They spring to life only for a genuine smile.

The Thai smiles means more—and less—than the western smile. It is a mask or, more accurately, many masks. The Thai smile can signify happiness but also anger, doubt, anxiety, and even grief. Thais will smile at a funeral, something that foreigners find disconcerting.

The Thais remind us that the smile is not private. Researchers have found that people, sane people at least, rarely smile when alone. The smile is a social gesture more than a reflection of our inner state, though it can be that, too.

I doubt that there could ever be a Thai Harvey Ball, the inventor of the famous smiley face. Thais would find such a generic smile silly. Okay, the Thais would say, it's a smile but *what kind* of smile?

Just as the Inuit are said to have many words for snow, the Thais have many words for smile. There is *yim cheun chom,* the I-admire-you smile, and *yim thak thaan,* the I-disagree-with-you-but-go-ahead-propose-your-bad-idea smile. There is *yim sao,* the sad smile. And my favorite: *yim mai awk,* the I'm-trying-to-smile-but-can't smile.

It's all fascinating, but I also find the Thais' variety pack of smiles disconcerting. It has undermined my belief that a smile, at its core, signifies happiness, contentment. I don't trust the Thai smile anymore. I don't trust *any* smile. I see deceit and misdirection everywhere and find myself staring at people's *orbicularis oculi* for signs of activity. Maybe I'm right to be paranoid, but then again maybe not. Sometimes, as Freud would say, a smile is just a smile.

Noi, like most Thais, believes in merit making. She keeps a running tally in her head. She knows that giving money to monks, or some other worthwhile cause, earns her major karma points, redeemable in a future lifetime. She's also crazy about Scott and often conveys her affection with a Thai expression: "I love you same as monkey loves banana." I find it very endearing.

In those rare moments when she's not watching TV, Noi is dispensing advice to Scott. She says things like "You're too serious." And "Don't think too much!" These are common Thai expressions, and they say much about this country and how it defines the good life.

I've always considered myself a thoughtful person. There's virtually nothing I won't think about, from the intensely profound to the astonishingly trivial. The only thing I haven't given much thought to is... thinking.

Like most westerners, I've never felt the need to question the value of thinking. To me, that would make about as much sense as questioning the value of breathing. Just listen to our language. *I think therefore I am. Think before you act. Think it over. Give it some thought. Let me think about it and get back to you. How thoughtful of you.*

Some people think (there's that word again) that our venal pop culture devalues thinking. That's not true. Pop culture devalues a certain type of thinking—deep thinking—but it values another kind: the shallow variety. Shallow thinking is still thinking.

The examined life, we're told, is the good life. Psychotherapy is built on this assumption—cognitive therapy, in particular. If we can only fix our faulty thought patterns, our corrupted software, then happiness, or at least less misery, will ensue.

I've spent most of my life trying to think my way to happiness, and my failure to achieve that goal only proves, in my mind, that I am not a good enough thinker. It never occurred to me that the source of my unhappiness is not flawed thinking but thinking itself.

Until I traveled to Thailand. Thais are deeply suspicious of thinking. For the Thais, thinking is like running. Just because your legs are moving doesn't mean you're getting anywhere. You might be running into a headwind. You might be running on a treadmill. You might even be running backward.

Thais do not buy self-help books or go to therapists or talk endlessly about their problems. They do not watch Woody Allen movies. When I ask Noi and other Thais if they are happy, they smile, of course, and answer politely, but I get the distinct impression that they find my question odd. The Thais, I suspect, are too busy being happy to think about happiness.

Indeed, I find myself questioning where all these years of introspection have gotten me: a library of self-help books and an annoying tendency to say things like "I'm having issues" and "What do you think that *means*?" A Thai person would never say things like that.

Thai culture, while rare in its distrust of thinking, is not unique. The Inuit frown upon thinking. It indicates someone is either crazy or fiercely stubborn, neither of which is desirable. The geographer Yi-Fu Tuan describes one Inuit woman who was overheard to say in a righteous tone, "I *never* think." Another woman complained to a friend about a third woman because she was trying to make her think and thus shorten her life. "Happy people have no reason to think; they live rather than question living," concludes Tuan.

On this score, the new science of happiness has been largely silent, and I suppose that's not surprising. An academic, after all, would no more question the value of thinking than a chef would question the value of cooking. Yet a few courageous psychologists have studied the relationship between introspection and happiness.

In one study, psychologists Tim Wilson and Jonathan Schooler had participants listen to a piece of music, Stravinsky's *Rite of Spring*. Some were given no instructions before listening to the music. Others were told to monitor their happiness, and still others to "try to be happy" while listening. It was these latter two categories that derived the *least* amount of pleasure from the music. Those given no instructions at all found the music most enjoyable. The inevitable conclusion: Thinking about happiness makes us less happy.

The philosopher Alan Watts, were he alive today, would nod knowingly when told of that experiment. Watts once said, "Only bad music has any meaning." Meaning necessarily entails words, symbols. They point to something other than themselves. Good music doesn't point anywhere. It just is. Likewise, only unhappiness has meaning. That's why we feel compelled to talk about it and have so many words to draw upon. Happiness doesn't require words.

When you get down to it, there are basically three, and only three, ways to make yourself happier. You can increase the amount of positive affect (good feelings). You can decrease the amount of negative affect (bad feelings). Or you can change the subject. This third option is one we rarely consider or, if we do, dismiss it as a cop-out. Change the subject? That's avoidance, we protest, that's cowardly! No, we must wallow in our stuff, analyze it, taste it, swallow it, then spit it out, swallow it again, and talk about it, of course, always talk about it. I've always believed that the road to happiness is paved with words. Nouns, adjectives, verbs, if arranged in just the right constellation, would enable me to hopscotch to bliss. For Thais, this is an alien and quite silly approach to life. Thais don't trust words. They view them as tools of deception, not truth.

The Thais have a different way, the way of *mai pen lai*. It means "never mind." Not the "never mind" that we in the west often use angrily, as in "Oh, never mind, I'll do it myself" but a real, just-drop-it-and-get-on-with-life "never mind." Foreigners living in Thailand either adopt the *mai pen lai* attitude or go insane.

"The whole world is fucked," declares Denis Gray, gesturing outside his office window at the concrete that stretches as far as the eye can see. Denis shows me a photo of the same perspective in 1962. It is virtually unrecognizable from the sea of skyscrapers that I see before me now. Just a few buildings and a car or two on the road. Denis would like to travel back to 1962, though, he concedes, most Thais probably would not. The Thais handle change very well, he says, but the old is not honored here.

Denis, an American journalist, has lived in Thailand for the past thirty-five years. He hates what the Thais have done to Bangkok, a city once known as the Venice of the east because of its elegant canals, long since paved over. But he loves Thai lightheartedness. Nearly every day, he says, he encounters a case of *mai pen lai*.

"The other day," he says, "my business manager and I were hashing out some problem with the accounts. We couldn't work it out, just couldn't get it resolved. The numbers wouldn't add up no matter how hard we worked the problem. And then she said, 'Denis, let's let this one go. We don't need to find a solution.' And so we did."

Denis is no Pollyanna; he admits the *mai pen lai* attitude has its drawbacks. It's sometimes used as cover for incompetence or plain laziness. But he believes it is, overall, a wiser approach to life's problems. After all, how can you pick up something new—a new career, a new relationship, a new outlook on life—without first letting go of the old? It's like trying to pick up a bag of groceries when your hands are already full. Most likely, everything comes crashing down, and you are left empty-handed.

I want to believe this, I really do, but part of me, the neurotic part, resists. I can't just let a problem go unsolved. To me, that seems like quitting, and quitting makes my skin crawl. Maybe if I spent thirty-five years in Thailand I'd come around to *mai pen lai,* too. Or maybe I would go insane.

Another thing that Denis likes about Thailand is the concept of *jai yen,* cool heart. The worst thing one can do in Thailand is to lose one's *jai yen.* This is why Thais have no patience for uppity foreigners, which is pretty much all foreigners.

"The Thais are great gossipers and schemers," Denis tells me, "but in thirty years I can recall maybe a dozen times that someone has lost their cool in the office." Wow. In an American office, people lose their cool twelve times *a day.* Denis has an unwritten law in his office: Don't explode. If you're upset with a colleague, observe a cooling-off period. Occasionally, he allows people to confront each other, to "be American about it." But not very often.

Later, I ask Kunip, a Thai school principal, about this notion of cool heart. We're sitting in the teachers' lounge, which has blond wood floors and reminds me of an airport business-class lounge. Kunip's skin is perfect and so is his white shirt and red tie. Personal appearance is very important to Thais. Not only do they dislike hairy armpits in their face, as Nick had pointed out, they don't like wrinkles or dirt either. Kunip answers my question about *jai yen,* cool heart, with a story.

A neighbor had a banana tree that had grown so fulsomely that it extended onto Kunip's property. Insects attached to the banana tree were infiltrating his house. This is where an American probably would have said to his neighbor, "Yo, do something about your frickin' banana tree! I've got bugs in my house." It's what I would have said.

But that's not what Kunip did. He broke off a leaf of the banana tree, just one leaf, thus subtly signaling to his neighbor his displeasure. A few days later, the neighbor's gardener showed up and pruned the banana tree. The conflict was resolved without a word being uttered.

"The relationship always comes first. It is more important than the problem," explains Kunip.

I try to wrap my mind around that. We in the west usually put problem solving ahead of relationships. In our search for answers, for the truth, we will gladly jettison friends and even family overboard.

But why, I ask Kunip, couldn't you just politely *ask* your neighbor to do something about his banana tree?

That would have been seen as unduly aggressive, he replies. Anger is "stupid, a crazy mood. That's why you have to stop it. We have a proverb about this: 'Keep the dirty water inside; show the clear water outside.'"

It sounds nice, this notion of cool heart, but how to reconcile it with the relatively high murder rate in Thailand? Or with the brutally violent national sport of *muay Thai,* kickboxing? Or with the unique skills mastered by the surgeons at Bangkok's Yanhee Hospital? They are expert, world-class, at reattaching severed penises. In fact, should you and your penis become separated, these are the surgeons you'd want to see.

It's not that they are more gifted than other surgeons. They just get more practice. Every couple of months, the Thai newspapers carry a story about a wife who, fed up with her husband's wayward ways, takes matters, and a knife, into her own hands. Lately, word has spread of the surgeons' remarkable skills, so the angry wives have upped the ante and adopted a new and even more effective threat: "And I'll feed it to the ducks." Those few words, spoken with quiet conviction, have caused many a Thai man to behave like a saint.

Yes, considering that they follow a religion that espouses the "middle way," Thais, conspicuously, seem to be missing a dimmer switch. They are either keeping their hearts cool or they're chopping off penises. Nothing in between.


People like to say that Bangkok isn't the "real Thailand," just as they say that New York is not the real America and Paris is not the real France. I think this is wrong. These cities did not materialize out of nothingness. They grew organically in the soil in which they were planted. They are not the exception to the rule but, rather, the rule on steroids. New York *is* America, only more so. The same is true of Bangkok.

I have arranged to meet a man who helped shape the Bangkok skyline. Sumet Jumsai, one of Thailand's best-known architects, has designed many of the city's most inventive buildings, such as the Robot Building, a structure that, yes, looks like a robot. He's a direct descendant of the Thai king Rama III. He grew up in France and England, went to Cambridge, and, I'm told, speaks flawless English. He seems like an invaluable cultural interpreter. I'm eager to meet him.

My taxi, though, is stuck in traffic. My driver doesn't seem to mind—he has many lives to live, but I have only one, and am going nuts in the backseat. I can't take this anymore. I pay the driver, hop out, and flag down a motorcycle taxi. A motorcycle taxi looks a lot like an ordinary motorcycle, except the drivers wear orange vests and charge a small fare to zip you around town. I settle onto the back and...whoosh!...he accelerates like a banshee. We weave in and out of traffic, the cars close enough to touch. This is the way to get around Bangkok and the best way, really, to see the city. At street level.

Modern western cities have been deodorized. They smell like nothing. Not Bangkok. It smells like everything. Freshly cooked pad thai, freshly cut marigolds, freshly produced human excrement. A feast for the nostrils. In the course of a few frenzied decades, Bangkok has grown from a sleepy city to a megalopolis that spreads far and wide in every direction. A steaming, throbbing city that knows no bounds. Literally. No one knows the precise boundaries of Bangkok, nor its exact population. That's how amorphous it is.

The age-old question of who is happier, city dwellers or country folk, remains unanswered. The research is inconclusive. I do remember, though, something that Ruut Veenhoven told me. In developing countries, such as Thailand, people living in cities are happier than those in rural areas. Why? Is it simply that cities provide economic opportunities lacking back in the village? That is part of the story, I think, but not the whole story. The truth is that when Thai villagers move to the big city, they are not really moving at all. They take the village with them and end up reaping the best of both worlds.

You see evidence of this everywhere in Bangkok, which is not so much a city as a collection of villages. In the *sois*, those narrow alleyways that crisscross Bangkok like hundreds of tiny capillaries, life is conducted, more or less, as it is in the village. The smell of noodles frying, the call of hawkers, the sense of fraternity. It's all there.

I arrive at Sumet Jumsai's office, shaken and exhilarated in equal measure from the motorcycle taxi. A security guard leads me through a garden to a small, pleasant office on the ground floor. It's cluttered with drawings and blueprints, as you'd expect in an architect's office. Sumet swivels in his chair to greet me. He's in his sixties, I guess, a bit stocky, and wearing a khaki safari shirt. A handsome, dignified man.

"Welcome, welcome," he says in unaccented English, guiding me to a chair. He promptly announces that he's "going through a naughty phase" and invites me to join him. Fortunately, his naughty phase consists of nothing more than a stiff drink.

He pours me a generous glass of whiskey, which I am pleased to see is labeled "Made in Bhutan." I take a swig, silently toasting the Bhutanese army. God bless them.

Sumet pours himself a glass of gin. I can tell it's not his first. "We Buddhists have only five commandments compared with your ten. Do not indulge in intoxicants is one of them," he says, sipping his gin.

I have lots of questions for Sumet, and I want to get to them before he slips from pleasantly drunk to incoherently drunk. I start with merit making. Is it really like a karmic bank account?

"Actually, yes. It's very straightforward. You accumulate

negative energy, which you offset by making positive merits." A spiritual calculus any accountant would love.

And what about *sanuk,* fun? Thais consider it very important, yes?

With this, his eyes light up, and he bolts upright in a sudden burst of sobriety.

"Ahh, *sanuk.* If it's not *sanuk,* it's not worth doing. People will resign from a good-paying job because it's not fun."

"But everyone likes to have fun. We Americans practically invented fun."

"Yes, but you Americans take your fun very seriously. We Thais do not. We don't believe in this work-hard, play-hard mentality. Our fun is interspersed throughout the day."

"What do you mean?"

"It could be a smile or a laugh during the workday. It's not as uptight as in America. Also, our patterns of holidays are different. We don't take the entire month of August off, like Europeans. We take a day off here, a week off there. Everything is interspersed."

Sumet reaches for a pen—a Ridiculously Expensive Pen, I notice. Clearly excited, he writes something down and shows it to me. I have no idea what it says. That's because it's Latin.

"It means 'you will be as I am.' Isn't that fantastic?" he says with an expulsion of air and a burst of energy that briefly alarms me. Maybe it's time for me to go. No, he's calmed down again, and he's telling me about his brother, who is a "good Buddhist." He meditates every day.

"Do you meditate?" I ask.

"No. I have a western mind. When I paint, though, it is a kind of meditation."

"Are you happy?"

"In a nutshell, yes. In Christian terms, I have sinned. But I have offset this with merit making, though not consciously. I have a weak spot for the oppressed."

As I down more glasses of Bhutanese whiskey, our conversation begins to meander. I try to discipline myself, to stick to the questions I've written down, but then, unexpectedly, I have a flash of *mai pen lai* and decide to let the conversation steer itself.

And so we talk about Bangkok. It's like a mini-Shanghai, he tells me, in the sense that everything changes every few months, so even residents must constantly relearn the city.

"Bangkok is a global city, designed like spaghetti. It's vibrant. Sure, Paris and London are vibrant, but you walk into a department store in Paris or London and people don't smile. Here, they smile, and the temples, oh, the temples and the *sois*, where you can get a divine pad thai for just a few baht."

Sumet asks me to stay for another drink, but I politely decline. As I stand to leave, I sense sadness in his eyes. Sumet, I think, has enjoyed our round of American-style introspection. He probably doesn't get to do it very often. I get the impression he could have talked, and drank, for many, many hours.

Some think of cities as godless places. Yet one of the original intents of cities was to provide places to consort with the gods, and it is in cities, not rural areas, where Christianity first took root. In Bangkok, the sacred and the profane exist side by side, like a divorced couple who, for financial reasons, decide to continue living together. Not the perfect arrangement, but not as contentious as it sounds, either.

I'm riding the Skytrain, the monorail that glides across Bangkok like a Disney ride. I look outside and see a Buddhist temple complex, gold and gleaming, sandwiched between two shopping malls. I get off and walk a few blocks to the Erawan shrine. A modern legend surrounds the shrine. Years ago, workers building a new high-rise hotel encountered a series of problems. Machinery broke down. Nothing seemed to go right. Then, someone had an idea. Build a shrine to appease the gods. They did, and the project went smoothly.

Today, Thais stop by the shrine for a quick hit of the divine. At first, it does not strike me as a particularly divine location, encircled as it is by a pantheon of western gods: Burberry's, Louis Vuitton, McDonald's, Starbucks.

Yet no one seems to notice the incongruity. The air smells of incense, or is that car exhaust? A man places a basketful of brown eggs at the shrine, an offering. Others kneel, motionless and silent. A sign says, "For security reasons please don't light large candles." People do anyway, and a security guard walks by and extinguishes them by waving his big straw hat.

Yes, it's a peaceful oasis in the middle of Bangkok, but a few years ago a crazy man used a hammer to destroy the shrine's gold statue. Cool hearts did not prevail. A crowd immediately set upon the man, beating him to death. The Thai media condemned the killing of the man and bemoaned the loss of the statue.

I continue my meander through Bangkok. Asian cities are tough nuts to crack. So much remains invisible in plain sight. Somerset Maugham observed this when he traveled the region in the 1920s. "They are hard and glittering... and give you nothing. But when you leave them it is with a feeling that you have missed something, and you cannot help thinking that they have some secret that they have kept from you."

I walk through the city's Chinatown. This is not like the museum-piece Chinatowns found in some cities but, rather, a thriving, living part of the city. The Chinese influence in Thailand stretches back many centuries and continues to this day.

I pass many shops—mostly machine-tool shops, for some reason. They are all spotless, which I didn't think was possible. There are mangy-looking dogs, people playing some sort of board game. The shops and many of the homes are open to public view, physical privacy being less important in this part of Asia than in the west. I feel like I possess X-ray vision and can see things normally hidden from view: a family cooking dinner, a man getting a haircut. I see a man sitting quietly in a shop. He's wearing jeans and is resting in a chair. His eyes are closed. I assume he is sleeping but then realize he's just finding a moment of peace in the chaos. He opens his eyes, and I look away, embarrassed.

In front of each shop, each home, is a spirit house. These look like elaborate, beautiful birdhouses. The idea is that by giving evil spirits a place to inhabit, a room of their own, they will stay away from your actual home. It's not unlike the in-law cottages that sit in the yards of many Miami homes. Same principle.

I pass signs for the Wrantoh Gem Center ("If it shines we have it") and for something called "Happy Toilet, Happy Life." Indeed, Thais may not *think* much about happiness, but they are nuts about the word. I see it everywhere. There's the Happy Massage Parlor, the Happy Pub, a dish called Double Happiness (tofu stuffed with noodles).

My wanderings have taken me to the United Nations office. It's big and officious looking, and, I notice, there is no spirit house outside. The United Nations brings to mind many things. Happiness is normally not one of them. But the good people at the UN, like the good people at the Peace Corps, are also in the happiness business, though of course the UN bureaucrats would never put it that way.

I'm here to meet a woman named Sureerat. A friend in the United States told me she might have some insights into Thai happiness.

She greets me, with a smile, and we walk to the canteen for a cup of coffee. Sureerat is in her mid-thirties, is single, and lives at home with her parents. That's not unusual for single Thai women, or men for that matter.

I ask her why Thais seem so happy.

"Thai people are not serious about anything. We don't take anything seriously. Whatever it is, we can accept it."

"What do you mean?"

"I'll give you an example. In the U.S., when you trip over something and fall, no one interferes. It's as if nothing happened. But Thai people? We laugh and laugh nonstop. We still run over and help, but we're laughing at the same time."

"So, you don't have any stress in your life?"

"I have stress. Of course I have stress. But there are some situations we can't control. You can't change things outside yourself, so you change your attitude. I think that approach works for Thai people. Like when you're pissed at someone, and you can't do anything about it. You feel you want to hit them, but you can't, so you take a deep breath and let it go. Otherwise, it will ruin your day."

She makes it sound so easy, like exhaling.

"I think America is one of the most stressed countries in the world. You think you need money to buy happiness. You hire people to do everything, even to mow your lawn. Here, even wealthy people do that themselves. We think it's fun."

There's that word again— "fun," *sanuk*. Does fun really hold a special place in the Thai heart?

"Absolutely, we laugh and joke during meetings. It's all very informal. That is when you get things done. If it's not fun, it's not worth doing."

Thais don't just have fun, they poke fun.

"We make fun of fat people here. You can call your friend 'hippo.' She might smack you, but it's all in good fun. You can't do that in the U.S., can you?"

No, I tell her, you can't.

Sureerat needs to get back to work—or to fun, I'm not sure which. We're walking past a bank of elevators when she spots a friend and says something to her in Thai. Afterward, she turns to me and says, "See, that's a good example. She's short, like a shrimp."

"So you call her 'shrimp'?"

"No," she says, as if I haven't been paying attention, "I call her lobster. Get it?"

I don't. The Thais, I conclude, are a fun-loving though not easily understood people.


Thais, even those who don't actively practice Buddhism, maintain a certain equilibrium that I find infuriating. They just don't get flustered, even when life hurls awfulness their way.

After the Asian tsunami in 2004, which killed thousands of people in Thailand alone, hardly anyone blamed the government.

They could have. They could have easily pointed to the lack of a warning system or the slow and chaotic response to the disaster. Certainly, that's what we would do, what we *did* do after Hurricane Katrina devastated New Orleans. We always need someone to blame, someone other than God, that is, since He's currently not accepting complaints. His in-box is full.

Thais accept what has happened, which is not to say they *like* what happened or want it to happen again. Of course not. But they take the long view: eternity. If things don't work out in this life, there is always the next one, and the next one, and so on. Periods of good fortune naturally alternate with periods of adversity, just as sunny days are interspersed with rainy ones. It's the way things are. In a worldview like this, blame doesn't feature prominently, but fortune—destiny—does, and I was curious about mine. Noi has arranged for me to visit a *jao,* or medium. She assures me that the *jao* is a good one from a good family. In Thailand, fortune-telling is a family business, a skill that is passed from generation to generation.

Scott is skeptical about all this but willing to come along. He's used to having his rational, atheistic mind assaulted in Thailand. Like he did on the morning he woke up and found people making paper cranes. Everyone was doing it, from street vendors to stockbrokers. What the heck was going on? It turns out that the king had proclaimed that people needed to cool hearts in the southern part of Thailand, where a Muslim insurgency has been raging for decades. So the prime minister came up with the perfect solution: paper cranes! Yes, they would make thousands and thousands of paper cranes and drop them from airplanes as a peace gesture. "They basically bombed the south with these paper cranes," says Scott, incredulously. "It was the most bizarre thing I've ever seen."

The three of us walk a short distance from Scott's apartment down a narrow *soi,* past the street vendors and the beauty salons and the stray dogs. We enter a nondescript house and go upstairs.

It is nearly empty of furniture. Just a ceiling fan and bare white linoleum floors. We walk past a few women who are sitting on the floor, eating and talking rapid-fire Thai, which is pretty much the only way Thai is spoken.

We're led upstairs to another room, also devoid of furniture, though not of deities. Along one wall is a small pantheon of Hindu gods. There's Hanuman, the monkey god, and Krishna and, my favorite, Ganesh, the elephant-headed god. He is the god of wisdom and poetic inspiration, two attributes I often find myself in need of. In one corner is a small statue of the Buddha, which I notice is elevated higher than anything else in the room, including ourselves. The floor is painted blue and green, a raucous pattern that resembles an unfortunate oriental carpet. The room is not air-conditioned, and I begin to sweat immediately.

We kneel on the floor and wait for the *jao* to arrive. Scott is even more skeptical now, which he tells me outright after Noi has gone off to buy some offerings for the spirits.

When Noi returns, she reaches into a plastic bag and pulls out two small cartons of milk, two straws, and two cans of Pepsi. She places all of this, along with thirty-nine baht (about $1.25), on top of a gold-colored tray. Scott whispers to me: "What happens if you use Coke instead of Pepsi?" I shush him, elbowing his flabby gut for good measure.

The *jao* arrives. She is a slim, middle-aged woman, unremarkable in appearance. She is wearing a red T-shirt and an orange scarf, which dangles over one arm. Her hair is tied in a tight bun. She sits lotus-style on a red blanket. There is a deck of cards next to her.

She lights candles at the Pepsi altar then asks me to recite something in Thai. Noi whispers it in my ear, slowly. My tongue wrestles with each strange syllable, but I manage to get through it.

The *jao*'s eyes are closed, palms pressed together at forehead level in the traditional Thai *wai,* a gesture that is part greeting, part prayer. She waves a stick of incense like a wand. Her lips move, but no sounds emerge. Noi whispers in my ear that she is "waiting for the good time, the auspicious time for the spirits to come." I hope it comes soon. My legs have started to cramp, and beads of sweat are streaming off my forehead and into my eyes, stinging.

Then something happens. The *jao*'s body starts to convulse wildly. She is channeling the spirit, Noi explains. Apparently, the spirit is a man, for the *jao*'s body language changes completely, from feminine to masculine. Once demure, her gestures are now gruff and bossy, and she repeatedly flings her hands forward in a vaguely aggressive manner. Before, Noi had referred to the *jao* as "she," but now she says "he." The transformation is complete.

She—sorry, he—reveals information about me, facts about my life—or more precisely, my lives. I learn that in a previous life I wrote a book about China, a book that was disrespectful and therefore not well received. Great, I think, I must be the first writer to get lousy reviews from a previous life.

"Be careful what you write about the Buddha," she/he says. "People will protest." With this last bit of advice, the *jao* spits up something red (betel nut, I hope) into the gold-colored bowl. She/he does this very aggressively, and I'm taken aback. "It's all part of the act," Scott whispers, and I elbow him again.

The pronouncements come rapid-fire. Noi struggles to keep up with the translation. The *jao* tells me some things that are simply wrong—that, for instance, I can speak Thai. (I can't.) She tells me some things that are generically true—that I don't believe in myself enough. She tells me embarrassing things—that I should please my wife, suggesting specific acts that I really don't want to get into here. And she tells me things that, I swear, she couldn't possibly have known. She says I have a daughter that is not my flesh and blood. It's true. My wife and I adopted a baby girl from Kazakhstan. I am speechless.

When it comes time for me to ask questions, I have only two. When will I be happy? *Where* will I be happy?

"It's best if you stay in your own country, but you don't need to worry too much about things. Don't be envious of what other people have." Sound advice.

Now she/he has a question for me. "Do you believe in God?"

Oh, no. I'm not sure how to answer. Lying to a *jao* seems like bad karma, and besides I don't know *what* I believe. At that moment, for some reason, Luba of Moldova pops into my mind, and I blurt out "feevty-feevty." The *jao* seems satisfied with this response, and everyone in the room breathes a sigh of relief.

"You must believe in Ganesh," she/he says. "You have one, right? A brown one."

"Yes, I do. How did you—"

"It is in the sitting, not standing position, yes?"

"Yes, but..."

She/he tells me I am neglecting my Ganesh. I need to give him flowers and bless him regularly. Then all of my problems will disappear. I promise to do so. Then the *jao* convulses again, and she/he becomes a she again. The session is over.

We step outside into the heat, and Scott and I buy a couple of beers from a small grocery store. We plop down on two small plastic chairs and review what just transpired.

"How could she possibly know those things?" I ask Scott.

Easy, says Scott. There's a rational explanation. A few of the answers were generic and could apply to anyone. He dismisses those with a wave of his hand. The others are harder to explain but still possible. Adoption is common in Thailand, so the fact that I adopted a daughter was an educated guess.

"And the brown Ganesh statue in a sitting position?"

"That's easy, too. Many foreigners own Ganesh statues, and most Ganesh statues are brown and in a sitting position." But the conviction has drained from his voice. I can tell he's just going through the motions.

This, I realize, is what life is like for most Thais. They are not in control of their fates. A terrifying thought, yes, but also a liberating one. For if nothing you do matters, then life suddenly feels a lot less heavy. It's just one big game. And as any ten-year-old will tell you, the best games are the ones where everyone gets to play. And where you can play again and again, for free. Lots of cool special effects are nice, too.


It's my last day in Thailand. I'm packing my bags while Scott fires off some e-mails and Noi, as usual, watches TV. They're showing footage of the king. Nothing strange about that. But it is old footage, from his youth, and it's on every channel. This is highly irregular, says Noi, and she should know, given the amount of TV she watches. My immediate fear is that the king has died. This would be bad for the Thais, who adore their monarch. It would also be bad for me. With the country hurled into a period of deep mourning, the airport might close, and I'm due to leave in a few hours. It's a selfish impulse, I realize, and I silently take note that, karmically speaking, I still have a long way to go.

"It's a coup," shouts Scott from the other room. My first reaction is, oddly, thank God. Only a coup. The king is alive. My second reaction is: a coup? In a country with Starbucks and KFC? In a country where fun is the national ethos and cool hearts prevail (usually)? But, sure enough, there are tanks on the streets, and martial law has been declared. Even the go-go bars have closed.

My journalist's instincts kick in, and I call NPR in Washington. I file a short news item, but honestly my heart's not in it. Coups don't really fit into my search for the world's happiest places, and this is just the sort of unhappiness I've been trying so hard to avoid.

I am determined to catch my flight. I manage to find a taxi. The driver is oblivious to the unfolding drama and just seems pleased that, for once, the highway to the airport is wide open. En route, we pass a billboard for some resort. There's a photo of perfectly white beaches and crystal-clear water and then, in bold letters, "Paradise Made Easy." I'm struck by two things. First, the irony of such a billboard in the middle of a coup, and second, the questionable statement itself. Is that really what we want? Paradise made easy? Shouldn't we have to work at paradise? Isn't that the whole point?

The airport terminal is deserted. I'm not sure if this is because of the coup or because it is 3:00 a.m. Wait. I see some fellow passengers. Actually, I hear them before I see them. They are speaking loudly, and in heavy New York accents.

"Excuse me," I ask, "do you know if the airport is open?"

They seem perplexed by my question.

"I think so," says one of the women. "Why wouldn't it be?"

"Haven't you heard about the coup?"

They perk up. "No, a coup? A real coup?"

"Yes, the army has declared martial law. There are tanks on the streets."

"Oh, my Gawd," says another of the women. "This is sooo fascinatin'. Harriet, did ya hear? There's been a coup."

"Really?" says Harriet, glancing toward me in awe, as if I had given the orders myself. "Now why do you suppose they would do that?"

I'm not sure what to tell Harriet. Military men the world over have been imposing their will for many centuries now. "It's complicated," I say, and Harriet seems satisfied.

The airport, it turns out, is indeed open. The coup is only a coup lite—with half the tanks and one third the disruption of a regular coup. Soon the tanks would retreat, businesses would reopen, and the girls at Suzie Wong's would be back onstage gyrating and performing unnatural acts with Ping-Pong balls.


A few weeks later, back in Miami, I spot a small news item. Thailand's newly installed prime minister, Surayud Chulanont, the civilian face of the junta, has announced that henceforth, official government policy will no longer focus on economic growth but, rather, the happiness of the people. It is largely a public-relations ploy—but, still, a military government with a happiness policy!

As the sublime absurdity of this news sinks in, I react in the only sensible way: I smile. A broad, authentic Thai smile. Really. If you were there, you'd know. You would have seen it in my eyes.

# Chapter 8

# GREAT BRITAIN

## Happiness Is a Work in Progress

A couple of years ago, an unusual experiment took place in a dreary English town named Slough (rhymes with "plough"). The experiment, like all grand experiments of our day, was made for television. The BBC retained six "happiness experts" and set them loose on Slough, hoping to "change the psychological climate" of the place.

When I first heard that phrase, I was instantly intrigued. It dawned on me that I had overlooked an important component in the happiness equation: change. Here I was skipping across the globe, looking for the world's happiest places, even visiting the world's least happy place, but all the while assuming that these places were static, immovable. They were either happy or not. But, of course, places, like people, change. Maybe not much, maybe not often, but surely they do. And here was a deliberate, ambitious attempt to take an unhappy place and make it happy—or at least *happier*. Could it be done?

I arrive, bleary eyed, at London's Heathrow Airport, my mood elevated by the fact that the United States and Britain enjoy a "special relationship," as Winston Churchill called it. I've always liked that expression, a chummy term of endearment that stands out amid the steely vernacular of international diplomacy. I was feeling special indeed, uncharacteristically relaxed, as I strolled up to the immigration official. We're pals, he and I. Even his clothes put me at ease. Instead of police or military uniforms, British immigration officials wear blazers, as if you were attending some fancy cocktail party and they were your host.

I hand the man in the blazer my passport, figuring this shouldn't take long.

"What is your purpose for visiting the UK?"

"I'm doing research for a book."

"And what exactly is this book about?"

"Happiness."

Until now, he has been glancing down at my passport, but now he looks me squarely in the eye. It is not the look of a pal.

"Happiness?"

"Yes, sir."

"In the UK?"

"Um, yes."

Clearly, my story is not plausible. Possibly a cover, and a flimsy one at that, for nefarious doings. He peppers me with questions. How long will I be in the UK? Whom am I staying with? Was this person British or American? Was I a terrorist? Okay, he didn't ask that last question, but it was implied. Finally, after twenty minutes of grilling, just when I fear the possible onset of a cavity search, he stamps my passport, reluctantly.

"Suspicion of happiness is in our blood," said English travel writer E. V. Lucas. Or, as one Brit told me, in colloquial American so I could understand, "We don't *do* happiness." No indeed. A stiff upper lip may come in handy when German bombs are raining down, but it gets in the way of a good smile.

In Britain, the happy are few and suspect. If you are English and, through no fault of your own, find yourself inexplicably joyful, do not panic. Remain calm and heed the advice of English humorist Jerome K. Jerome: "Don't show [your happiness] but grumble along with the rest." For the British, happiness is a transatlantic import. And by "transatlantic" they mean American. And by "American" they mean silly, infantile drivel. Confectionary.

I step outside the terminal to a dreary London day and take a taxi to visit my friend Rob and his wife, Nancy. Rob, as you recall, is the Closet American, the man of a thousand refills. He's back in London now, working as a "foreign" correspondent in his own country. That seems right to me. There's no one better suited than Rob, an insider/outsider, to explain Britain to an American audience. Rob speaks both languages.

Rob's house is nice and cozy and exudes that worn charm that the English do so well. Nancy had a "proper" English upbringing. This means she is chronically polite and bakes her own bread and heats the dinner plates in the oven. Like her husband, though, she doesn't quite feel comfortable in her English skin, and the couple escapes to America every chance they get.

The three of us sit down over a bottle of wine, and, as inevitably happens when Brits and Americans get together, the conversation turns to the differences that bind us, differences not immediately apparent because of the common language that divides us.

"In America," says Nancy, "every conversation is held as if it might be your last on Earth. Nothing is held back. I always want to say, 'I'm sorry, but I just met you. I don't know you. I really don't need to hear about your hysterectomy.'"

Nancy, though, never actually says that. It would be offensive, and the English go to great lengths to avoid offending anyone, any time, and in any way. Nancy finds this English reserve as disconcerting as American loquaciousness.

"Here, people cut themselves off from a happy little center," she says. "I was standing in a queue at the Tate Gallery the other day, and I started to chat with people—you know, small talk, like 'Terrible queue, isn't it?'—but nobody said anything. They just looked at me like I was crazy. In the UK, we don't want to bother anyone. When someone dies, we don't call the relatives to offer our sympathies because we're afraid we might disturb them. We don't want to be too loud, too American."

Being too American, or American at all, is pretty much the

worst thing a Brit can be. "American" is synonymous with pushiness, tactlessness, and puppy-dog earnestness. Americans buy self-help books as if their lives depend on them. Brits, as a rule, do not. Such pap is seen as a sign of weakness. One Brit quipped that if his countrymen were to embrace a self-help book, it would probably be something like *I'm Not OK, You're Even Less OK.*

For the English, life is about not happiness but muddling through, getting by. In that sense, they are like the ancient Aztecs. When an Aztec child was born, a priest would say, "You are born into a world of suffering; suffer then and hold your peace." There is something noble in that attitude, that quiet suffering. True, Aztec civilization died out centuries ago, leaving only a few ruins now trampled on by sunburned American tourists. But never mind. At least they had the decency not to whine about their demise. You have to respect that in a dying civilization.

At this point, Rob interjects, feeling compelled, I suspect, to defend his homeland. The British, he declares, possess a "latent happiness." It's there, lurking deep in their bowels. You just can't see it. Or feel it. Or hear it. Or detect it in any way known to man. But it's there, Rob assures me.

The same year that Thomas Jefferson penned the "pursuit of happiness" line in the Declaration of Independence, in London Jeremy Bentham, a young, unhappy lawyer (is there any other kind?) was writing his treatise on "the greatest happiness of the greatest number" and working on his "felicific calculus."

Bentham's philosophy, utilitarianism, lacks the gung-ho optimism that Americans savor. Like the British themselves, utilitarianism is practical and devoid of any mawkishness. But the goal is the same: a happy nation, latently or otherwise.

I decide to visit Jeremy Bentham. He resides at the campus of University College London. The buildings are all old and regal. They look like cathedrals more than classrooms. Bentham is in one of these buildings, but which one?

I find an information desk and approach the young blonde sitting behind the counter.

"May I help you?"

"Yes, I'd like to see Jeremy Bentham."

"Do you have an extension?"

"Oh, no, he's not alive anymore."

Her eyes grow wide. "I'm sorry I can't help you, sir," she says, clearly calculating whether I am a harmless loony or a dangerous loony.

"No. You don't understand. He died about two hundred years ago, but he's still on campus."

Dangerous loony. She's about to call security when a grad student intervenes on my behalf.

"You're looking for the auto-icon," he says.

"The what?"

"The auto-icon." That is, it turns out, what the now-dead Jeremy Bentham is called. The grad student gives me directions to another building, and there I find him, sitting quietly in one corner. He looks good for his age.

He's sitting on a wooden chair, the same chair where he wrote his happiness papers, and wearing the same clothes he wore when he died in 1832: black vest and sport coat and a wicker hat. Underneath the clothes is his real skeleton. This is the way Bentham wanted it.

Bentham loved good philosophical banter, and he didn't see why death should interfere with that. His will included these instructions: "If it should happen that my personal friends and other disciples should be disposed to meet...the founder of the greatest happiness system...will from time to time come to be conveyed to the room in which they meet." To this day, rumor has it, Bentham is wheeled into university meetings, where he is listed as "present but not voting."

For Bentham, happiness was a mathematical proposition, and he spent years fine-tuning his "felicific calculus," a wonderfully disarming term. I, for one, never associated calculus with felicity.

It's simple math, though. Add up the pleasurable aspects of your life, then subtract the unpleasant ones. The result is your overall happiness. The same calculations, Bentham believed, could apply to an entire nation. Every action a government took, every law it passed, should be viewed through the "greatest happiness" prism. Bentham, for instance, reasoned that giving ten dollars to a poor man counted more than giving ten dollars to a wealthy man, since the poor man derived more pleasure from it.

Bentham's theory is intriguing but flawed. For instance, he didn't distinguish, qualitatively, one pleasure from another. The pleasure accrued by helping a little old woman across the street was for him on par with the pleasure a sadist derived by beating that same old woman senseless. For Bentham, pleasure was pleasure.

Another pitfall: Utilitarianism is interested only in making the *majority* of people happy. It is concerned with the happiness of the many, not the misery of the few, which is fine if you are lucky enough to be among the happy many, but not so fine if you find yourself among the miserable few.

To this day there persist in Britain Bentham-ite tendencies, a willingness to accept government intervention into people's lives for the common good. The British happily pay a licensing fee to the BBC for every TV set they own. The mayor of London, Ken Livingstone, recently imposed a congestion fee for drivers to enter central London during peak hours. It is classic utilitarianism. A relatively few people—drivers who want to enter central London—are rendered considerably less happy so that the vast majority of Londoners are made a little more happy. Now New York has latched onto the idea, though it has proved more controversial than in London. That's not surprising. Americans are less utilitarian than the British.


These days, talk of happiness is popping up everywhere in Britain. "We should be thinking not just what's good for putting money in people's pockets but what is good for putting joy in people's hearts." Those words were uttered not by some Americanized fruitcake or far-left politician but by the leader of Britain's Conservative Party, David Cameron, a man who aspires to the prime minister's office.

Speaking of which, let's not forget the former prime minister, Tony Blair, the most optimistic, happiness-prone leader the British have ever known. Blair possessed a fierce optimism that was borderline American. For starters, Blair smiled, something his predecessors proudly avoided. Blair was intrigued by the emerging science of happiness and toyed with the idea of converting theory into policy. In 2002, his Strategy Unit convened a "life-satisfaction" seminar. Some (not Blair) called this group the Department of Happiness.

The group published an analytical paper suggesting—just suggesting, mind you—ways in which government might boost national happiness. Among the proposals: a happiness index, akin to Bhutan's Gross National Happiness; teaching "happiness skills" in schools; encouraging "a more leisured work-life balance"; and imposing higher taxes on the wealthy.

It was the last suggestion, as you can imagine, that got the most attention. The notion of higher taxes as a path to happiness was first proposed by British economist Richard Layard. The wealthy, Layard argues, incite envy in others, spewing a sort of "social pollution." So, Layard reasons, just as we levy fines on industrial polluters so, too, should we fine these envy generators, the wealthy. Not surprisingly, the idea has met some resistance. "Beware the Happiness Brigade" screamed a typical headline. Others wondered why the wealthy should be punished just because some people can't get a handle on their envy issues.

Libertarians went ballistic: Bureaucrats can't manage to fix potholes, how are they going to make us happy? Besides, the major factors that determine our happiness—friendship, sex, trust—are largely beyond government's control anyway.

I'm sympathetic to these concerns, and I'm not advocating a

Department of Happiness in any government, but let's not forget that government is already in the happiness business. Every time it offers tax incentives for married couples or mandates the wearing of seat belts or strives to increase gross domestic product, it's sticking its nose in our happiness. Besides, what *is* the role of government if not to make the citizenry happier?

The BBC producers did not choose Slough by accident. The town, just outside London and underneath a flight path to Heathrow Airport, is a one-word punch line in Britain. The name itself is trouble. "Slough" means, literally, muddy field. A snake sloughs, or sheds, its dead skin. John Bunyan wrote of the "slough of despond" in *Pilgrim's Progress*. In the 1930s, John Betjeman wrote this poem about Slough:

> *Come friendly bombs and fall on Slough!*
> *It isn't fit for humans now,*
> *There isn't grass to graze a cow,*
> *Swarm over, Death!*

Then he got nasty. To this day, the residents of Slough rankle when anyone mentions the poem. The town's reputation as a showpiece of quiet desperation was cemented when the producers of the TV series *The Office* decided to set the show in Slough.

The unspoken assumption now is that if these six experts can make Slough happy, they can make *anyplace* happy. The series aired before I arrived in the UK, so I procure the DVDs and sit down in Rob's living room to watch *Making Slough Happy*. The screen fills with an aerial view of a large town: "the much-maligned Berkshire town of Slough," a narrator informs me gravely.

We're introduced to the happiness experts who are, to a man and woman, insufferably chipper. The narrator, in a voice-of-God tenor, explains the experiment. The happiness experts have selected fifty volunteers from Slough. They will undergo twelve weeks of intensive "happiness training." Then, they will spread the happiness virus throughout the town, thus changing the "psychological climate of Slough." That's the idea, at least.

This ought to be interesting. I pour myself a glass of wine and lean back in the chair. The first task is to take the volunteers' "happiness temperature." The Sloughites, it turns out, are about as happy as the rest of Britain, which is to say fair to middling— well below the supremely content Swiss and Danes but comfortably above the mopey Moldovans.

In the effort to boost happiness levels, no exercise is considered too far-fetched or embarrassing. Or American. The Sloughites hold hands. They hug one another. They hug trees. They perform something called biodanza. They do tai chi. They do yoga. They laugh uncontrollably. They submerge themselves in flotation tanks. They dance in the aisles of a supermarket.

I hit the pause button. I can't take it anymore. Watching Brits shed their inhibitions is like watching elephants mate. You know it happens, it must, but it's noisy, awkward as hell, and you can't help but wonder: Is this something I really need to see?

Deep breath. I reach for the remote. Click. Each of the Slough fifty is handed a happiness manifesto. It contains ten mostly commonsense tips, like phone a friend or count your blessings or, my favorite, cut your TV viewing by half. The irony—that the manifesto itself is part of a TV program—seems lost on all involved.

In one episode, a few of the Slough fifty hop into a limousine and visit a lottery winner. She tells them that—surprise!—her life isn't necessarily happier, only more comfortable. Her brother died recently, and she says she'd gladly give up every dollar of her lottery winnings to have him back.

Click. Another episode. One of the happiness experts, a toothy psychologist named Richard Stevens, is vacuuming a floor with a maniacal look in his eye while uplifting music plays in the background. "You can vacuum with care and love," he tells one of the Slough fifty, who looks incredulous. Then there's eighty three-year-old Rex Burrow, who says he still has "much to do" in life. I don't think he means vacuuming, though I could be mistaken.

One of the more interesting experiments was the "graveyard therapy." (Once again, death intrudes into a book about happiness.) Stevens organized a trip to a local cemetery so that participants could realize that "we are all going to end up dead, but for the moment we are alive." Some of the participants found the exercise uplifting. Others found it creepy. One woman broke down in tears.

Finally, the big moment. The twelve weeks are over. It's time to see if the Slough fifty have boosted their happiness levels and, perhaps, changed the psychological climate of this much-maligned Berkshire town. First, there is the requisite dramatic tension—some hugging, some crying, some mood music. Stevens, glasses perched on the bridge of his nose, reviews the data, while the rest of the happiness experts look on in anticipation. The envelope, please. And...it's a huge success, Stevens declares. The Slough fifty have boosted their happiness levels by 33 percent. Stevens has never seen anything like it. The group had started with happiness levels on par with that of China. Now they've surpassed even Switzerland and Denmark. If Slough were a country, it would be the happiest in the world. Champagne is poured, a toast proposed: "To increased happiness everywhere." Hear, hear. Clink glasses, roll credits.

That's the TV version of Making Slough Happy. And, as we know, any overlap between TV and reality is purely coincidental. I can't help but wonder: Did these happiness experts really change the psychological climate of Slough, or did they just tickle fifty of its residents for a while?

I call Richard Stevens. He sounds surprisingly brusque on the phone, borderline rude, not at all like the cheery, happy vacuuming, tree-hugging fellow on TV. Maybe he's having a bad day. Even happiness experts get the blues. He does agree to meet me, though.

He's wearing a white shirt and jeans. He is tan, suspiciously so. One does not tan naturally in Britain. It just doesn't happen. Some sort of technology is required—either a tanning salon or an airplane. Stevens explains that it's the latter; he's just returned from a beach holiday in India. I silently wonder why he was so grumpy on the phone. His apartment is spotless, bright, and airy. There's a piano in one corner, and above it a picture of a woman standing next to a young-looking Bill Clinton.

Stevens explains how he cobbled his "happiness tool kit" together from a variety of sources: Buddhism, evolutionary psychology, the new positive-psychology movement, South American dance. He and the other happiness experts had many obstacles to overcome. At first, the Slough town council wasn't cooperative, and frankly I can't blame them. They'd been kicked in the backside many times in the past and weren't about to bend over again, not even for the BBC.

Stevens explains that some of the exercises went over better than others. The biodanza proved tricky. Too sensual for your average Brit. The laughter yoga fell flat. This is where people get together and laugh, unprompted by jokes or humor of any kind. The idea is to trigger a physiological reaction and spread contagious laughter. Completely irrational, the laughter clubs started in India. I tried it once in Bombay. We gathered at a park early in the morning and stood in a circle. Under the tutelage of a cardiologist named Madan Kataria, we started laughing, just like that, for absolutely no reason. It worked. I couldn't stop laughing. I'm laughing now, as I replay the event in my mind. Not the Brits, though. They prefer their main course of laughter served with an aperitif of humor.

I ask Stevens if it is possible, given enough time and resources, to really change the psychological climate of a place. He thinks for a moment before answering, no doubt aware of the fact that happiness levels are stubbornly stable.

"I suppose it is possible," Stevens says. "There are all sorts of things I'd love to do—work with the schools for instance, build up the sense of community." All of which is worthy. None of which makes for good television.

Stevens urges me to go to Slough and judge the results for myself. I was afraid he might say that. My last trip to an unhappy place, Moldova, left me in a funk for weeks afterward. I fear Slough may send me deeper into the abyss.

To steel myself, I go to see Tim LeBon, a "philosophical counselor." He uses the teachings of the ancients to help people with their twenty-first-century problems. Relationship trouble? Jerk for a boss? Tim dips into the deep well of philosophy and channels Aristotle or Plato or, if he's feeling ambitious, Nietzsche.

Tim had heard about my quest for the world's happiest places and, like the immigration official at Heathrow, wondered what the hell I was doing in Britain. We meet at one of the happiest of British institutions: the local pub. It's called Queen Boadicea, and it's smoky and crowded and cozy. We manage to find an open sofa and order a couple of pints.

Tim has several clients. All foreigners. The British don't *do* therapy, philosophical or any other kind, for the same reason they don't buy self-help books. It's seen as weakness. Tim tells me an apocryphal story. He went to his local library in search of an American self-help book called *Changing for Good*. The nearest he could find, though, was *Changing for Dinner*, a book about English etiquette. "That kind of sums it up right there," says Tim, staring forlornly into his beer.

Woe be the British therapist. Tim's friends don't understand what he does for a living. Strangers are downright alarmed. They recoil in horror, as if he's just confessed to being a pedophile. Or an American.

On the one hand, I understand their skepticism. I've had plenty of experience with therapists myself, and I can't say it's made me any happier. At the same time, the British reserve makes me uneasy. Not once has anyone here told me to "have a nice day." I get the distinct impression they don't want me to have a nice day or, at the very least, don't care if I do. Maybe there is an undercurrent of warmth here, a subterranean channel of human affection, but if there is it is buried very, very deep.

I feel sorry for the Brits, deprived as they are of the salutary benefits of the self-help industrial complex. Isn't there something we can do for these sad souls? Perhaps a New Age Marshall Plan. I picture planeloads of Deepak Chopra and Wayne Dyer books and CDs dropped by airplane over the English countryside, with little parachutes slowing their descent to earth, of course, for there is nothing more painfully ironic than being clocked on the head by Deepak Chopra and knocked unconscious. Loudspeakers could broadcast Marianne Williamson in the Tube. Yes, it would be another Blitzkrieg, though this time the bombs would be friendly, armed with payloads of glorious self-renewal.

Tim also teaches a course in positive psychology, but he is not a true believer. Sometimes, he tells me, people choose not to be happy, and that's okay. Freud was dying of cancer, not far from this pub actually, yet he refused morphine. He wanted to continue to work and didn't want to have his mind clouded. If you believe that pleasure, or at least the absence of pain, is man's highest ideal, then Freud's decision made no sense. Yet happiness, as Tim sees it, is more than simply an uninterrupted series of pleasurable moments, and that's a point he feels the positive-psychology movement misses.

Tim also finds positive psychology's emphasis on optimism troubling. Optimism is sometimes a wonderful thing, but not always. Tim gives me an example. Let's say you're on a flight, and there is a problem, an engine has caught fire. Would you want an optimistic pilot at the controls? Perhaps, but what you really want, Tim says, is a wise pilot. Wisdom born from years of experience.

"Part of positive psychology is about being positive, but sometimes laughter and clowns are not appropriate. Some people don't want to be happy, and that's okay. They want meaningful lives, and those are not always the same as happy lives."

I can't argue with that. Tim, I realize, neatly combines American optimism and British circumspection in one package. I bet he's a good therapist.

Slough lies a few miles west of Heathrow Airport, just outside the M25 motorway, London's equivalent of the Washington Beltway. This places Slough squarely in no-man's-land, neither part of London nor divorced from it entirely. Not a happy space to occupy, as anyone in mid-divorce can attest.

I stroll down High Street. It is pleasant enough. It's a pedestrian-only zone, which immediately endears it to me. Traffic has never been associated with happiness, and that holds true for both drivers and pedestrians. There are the usual fish-and-chips shops and curry shacks, plus an inordinate number of pawnshops and betting centers. The colors are muted and range from deeper to lighter shades of gray. The people seem gray, too, and slightly disheveled. The word "frumpy" springs to mind. Yes, that's it, Slough is frumpy.

Slough has more than its share of "yobs," the British term for young men who look like trouble. (Yob is "boy" spelled backward.) I had been warned about this. I can't take the threat seriously, though. To me, a yob sounds like a stuffed toy I might buy for my two-year-old, not a social menace.

I pick up the local rag, the *Slough Observer,* and scan the headlines. There's a story about growing resistance to "supermarket creep," which I learn is not that weird guy eyeing women in frozen foods but, rather, the abundance of megastores that are driving the mom-and-pops out of business. There's a story about a feud that's broken out between rival taxi companies; apparently, they're fighting over who has the right to pick up passengers at the train station. There's a story about language courses for new immigrants and who should pay for them.

Slough, like much of Britain, is multicultural. On the one hand, this is welcome news. The immigrants have spiced up bland

British cuisine, as well as the bland British personality. On the other hand, this influx of immigrants has brought problems. Most notably, Islamic terrorists. This is where political correctness and happiness research part ways. Diversity, that much heralded attribute, does not necessarily make for a happy place. The world's happiest nations—Iceland, for instance—tend to be ethnically homogenous.

My first objective: Get underneath the skin of Slough. Peel back its copious layer of gloom and see what lies beneath. To accomplish this, I'll need to dip into my journalist's bag of tricks. We journalists are seducers, except it's not sex we're after (usually). It's sound bites and quotes and information. Like all great seducers, we tailor our overtures to the conquest at hand.

As a radio journalist, my task has been complicated by the necessity of a microphone. You'd be surprised how many people around the world suffer from microphobia. The Japanese have a severe case. I remember once whipping out my microphone at a Tokyo department store. Judging from the look of sheer horror in people's eyes, you'd think I'd just unholstered a semiautomatic pistol or dropped my pants.

In Arab countries, it's crucial to graciously accept many, many cups of tea before asking anything that might be construed as a substantive question. In India, I found that flattery was the way to get people to talk. In America, microphobia is extremely rare, and no such foreplay is necessary. If anything, the challenge is getting people to *stop* talking.

I wasn't quite sure how to handle the British. I briefly toy with the direct approach—"Hi, my name's Eric. I'm from America. Are you happy?"—but quickly dismiss that idea, which no doubt would elicit a response in which the words "sod" and "off" feature prominently

Instead, seasoned journalist that I am, I decide to drop by the local barbershop. This is a time-honored tradition among journalists, nearly as time honored as interviewing your local cab driver, but I was reluctant to get in the middle of Slough's feuding taxi drivers.

Sabino's Barber Shop looks like a local institution. In other words, it looks old. And a bit musty. My plan is to pass myself off as just another customer looking for a haircut. It's a brilliant plan, except for one minor detail: I don't have any hair. No problem. I unsheathe another weapon from my journalist's arsenal: humor.

"Don't suppose you offer discounts for the folliclely challenged?"

"No, but we do charge a search fee."

Nice parry, old boy. English humor at its best. The witty bloke is Tony. Thick, black hair. A gut the size of a small refrigerator. Tony has lived in Slough all of his life. A fine place, he says. You can always find work here if you want. Or not. There's always the dole. Tony gets a bit defensive when I mention the "friendly bombs" poem. That was a long time ago, he says, and besides, one of the poet's daughters has since apologized on his behalf. Case closed.

"So, what exactly is so nice about Slough?" I ask, as Tony scans my head for anything resembling hair.

"Well, we're centrally located. You can get anywhere from here. It's just twenty minutes to London or Reading. Windsor Castle is very close, too."

Alarm bells go off inside my bald head. It's never a good sign when the best thing to recommend a place is that it's near other places. Just ask the residents of New Jersey. Tony and I talk awhile longer, as he goes through the motions of a haircut, and then I get up to leave.

I'm walking out the door when Tony recommends I visit the Slough Museum. "Make sure you set aside enough time—a good twenty minutes. You wouldn't want to miss anything." I can't tell if Tony is being sarcastic or not but decide to give him the benefit of the doubt.

I find the Slough Museum on one end of High Street, looking forlorn and neglected. I walk inside, pay a small fee, and stroll around the exhibits, such as they are. I learn valuable Slough facts. For instance, as early as the seventeenth century, Slough was a popular rest stop for carriages traveling between London and Bath. In other words, even back then, it was a place near other places. I learn that Slough's farmers had "such a plentiful supply of horse manure they didn't have to leave their fields fallow." Okay. What do we have so far? Historically, Slough was a pit stop full of manure.

Another exhibit features an old black-and-white photo of army trucks lined up as far as the eye can see. I read the placard: "During World War I, Slough was used as a repair depot for military vehicles, earning it the nickname of 'The Dump.'"

You have to say one thing about Slough. It's consistent. Wait, wait, there is more. Neatly arranged behind a glass display case are some of the products made in Slough: socks, matchbox covers, Air Wick air fresheners (because of all that manure, no doubt), nail cream, Mars bars. Radar was supposedly invented in Slough, too. How ironic, I think, given that Slough hardly appears on anyone's radar.

My twenty minutes are up. I need a drink. Once again, for research purposes. If you want to get to know an English town, you need to spend time at the local pub. Don't take my word for it. Anthropologist Kate Fox says so. She spent years scrutinizing her fellow citizens as if she were studying some Stone Age tribe in Papua, New Guinea. In her book *Watching the English,* she describes the importance the natives ascribe to their drinking ritual: "It would be impossible even to *attempt* to understand Englishness without spending a lot of time at pubs."

The pub is the one place where Brits discard their native shyness. The entire enterprise—"pub" is, after all, short for "public house"—is designed to encourage people to interact. That's why there's never waitress service at an English pub; instead, patrons are forced to order their drinks at the bar, where they invariably encounter others doing the same. Conversation ensues—awkward, roundabout, stuttering British conversation but conversation nonetheless.

The English penchant for strict rules of behavior extends into the pub. The one that sticks with me is this: Don't introduce yourself right away. It's considered "cloyingly American," says Fox. I make note of that, and also of the fact that in the UK the word "American" is often preceded by the word "cloyingly."

Finding a pub in an English town is as easy as finding a church in Alabama. Slough offers several choices. I like the looks of the Herschel Arms, named after Slough's most famous son, Sir William Herschel, astronomer to King George III.

Despite its English pedigree, the Herschel Arms is owned by a witty Irishman named Tom. There's bric-a-brac everywhere. An old sign for "Baldwin's Nervous Pills," which claims to cure "nervousness, irritability of temper, fear and dread." There's an old 1930s radio and another sign that says: "Avoid hangovers. Stay drunk."

I plant myself at the bar and, following Fox's advice, place a five-pound note in my hand. "It is acceptable to let bar staff know that one is waiting to be served by holding money or an empty glass in one's hand," she advises. On second thought, maybe this wasn't necessary, since I'm the only one in the pub so far.

The beer arrives warm, of course, yet drinkable. I'm soaking up the overtly old-world atmosphere when I glance out the window and see an Islamic bookstore with a sign on its storefront glowing bright and clear: "There has come to you from Allah a light and a clear message." Allah and pubs, cheek by jowl. I take a sip of my warm beer and silently toast the new Britain. God help it.

I've come here to speak with actual Sloughites, yet I'm nervous at the same time. Kate Fox has scared me with her observation that "every pub has its own private code of in-jokes, nicknames, phrases and gestures." How could I possibly know what they are?

Just as my anxiety is peaking, in walks a lanky man, dignified looking. Late sixties, probably. He's wearing a perfectly tailored blazer with a handkerchief folded neatly in the pocket.

"Bloody awful weather we're having."

"Yes," I say, "bloody awful."

The last two words sound ridiculous coming out of my American mouth, but the man either doesn't notice or is too polite to say anything.

He leans toward me and says, "Did you know that this pub is named after William Herschel? He was an astronomer."

"Yes, I've heard that."

"Did you know he discovered one of the planets?"

"No, really, which one?"

"Uranus."

There's an awkward pause. I try not to snicker. I take a sip of beer. Suppress another snicker. Finally, he steps in and saves me.

"I know. Typical, isn't it?"

With that, we share a good, hearty laugh.

The ice properly broken, I gingerly ask the man about Slough, careful not to offend his native sensibilities.

"So I take it you're familiar with Slough's, er, reputation."

"It's well deserved. This is a godawful place. Total crap."

So much for native sensibilities. He had heard something about *Making Slough Happy* but is deeply skeptical. He expresses this skepticism not by subtle English body language but by more scatological references.

"Look, if you have something fundamentally shitty, you can't do much with it, can you?" With those few choice words, the man has dismissed the entire happiness experiment and much of the positive-psychology movement. I'm not sure how to respond, so I switch to a safer topic.

"Nice pub, isn't it?"

"Oh, it used to be. But now it's a bit over the top with the décor. And they serve food, you know. It's all about the food now." He says this last part with moral revulsion, as if the pub had taken to serving heroin with the beer, instead of onion rings.

We talk and drink. I order a round, which endears me to him, just as Kate Fox told me it would. A good hour into our conversation, we introduce ourselves. His name is Geoffrey, a morsel of information that I find as precious as any CIA intelligence. In Britain, finding out someone's name isn't pro forma. It's an accomplishment.

Much beer is drunk and laughs shared, over what exactly I can't recall. I've never seen anyone laugh quite like that before. His body stiff and erect, like a soldier's, Geoffrey tilts his torso backward, so that it is at a forty-five-degree angle to his legs. It is a highly controlled laugh and, in that sense, a very English laugh.

Even in the inebriated atmosphere of the pub, the British remain economical with their emotions. Personal information is doled out judiciously, like premium chocolate or fine wine. As any economist will tell you, scarcity creates value. So when a Brit opens up, exposes their wounds, where it hurts, this is more valuable, more meaningful, than when an American does it. For the first time since I arrived in Britain, I appreciate the virtue of reticence.

I learn much about Geoffrey. I learn that he prefers warm weather over cold, that as far as he's concerned "global warming is a good thing." I learn that he is, in fact, flying to an Egyptian beach resort next week and that he "doesn't give a fuck if the plane crashes" because he's had a good life. I learn that Geoffrey's wife died three years ago and, though he doesn't quite say so, that he misses her very much.

I suspect this is the reason Geoffrey stays in Slough, though of course he would never confess to such a maudlin sentiment. The relationship between death and geography is complicated. Sometimes, when unspeakable tragedy strikes—when someone loses a child, for instance—they feel obliged to flee the scene immediately, hoping that by changing physical location they might lighten the unbearable grief pressing down on them. Other times, though, we feel compelled to stay. The place is all that remains, and to leave would feel like a betrayal. That, I think, is the case with Geoffrey. He doesn't love Slough, but he loved his wife, loved her *here*, in this much-maligned Berkshire town, so here he stays.

Sure, he's thought about leaving, Geoffrey tells me, but he

can't bring himself to do it. "I mean, in the end, you come home because this is where you live." That last line strikes me as profound, though in my beer-addled state I can't pinpoint why. It is only the next morning, after I have stumbled back to my hotel and collapsed into a deep, Slough sleep, that it dawns on me. *You come home because this is where you live.* It was Geoffrey's matter-of-fact, proscriptively English way of saying what we all know to be true: Home is where the heart is.

I wake to fresh snow. It's beautiful, coating the trees and the ground in a blanket of white. Apparently, though, snow is a rare event in the London area, and the few inches of powder have triggered a national emergency. All across southern England, people are wheeling out their stiff upper lips for the Big Snow Event, as a local newscaster breathlessly calls it. You'd think the Germans were firebombing London again. Schools are closed. Airports are closed. But, the breathless announcer reassures me, people are determined to continue with normal life. Otherwise, the snow wins, and we can't have that.

I, too, am determined to stand firm in the face of the fluffy white flakes. I decide to keep my appointment with Heather White. She is one of the Slough fifty, and I'm curious to see if the TV experiment has had a lasting impact on her happiness. Heather lives on Shaggy Calf Lane. When she told me this on the phone, I smiled. It sounds like something out of a fable.

In person, though, Shaggy Calf Lane turns out to be just like any other English street. No calves in sight, shaggy or otherwise, just lots of small cars driving on the wrong side of the road. I walk up to Heather's front door and ring the bell. I had prepared for our meeting by reading up on the natives' greeting habits. What Samuel Johnson observed more than two hundred years ago holds true today: "When two Englishmen meet their first talk is of the weather." Not just any talk but reassuring, comforting talk. "You must never contradict anyone when discussing the weather," warns George Mikes, a Hungarian humorist. Right. Got it. Luckily for me, I had actual weather, the Big Snow Event, to talk about.

"Quite the weather we're having," I say to Heather White as she greets me at the door.

"Oh, I don't know. It's not so bad."

This throws me off balance. She's not following the script.

Heather is wearing a wool vest and chunky glasses. She is eighty years old, but her mind is nimble and sharp, and she says she feels like she's thirty-five. Heather hails from a proud British military family. Her father was Winston Churchill's commanding officer when the two served in India. Heather herself received a medal when, as a thirteen-year-old bicycle courier, she was wounded by shrapnel during World War II.

She invites me inside, shooing Lizzie, her bull terrier. She shows me to a sitting room, which is filled with drawings of bull terriers and lots of books: an Indian cookbook, a biography of Jane Austen, an English translation of the Koran. Heather White is a woman of many surprises.

Heather has spent most of her life in Slough, but like Geoffrey she has a few reservations about the place, which she expresses in classic English understatement.

"Slough is crap. Total crap. I hate it."

Heather doesn't like what's happened to Slough in recent years. Doesn't like the housing projects. Doesn't like the traffic. Doesn't like the shopping malls. Doesn't like the Asians, except for her neighbors, who are from Pakistan and are very nice.

I point to a photo of a man on the wall. As I suspect, it's Heather's husband. He died several years ago, she says, and was "a real boffin."

"I'm sorry to hear that," I say.

Heather looks at me like I'm daft. A boffin, it turns out, is what Brits call a clever inventor. Indeed, he was a clever man in many ways. When he and Heather were courting, he wrote her love letters in ancient Greek. She had to find a friend to translate.

Heather White is happy, though I suspect she was happy before the happiness experts descended on Slough. Not coincidentally, Heather White is a nurse, one of the professions that the University of Chicago researchers found to be among the happiest. Technically, Heather's retired, but she's always going to the hospital to help out with one thing or another. Heather is needed. Heather looks forward to Monday morning.

Heather had never heard of "the science of happiness" before the producers of *Making Slough Happy* approached her. She decided to try it on a lark. Heather thought the experiment was fine but wonders why they didn't include exercises involving dogs and gardens, the two pillars of English happiness. Especially dogs. "You take dogs into the hospital, and the patients heal better. I've seen it. Dogs are the key to happiness."

One exercise she especially enjoyed was photography. Her assignment was to photograph the faces of Slough, photos that would eventually be assembled into a giant mural and displayed on High Street. Heather had hardly taken a photo in her life. But she's a fast learner and, it turns out, quite a good photographer. Only one problem: The people of Slough don't smile and don't like having their pictures taken. So Heather pointed her camera downward and photographed manhole covers instead. Snap, snap. It's amazing how many different manhole covers there are. Snap. Each one is different, like snowflakes. Only not as beautiful. Heavier, too.

One of her fellow participants lent Heather a book about positive psychology. It was so "typically American," she says. So sugary. Heather White takes her tea and her life straight up, no sugar.

"Do you ever feel down, Heather?"

"Oh, yes, of course. If I do, I just have a good moan and get on with it."

Ahh, a good moan. That's the thing about the Brits. They don't moan or whine or complain. Until they do. Then get out of the way.

Britain is a great place for grumps like myself. There are lots of fellow grumps to hang out with. There are books for grumps and even a TV series. It's called *Grumpy Old Men*, and it's hugely popular.

I picked up the companion book to *Grumpy Old Men* and flipped to the foreword, written by a grump named Arthur Smith. He begins by observing that "life is shit organized by bastards." Then he gets negative.

Arthur, like most Brits, I suspect, derives a perverse pleasure from his grumpiness. How else to read this description of how he feels in midmoan? "As I railed on and on, I became increasingly energized and excited by my own misery and misanthropy until I reached a kind of orgasm of negativity." Wow. Now that is grumpiness par excellence. He's taken Hilmar the Happy Heathen's "enjoyment of misery" to a whole new level. The Brits don't merely enjoy misery, they get off on it.

I can relate. After all, my last name is pronounced "whiner," and I do my best to live up to the name. I have the embarrassing tendency, for instance, to sigh heavily. I do this constantly, while writing, driving, and even in meetings. People assume I am bored or agitated, but that's usually not true. It's just my way of relieving the grumpy pressure that has built up inside of me. A good sigh, like a good moan, is a self-correcting mechanism. But here in Britain, land of the grumps, I am out of my league. Once uncorked, British grumps are a force of nature, remarkable for, if nothing else, their sheer staying power.

Like me, Heather White is an amateur grump. She'll just moan for a few minutes then return to her natural state of contentment. She counts her blessings: her dog, her garden, her friends. And now a degree of fame, since the program aired. Heather has no desire for riches, though. She wouldn't know what to do with all that money. "I've seen plenty of people with money who are miserable. It's people, not money, that make you happy. Dogs, too."

Heather offers to drive me back to my hotel. I'm fastening my seat belt when she picks up on my trepidation. "You're not afraid of my driving, are you?"

"No," I lie.

She turns out to be a darned good driver, skillfully navigating the snow-covered roads while quietly humming to herself. At that moment, I realize that Heather White is latently happy.

I've arranged to meet Richard Hill in front of a Chinese restaurant. From a block away, I can tell that he is not well. He's walking slowly, cautiously. He's stooped over and pale, though he's only in his early fifties. As I get closer, I can make out his crooked, yellow teeth.

We sit down at a coffee shop, and Richard orders a huge cup of cappuccino. It's more of a bowl, really, a very large bowl. The kind of beverage one should not drink without a life preserver.

Richard is unloading three packets of sugar into his cappuccino and telling me how, at the age of thirty, he had his first heart attack. It wasn't far from here. He was at a friend's house, watching TV, when the pain hit like a tsunami. He's had two more heart attacks since. Richard suffers from severe angina. His body produces too much cholesterol. Exercise and diet don't help. He's too sick to work. He's had two bypass operations and takes drugs to control the condition, but he knows that his life is more precarious than most.

"I could drop dead at any moment," he tells me, matter-of-factly, as he pours yet another packet of sugar into his cappuccino.

I'm just sitting there, wishing I had signed up for that CPR course at the Red Cross, when Richard, a Welshman, explains how he landed in Slough. He was recuperating from that first heart attack when he decided he quite liked Slough and would call it home. "A brilliant town," he says, and he means it. It's multicultural, and Richard figures that's a good thing. He can go to India or Pakistan or Poland without ever leaving Slough.

Richard caught wind of *Making Slough Happy* and couldn't resist. He considers himself reasonably happy, but here was a chance to make himself even happier—for free—and appear on television, to boot. What's not to like?

Richard found the happiness manifesto a bit sappy at first, but it's grown on him. Some eighteen months since the experiment ended, he still turns to it regularly, even if just for obvious things, he says, such as counting your blessings and being grateful for five things every day.

I can't imagine what this sickly, unemployed man can be grateful for, so I ask.

"That I'm still alive. That's the big one. That I didn't have a heart attack in the middle of the night and die. It's not a theoretical fear. I have come close to death. It's something you have to experience. It's not an intellectual thing."

"But your health problems, they must make you less happy."

"No, they've made me happier."

"Happier?"

"Yes. Let me put it this way. When was the last time you had your heart checked?"

The question makes me nervous. It happens to be my birthday, and I'm now comfortably (if that's the word) in the heart-attack years.

"My two-year-old daughter checked my heart with her toy stethoscope, does that count?"

"No. When is the last time you had an angiogram?"

"What's an angiogram?"

"The point is you don't know the condition of your heart, while I know *exactly* the condition of my heart. I know it's in reasonably good working order, even though I get chest pains and everything. I could pack up, but so could anyone else. I went through a phase where I lost all my ambitions because of my heart problems, and I couldn't be inspired to do anything because I could drop dead tomorrow. Then my cousin died suddenly, and he had been perfectly healthy. Fifty-one years old. A very athletic farmer. And I got to thinking, yeah, I could drop dead, but so could anybody else. At least I know the condition of one of my vital organs."

"But aren't you afraid of dying?"

"No. I'm afraid of a painful illness that leads to death. But I'm not afraid of dying of a heart attack. I've come close a couple of times and if that's what dying is like, that's okay with me."

I steer the conversation back toward the *Making Slough Happy* experiment, but death continues to tail us. Richard tells me that the graveyard therapy was a highlight for him. He wandered around the cemetery, as instructed, and found a tombstone for a boy who was four years old. "And I got to thinking, it's tragic for the people left behind, but that boy had no sense of his own mortality, so, providing he didn't suffer, he had a wonderful life, I'm sure."

Richard agrees with my theory that British culture hinders happiness. The most obvious manifestation is the lack of hugging. The British don't even hug their own mothers. Once, when he was ten years old, Richard visited Canada and discovered a brave new world of hugging. He started giving his mom a hug every time he saw her. Hugging, he says, "really lifts your spirits."

I present Richard with a proposition. If I give him five years and fifty million dollars and asked him to make Slough happy— *really* happy, not television happy—what would he do?

"Well, you need to point out to people that you don't need the money. Just put the happiness manifesto into action. Chat with someone who is down. Appreciate the moment. That's it. Like this cappuccino. If it was bad, we'd be quick to complain. But if it was excellent, if it exceeded our expectations, would we write and compliment the café? No, we wouldn't."

Richard has finished his cappuccino, which was excellent, by the way. We step outside. The sky is gray. It looks like another cloudy day to me. But Richard Hill, signatory to the happiness manifesto, a man hovering between life and death, looks up at the sky, spots patches of blue, and declares it a partly sunny day.


Toothpaste or toilet paper? That was the grim choice facing Veronica Puglia. She was recently divorced, living on the dole, and had only enough money for one of those items. Which would it be: toothpaste or toilet paper? I'll tell you later. First, more about Veronica. She's the daughter of Polish immigrants. Her maiden name means "nutty center" in Polish, a fact she evidently takes pride in. One day, one of her daughters handed her a flyer for *Making Slough Happy*. They were looking for volunteers. Veronica was intrigued. She wondered if such a thing was possible, to make an entire town happier. She wouldn't mind being a bit happier herself.

It worked. The experiment made her happier, but it wasn't the science of happiness that did it. No therapeutic breakthrough, no clap-of-thunder revelation. It was old-fashioned socializing. Getting out and meeting people.

Veronica was one of the volunteers who met with the lottery winner. She doesn't buy the research about lotteries and happiness and hedonic adaptation. Show her the money, she says. Others may squander their winnings, but *she* would know what to do with the millions. She would be happy. Winning would give her choices, and choices are good, Veronica reckons. Well, most choices. Not between toothpaste or toilet paper, but as a lottery winner, that's one choice she would never have to make again. If she won, she'd open a pub, she tells me and, yes, I can see it. Veronica would make an excellent publican. The kind that makes you feel like the pub is a second home.

Veronica's life, her life circumstances to be more precise, have grown worse since the experiment ended. She was laid off from her job teaching résumé writing at a local school, so she's back on the dole, watching every pence, barely making ends meet. Life is bloody tough, she tells me.

"So, Veronica," I ask, gingerly, "how happy are you these days? On a scale of one to ten."

"A six," she says, but I can tell she's not satisfied with her answer. She's cogitating.

"No, that's not right. I only said that because that's what I *think* I should be, given my life situation, being on the dole and divorced and all. But, actually, I'm an eight. No, an 8.5. Yes, that's

what I am. An 8.5." She has her health and two beautiful daughters. And every Monday night, she and a few of the Slough fifty
meet down at the Red Lion Pub for quiz night.

So what was it: toothpaste or toilet paper? Veronica figures
there are two types of people in the world: Toothpaste People
and Toilet Paper People. Veronica? She's a Toothpaste Person.
You can always find a stand-in for toilet paper—paper napkins,
for instance. But not toothpaste. Toothpaste, unlike toilet paper,
does more than perform a necessary function. It also makes your
mouth feel good, makes *you* feel good. Yes, Veronica is a Toothpaste Person.

Dusk is settling over Slough. I'm walking back to my hotel. I decide to stop at a church cemetery and try a little graveyard therapy.
I trudge through the slushy, unkempt grounds, stopping at each
tombstone and saying each name aloud. For me, something isn't
real unless I say it aloud. A thirteen-year-old boy. An eighty-four-
year-old man. A nineteen-year-old girl. I know this is supposed to
make me feel lucky to be alive, but I can't muster that sentiment.
I'm cold and tired and feel silly standing in a cemetery, talking to
myself.

Then I come across the gravestone for one Ellen Greenway,
who died on the twenty-fifth of March, 1914. She was exactly
my age when she passed away. I can relate to Ellen. She is not
an abstraction. Right there, standing amid the slush and weeds,
shivering from the cold, I make a promise to myself: I will remember that every day from this moment on is gravy. Pure, fat-laden,
creamy, heart-attack-inducing gravy.

The TV experiment was fine, but how, I wonder, would we go
about really making Slough—or any place else—happier? Is it simply a matter of eliminating problems? Reduce crime, get rid of
those ugly housing projects, clean up air pollution, and happiness

will flow like warm beer from the tap? George Orwell was skeptical of this approach: "Nearly all creators of utopia have resembled the man who has a toothache and therefore thinks happiness consists in not having a toothache."

He's right. Surely, happiness is not merely "the absence of suffering," as that über-pessimist Schopenhauer believed, but the *presence* of something. But what? And can you make places change or, like the old joke about psychiatrists and lightbulbs, does the place have to *want* to change first?

In Slough, I can't avoid the facts. The viral theory of happiness never took hold. The Slough fifty may have learned a thing or two about happiness, but the message never spread very far. Does that mean that the viral theory is flawed? I don't think so. It's simply a matter of numbers. Plant enough happiness seeds—people like Richard Hill and Heather White and Veronica Puglia—and eventually the laws of exponential growth kick in. A tipping point is reached, and happiness, I believe, will spread like a California brush fire.

So what to do in the meantime? I suppose we continue planting seeds. Besides, it is the planting that matters, not the harvest. As many philosophers have noted, happiness is a by-product. Happiness is, as Nathaniel Hawthorne observed, the butterfly that alights on our shoulder, unbidden.

So, instead of actively trying to make places, or people, happier, perhaps we'd be better off heeding the advice of Canadian author Robertson Davies: "If you are not happy you had better stop worrying about it and see what treasures you can pluck from your own brand of unhappiness."

Put that way, I see frumpy old Slough in a whole new light. It is no longer a much-maligned Berkshire town, the butt of jokes, but rather a treasure trove of unhappiness, just waiting to be plucked.

# Chapter 9

# INDIA

## Happiness Is a Contradiction

Some places are like family. They annoy us to no end, especially during the holidays, but we keep coming back for more because we know, deep in our hearts, that our destinies are intertwined.

For me, that place is India. I hate it. I love it. Not alternately but *simultaneously*. For if there is anything this seductive, exasperating country teaches us it is this: It's possible to hold two contradictory thoughts at the same time and, crucially, to do so without your head exploding. Indians do it all the time.

As he boarded a flight for Bombay in 1958, Hungarian-born writer Arthur Koestler said he wanted "to look at the predicament of the West from a different perspective, a different spiritual latitude." Yes, that's it! I thought, when I read those words. A different spiritual latitude or, as author Jeffrey Paine puts it, "an alternative track through modernity"—and, he might have added, directly to happiness.

When Koestler disembarked in Bombay, though, the heat and the stench of raw sewage made him feel as if "a wet, smelly diaper was being wrapped around my head by some abominable joker." One might conclude that India disappointed Koestler, but I don't think that's true. India does not disappoint. It captivates, infuriates, and, occasionally, contaminates. It never disappoints.

I always wanted to be a foreign correspondent, and India was certainly foreign. So when NPR offered me the chance to live and work there, I jumped at it, even though I had never set foot in India. I knew little about the country beyond the usual clichés of snake charmers and desperate poverty.

So on one December day in 1993, contrary to all common sense, I arrived at Indira Gandhi International Airport in New Delhi, hauling two trunks stuffed with tape recorders and notebooks and a few articles of climatically inappropriate clothing.

As a correspondent, I covered weighty topics like economic reforms, nuclear proliferation, and an outbreak of bubonic plague that belied India's claims that it was on the path to modernity. Of course, I was aware of the *other* India—the India of gurus and miracles—and occasionally this India rose to the level of news, like that morning I awoke to find the "milk miracle" sweeping the nation.

Wandering the narrow streets of Delhi's Paharganj neighborhood, the backpacker district, I'd see the lama lickers, disheveled travelers who scrimped every *rupee* and rarely bathed. But they had a luxury I did not have: time. They spent months lounging on beaches in Goa, getting stoned, or hiking the Himalayas, getting stoned. When they weren't getting stoned, they dabbled in spirituality by attending one of India's many ashrams. What exactly transpired inside these spiritual retreats remained a mystery. I heard stories of group sex and enlightenment, too. As a serious journalist, though, I couldn't justify a trip there. I left India after two years without once stepping inside an ashram. I felt cheated.

And so I've returned to India, this time with a different agenda, a happiness agenda. And with a question I desperately needed to answer: Why do so many presumably sane westerners leave their wealthy, functional nations behind and travel to a poor and dysfunctional nation in search of bliss? Are they romanticizing the east, falling for charlatans with flowing beards? Or did the nineteenth-century scholar Max Mueller get it right when he said that, by going to India, we are returning to our "old home," full of memories, if only we can read them?

\*   \*   \*

Every time I return to India—about once a year—it is different yet the same. Yes, there's now a McDonald's at my favorite market in Delhi, but around the corner is the shop that sells statues of Ganesh. Yes, there are cellphones and ATMs and Internet cafés, but none has made a dent in the bedrock of Indian culture. These latest foreign intruders are no different from the Mughals or the British or any of the other interlopers who over the centuries tried to subdue the subcontinent. India always emerged victorious, not by repelling these invaders but by subsuming them.

The Taj Mahal is today considered the quintessential Indian icon, yet it was built by a seventeenth-century Mughal emperor who at the time wasn't Indian at all. He is now. Likewise, McDonald's caved to the Indian palate and, for the first time, dropped Big Macs and all hamburgers from its menu, since Hindus don't eat beef. Instead, it serves McAloo Tikki and the McVeggie and a culinary hybrid, the Paneer Salsa Wrap. McDonald's didn't change India, as some feared. India changed McDonald's.

And so it is with western travelers who seek their happiness here. Even before the Beatles meditated with the Maharishi Mahesh Yogi on the banks of the Ganges, foreigners have been drawn to India. Annie Besant, E. M. Forster, Christopher Isherwood, Martin Luther King Jr., and many others. Some came in search of solutions to political problems back home. Others wanted to transcend their pedestrian, earthly existence, if only for a moment, and taste the eternal. Some just wanted to chill. This despite the fact that India is not a particularly happy place, according to Ruut Veenhoven and his database. Looking for bliss in a land of misery? A contradiction? Yes. And no.

I'd heard of a new, popular guru named Sri Sri Ravi Shankar. He has long, silky black hair and a serene smile. He is a mainstream guru, if such a thing is possible.

278 THE GEOGRAPHY OF BLISS

Sri Sri's ashram is located just outside of Bangalore, India's Silicon Valley. Bangalore is New India, the India of call centers and shopping malls—"India Shining," as one political party calls it. Many of the city's software engineers and call-center workers—cybercoolies, as they're called—escape to the ashram whenever they can. New India turns to Old India for salvation or, at least, for a bit of downtime.

Driving to the ashram in a taxi, we pass cows, dogs, meat hanging from hooks, tailor shops, a gleaming office building for Oracle, a sign for "Speak Easy English." We pass an auto-rickshaw, one of those three-wheeled menaces that buzz around India's cities like swarms of killer bees. Its black exhaust makes me cough. I see a sign for "Asia's Most Advanced Super Specialty Hospital." The disease and the cure. India has it all. One-stop shopping.

Finally, we arrive at the ashram, entering through a white archway, and suddenly we're in a little Garden of Eden, lush and green with fresh mangos and bananas growing everywhere. It seems blissfully quiet. Perhaps that is the secret of the Indian ashram. Maybe they're not exceptionally peaceful places but only seem so compared to the cacophony outside their gates.

Reception is basic, not as friendly as I expected. Nobody hugs me or, for that matter, seems to care much that I'm here. Sri Sri Ravi Shankar, or Guru-ji, as he's called respectfully, is everywhere. There's a big photo of him behind the reception counter and another one across the room. He's also on a big projection TV.

An officious woman hands me a form and asks me to fill it out. One question asks if I have ever sought psychological counseling. I lie and check no. Under occupation, I write consultant. Another lie, in case they don't like the idea of a journalist sniffing around their ashram. I briefly wonder if lying on my ashram application form is a bad idea, karmically speaking, but that thought vanishes just as quickly as it arrived.

The ashram is entirely self-contained, a cruise ship for the soul. There is no reason to leave. Everything you need is here: food, laundry, ATM, pharmacy, Internet café. Everything, I was quickly learning, except for irony, which is scarce indeed.

I walk down a manicured path, lugging my suitcase. A sign says "Please only touch the flowers with your eyes." I pass a few people. They seem calm, alarmingly so. I say hello. They respond with *"Jai Guru Dev."* A strange greeting, I think. Later, I learned it means "Victory to the Big Mind." I'm not sure who has the big mind, us or Guru-ji.

I change into loose-fitting clothing, ashram wear, and walk down a steep path to the dining hall. I take off my shoes and leave them outside with the dozens of others. A man plops supervegetarian food (no dairy or onions or garlic) on my plate, and I take a seat. Except there are no seats to be taken. Everyone is sitting on the floor. Some people are natural floor sitters, their legs curling into the lotus position with consummate ease. I am not one of these people.

A holy man, or *sadhu,* sits next to me. He is dressed in saffron, with a long, flowing beard and a vertical slash of charcoal on his forehead. *"Jai Guru Dev,"* he says. He prays silently, palms together, then begins to eat. He does so expertly, scooping up the rice and lentils in easy, fluid motions. I am less graceful. I spill half my food on my lap. More food dribbles down my chin. A few lentils find their way into my mouth, purely by chance. I feel ridiculous. I can understand someone who has eaten with their hands all their life struggling with the transition to knife and fork, but what could be more instinctual, more human, than eating food with one's hands?

Someone comes up to me and taps me on the shoulder. For a moment, I think he might be dispensing spiritual advice—this is an ashram, after all—but his advice, it turns out, is far more practical. He informs me that I should use only my right hand to eat with. The left hand is used for other bodily purposes.

I see some people wearing T-shirts that say "Commitment to service is the key to happiness." Actually, the research backs them up. People who volunteer regularly are, statistically, happier than those who don't. I briefly consider pointing this out to them but then drop the idea. An Indian ashram is no place for statistics.

Walking out of the dining hall, I notice a bulletin board with posters highlighting Guru-ji's expanding empire of bliss. There's the Sri Sri Journalism School and the Sri Sri School of Management. Instantly, the term "management guru" springs to mind. I chuckle to myself, except it's not to myself. It's out loud. No one cares, though. That is the beauty of life in an ashram. You can suddenly burst out laughing—or crying or regressing to infantile behavior or hopping madly on one foot—and no one bats an eye. It's okay. At the ashram, everything is okay. Except, I was to learn, disrespecting Guru-ji. That is definitely not okay.

The ashram's main temple looks like a giant three-tiered wedding cake with a big blue lightbulb on top. Inside, it's all white marble and arches. On the stage is a picture of Guru-ji. It's huge, at least four feet high, resting on a sort of throne and looped with a big garland of flowers. The white marble is cool and feels nice on my bare feet.

The overall effect, though, is borderline lurid—too many pink, flowery things on the ceiling, and the entrance to the temple is bookended by two five-foot-high swans. That, along with the trash cans shaped like bunnies, create a vaguely Disney-like atmosphere.

There's a small musical troupe sitting on the floor near Guri-ji's photo. *"Shiva om, Shiva om,"* the singers chant. People around me start to move, slowly at first, but as the tempo increases, the dancing grows feverish. Some people start twirling and spinning wildly. Others hold hands. And me? I resort to my default mode and simply observe. It disturbs me that I can't loosen up, not even here. Then again, I just arrived, I tell myself. Give yourself time.

It's mostly Indians at the ashram. Stressed-out IT workers from Bangalore. One woman came to town from a neighboring state. She was hoping to enroll in an Oracle software course, but it was full so she enrolled at the ashram instead. Software or spirituality. In India, they are interchangeable.

There are a few foreigners here, too, and I meet two: Elsa from Portugal and Eva from the Dominican Republic. They are ashram hopping. They just spent two weeks at Sai Baba's ashram, not far from here. Living conditions there were much rougher, they tell me. The rules were strict and enforced by burly men wearing white scarves. And there were none of the luxuries found on this ashram. I can't imagine of which luxuries they speak. My shower has no hot water, and at dinner everyone washes his or her own dishes, which is fine but hardly luxurious. Yet what they sacrificed in material comfort they gained in spiritual payoff.

"We saw amazing things," says Elsa, somewhat mysteriously.

"Swami calls you. You don't go to him. He summons you," says Eva.

Eva seems flummoxed by the paucity of information at this ashram.

"No one has told us where to go," she says to one of the ashram officials, an edge of panic creeping into her voice. "We have been given no information." She seems awfully tense for someone who just spent two weeks at an ashram—and besides, isn't the whole idea to find information for ourselves and not be told what to do?

Today is our first session. There are about thirty of us in the class, called the Art of Living, and just a few foreigners: myself, Elsa, and Eva. We're sitting on the floor, of course. Our teacher is an Indian woman named Ami. She's a former corporate executive. Now she and her husband travel the world, spreading the word of Guru-ji. She's sitting lotus-style on a raised platform so that she is slightly higher than the rest of us. She's wearing a long flowing *salwar khameez* and a smile that is the most serene I've seen since Thailand.

We start by introducing ourselves. No problem, I think. Except we're supposed to say "I belong to you" to everyone in our class, one at a time. This makes me uncomfortable. I just met these people. How can I belong to them? I go through with it, mumbling the "I belong to you" part. Next, we're told the ashram rules.

Rule number one: wear loose clothing.

No problem.

Rule number two: no alcohol for the next three days.

Slight problem. I'll miss my evening glass of wine but figure I can go for three days without and compensate later.

And the last rule: absolutely no coffee or tea or caffeine of any kind.

Big problem. This rule hits me like a sucker punch and surely would have knocked me to the floor had I not been sitting there already. I'm eyeing the exits, plotting my escape. I knew enlightenment came at a price, but I had no idea the price was this steep. A sense of real panic sets in. How am I going to survive for the next seventy-two hours without a single cup of coffee?

Ami doesn't smell my fear or at least doesn't let on. She's moving on to the next exercise: a guided meditation. I've dabbled in meditation in the past but have always found the silence unsettling. In radio, silence is something to be avoided at all costs. Sure, I'd insert a second or two of silence for dramatic effect, but any more than that is a signal that something has gone terribly wrong. That's why it's called dead air.

And counting breaths? Can't do it. In my mind, each breath brings me one step closer to death, and why would you want to count down to your own death?

Ami pushes a button on a CD player, and Guru-ji's voice, high-pitched and serene, fills the room. "You are at peace with your environment now. Be grateful for this wonderful body, this instrument."

*My* instrument is a bit out of tune, and as for wonderful? Yes, in 1987. But I get the idea. We should be grateful to be alive. Our eyes are supposed to be closed, but I cheat and open them for a second. Ami's smile is radiant; she's glowing. There's no other word for it. That should be proof enough that Guru-ji is on to something, that the ashram is for real, yet I can't seem to jettison my doubts.

At the same time, some of Guru-ji's words, channeled through Ami, ring true: "We keep postponing happiness. We can only experience happiness now. The present moment is inevitable." I like that last bit a lot. It's much better than that old dharma refrain, "Be here now," which always struck me as too much of an imperative, an order. "I said, 'Be here now, God damn it!'" But if the present moment is inevitable, then, well, I might as well embrace it.

Ami continues: "Ask a child to choose chocolate or peace of mind, and they will choose the chocolate. But an adult? Probably the peace of mind." Unless that adult lives in Switzerland, I think. There, chocolate *is* peace of mind.

We're on a break, so I take the opportunity to chat with a few of the Indians in my class. Most work in the IT field, and they put in long hours. The Art of Living course appeals to them (even the acronym AOL says high-tech) because it gives them a jolt of spirituality without requiring a lifelong sacrifice. They don't have to become *sanyasis,* those who renounce all their worldly possessions and pursue a purely spiritual life. All Guru-ji requires from his disciples is a three-day weekend.

I tell them about my search for the world's happiest places, about Ruut Veenhoven and his database. If anyone would understand, surely it is these people of the microchip. Yet I am met with furrowed brows and looks of incredulity.

"Why would you want to quantify happiness?" asks Binda, a software engineer.

It's a disarmingly simple question, and I don't have a good answer. I've spent much time pondering whether we *can* measure happiness but not much thought to whether we *should* measure it.

Many of these people have lived abroad, but they keep coming back to India. Why?

"Unpredictability," they say, almost in unison.

It's a surprising answer. We in the west think of unpredictability as a menace, something to be avoided at all costs. We want our careers, our family lives, our roads, our weather to be utterly predictable. We love nothing more than a sure thing. Shuffling the songs on our iPod is about as much randomness as we can handle.

But here is a group of rational software engineers telling me that they like unpredictability, crave it, can't live without it. I get an inkling, not for the first time, that India lies at a spiritual latitude beyond the reach of the science of happiness.

At dinner, I find Eva and Elsa engaged in a decadent activity. They're sitting on chairs. Flimsy plastic chairs, but, still, they're off the floor, and that seems like the height of luxury. A handwritten sign says the chairs are reserved for "the elderly and international visitors." Nonfloor people. I am grateful when they ask me to join them.

Eva tells me that at the other ashram we couldn't be talking like this, on the floor or anywhere else. Men and women were segregated. "Sai Baba wants you to focus on your spiritual development and not on your"—she pauses and makes a sweeping motion toward her pelvis—"not on your body consciousness." That's no problem, I think. The daily cold shower has pretty much taken care of my body consciousness.

Today is the big day. We're going to learn the *sudarshan kriya* breathing technique. This is the centerpiece of the course, the HOV lane to bliss. We take our places on the floor, and, once again, I contort myself into the lotus position. Ami tells us to remove any leather we're wearing, even watchbands, since "leather is dead skin, and it restricts the flow of *pranha*." *Pranha* means "energy," and it's a word that, along with "toxins," you hear a lot at any ashram. I don't deny the presence of either, but the terms are used so loosely as to be virtually meaningless. I cringe every time I hear them.

Everyone is a bit nervous. We've heard about this breathing technique, but the details have been kept secret. Ami tells us to "let your feelings go, don't hold back, and if you hear someone laughing or crying, don't stare. That is *their* experience. *They* are having an experience, not you." This concerns me. What are we about to do that would provoke such strong emotional reactions? I'm really not in the mood for this. It's been twenty-four hours since I've had a caffeine fix, and I'm feeling awfully grumpy.

We do the exercise, and it's really nothing so bizarre—sort of like snoring only when you're awake. Afterward, we lie on our backs for ten minutes. The woman next to me is moaning and sounds like she's in pain. I'm a bit worried and briefly consider opening my eyes to see what's going on, but that is *her* experience, so I don't.

Finally, we're told to open our eyes and return to the lotus position. Afterward, we share (another popular ashram word) our experiences. Eva pipes up first: "I've never experienced anything like that before. I saw many faces, including that of Guru-ji. He must be here with us now." Everyone applauds.

"I lost control," says someone else.

"I no longer have a headache," says a third, to more applause.

"I went away. I don't know where I went, but I was gone," says someone who has clearly returned from wherever she went.

Elsa, though, had the most dramatic experience. "I saw fireworks in my mind's eye with blues and reds, every color of the spectrum. And I felt sparks in my lower legs, as if electricity was shooting up them."

I experienced no such pyrotechnics. Yes, I feel a bit lightheaded, a bit moody, but that might be due to the lack of caffeine and circulation to my legs, thanks to all this sitting on the floor. What is wrong with me? Where are my spiritual fireworks?

Then there is Satish, a skinny software engineer. He fell asleep during the exercise and is still sleeping after we have shared. Someone shakes Satish, but he's in a deep, deep sleep and won't wake. The session is over. It's time to leave, but he's blocking the only exit. What to do? Ami tells us to just step over him and not disturb his experience. As I gingerly step over Satish's prone, snoring body, I can't help but think how lucky he is. He's having the best experience of all.

*   *   *

Over lunch, Eva and Elsa are ecstatic about the session. "If everyone meditated for ten minutes a day, the world would be a better place," says Eva. She's very sensitive to world events. She stopped watching the news years ago. She takes it all too personally. She tells me she developed a cyst in her breast during the Iraq war, which is really more information than I need.

My alarm chimes at 6:00 a.m. Another day. Another experiment in caffeine withdrawal. My head is pounding, my *pranha* dangerously low. It's all I can do to drag myself to the morning yoga. I am one grumpy ashramite.

I feel a bit better after the yoga. Blood circulation has returned to my extremities. Our second *kriya* breathing experience is more exciting for me. Afterward, I feel extremely giddy in a way I haven't felt since I smoked that Moroccan hash (for research purposes) all those months ago. As we lie on the floor, palms up, in what's known as the *shavasan* or "dead man's pose," images flutter through my mind. I see Ami naked, and that's okay. I feel like I'm dying, and that's okay, too. I'm having an experience.

Another exercise. We're separated by gender and told to stare into a partner's eyes "with childlike innocence." My partner is a hairy middle-aged Indian beverage salesman. Staring into his eyes makes me extremely uncomfortable. Finally, the exercise is over, and we pair up again with a different partner. This time we are told to tell our life stories, and I realize I'd rather talk to someone for five hours than stare into their eyes (with childlike innocence) for five seconds.

Next, we're shown a short video about Guri-ji. We hear testimonials from a former terrorist, a prisoner, a tsunami victim, an HIV-positive person, all attesting to Guru-ji's powers and talking about how he and his Art of Living organization changed their lives. Sri Sri is portrayed as a multinational guru, a player on the world stage, who regularly addresses such august institutions as the American Psychiatric Association.

At the ashram, Guru-ji is spoken of often and always in reverential terms. Ami flutters her eyes and blushes like a schoolgirl in love whenever she mentions his name. Like all gurus, Sri Sri's early years are replete with tales of wonder. He was supposedly reading the *Bhagavad-Gita*, a Hindu holy text, at age four. When he started his ashram many years ago, the land was barren. But, explains Ami, "Guru-ji himself would get water from the well and he said, 'It is so lush and green and beautiful. Can't you see it?' And it happened. Everything, including this building, came to be just as he said it would. Guru-ji's grace is here, I assure you."

I have to be honest: All this guru worship turns me off. If I wanted to worship someone, there's always my wife. I didn't need to come to India. Fawning over someone else is just as counterproductive, and annoying, as fawning over yourself. Narcissism turned inside out is still narcissism.

I had had a chance to see Guru-ji in person. A few days before traveling to the ashram, I had been in Delhi, visiting friends, when I noticed a small ad announcing that Sri Sri Ravi Shankar was giving a lecture, "Success without Stress." I couldn't miss this.

I arrive early, but there is already a long line. We are searched perfunctorily before entering a large auditorium. At the entrance is a wooden box where we can deposit questions for Guru-ji. I write down a question, fold the piece of paper, and drop it in the little slot.

One cannot listen to a guru on an empty stomach. I go to the snack bar to buy some popcorn and then take a seat up front. On the stage is a white sofa, draped in gold-colored fabric, with end tables on either side. Behind the sofa is a large sign. "Success without Stress," it says, "a talk by his holiness Sri Sri Ravi Shankar." Underneath are the logos of the fifteen corporate sponsors. Apparently, it requires a lot of cash to keep the guru machine humming along.

Guru-ji is late. The audience is starting to grow restless when suddenly the lights are dimmed and a small troupe, sitting on the floor, begins to chant. *Shiva om, Shiva om.* The pace quickens, and the audience begins to clap rhythmically. *Shiva om, Shiva om.* A voice intones, "Before you came there was darkness, now there is light." *Shiva om, Shiva om.* Then Guru-ji enters, and the audience is hooting and hollering and standing, as if he were a rock star.

The overhead lighting illuminates Guru-ji like a ray of sunlight. He's wearing a flowing white robe. Wrapped around his neck is the biggest garland of flowers I've ever seen in my life. It must weigh fifty pounds. I'm surprised he can stand with that thing around his neck. Guru-ji lights the ceremonial lamp, as suited businessmen and dignitaries look on admiringly. Guru-ji is talking now. His lips are moving, but we can't hear him. A murmur of concern spreads through the audience. What is wrong with Guru-ji? How can we heed the wisdom if we can't hear the wisdom?

Guru-ji is fiddling with something on his robe. He taps it. Nothing. He taps again. Still nothing. More fidgeting. He taps again, and this time a low-pitched thumping sound fills the auditorium, followed by the high-pitched, wise voice of Guru-ji.

"The whole thing depends on a tiny little button," he says, with a knowing gleam in his eyes.

The audience laughs and applauds. When a guru says something like that, his words are imbued with deep significance, while if you or I said it people would just assume we're talking about a tiny little button and nothing more. Thus, just as some people are famous for being famous, gurus are wise for being wise. They can't go wrong.

Guru-ji tells us to greet the person next to us, and we do.

"Did you really greet them, or was it a formality?" he asks. "Were you like a flight attendant saying, 'Have a nice day'? You don't really mean it." A titter of laughter ripples through the crowd.

Guru-ji tell us that a baby smiles four hundred times a day. Adults only seventeen times. Married adults even less, he says, and the crowd breaks into laughter again.

"What is life with no smile, no laughter? A stressed person cannot smile."

Guru-ji moves from one end of the stage to another, including the entire audience in the event, like any good speaker. He tells us that we need to create a space for imperfection in our lives.

"Why do we lose our temper? Because we love perfection. Create a little room for imperfection in your life. Are you still with me?"

"Yes!" shouts the audience, in perfect unison.

The lights are dimmed, and we're told to massage our jaws and eyebrows. It feels good. Then, we're instructed to make the "*om*" sound. The word is Sanskrit, the language of the ancient Hindu texts. It is a language based on vibrations. In Sanskrit, you don't merely hear words, you feel them.

Hearing and feeling about one thousand people saying "*om*" at the same time is something to behold. The whole room feels as if it is vibrating. I like this, I think, yes, I like this, and it dawns on me how much I associate India with sounds—the singsong call of a street hawker, the bleating horn of an auto-rickshaw, the chanting of a Hindu priest. Every sound, not just the holy ones, is a vibration. And a vibration is, of course, motion. Air pressing against air. Nothing more. Yet this simple act of physics can result in Mozart's piano concerto or a freeway at rush hour or a lover's whisper or the pop-pop of a semiautomatic weapon.

It's question time. A woman pulls a small piece of paper out of the wooden box. The very first one is my question. I can hardly believe it. There must be dozens, if not hundreds, of questions in that box. What are the odds of her choosing mine? It must be a sign. In India, everything is a sign.

She reads it aloud. "Is happiness the highest ideal, or is there something greater we should be striving for?" This is a question that has been nagging me for a while now. Here I am traveling thousands of miles looking for the world's happiest places, assuming that happiness is, as Aristotle believed, the summum bonum: the greatest good. But is it? Or is there a more important destination?

Guru-ji doesn't hesitate. "Yes, there is something higher than happiness. Love is higher than happiness."

The audience applauds.

Guru-ji waits for them to settle down then elaborates: "Not only does love trump happiness, but in a competition between truth and love, love wins. We must strive for a love that does not bring distortions."

I'm not sure what he means by that last part. But there will be no follow-up questions here. We've already moved on to the next one: "What happens to us after we die?"

This is a big one, *the* big one, and everyone, including me, is on the edge of their seat.

Guru-ji pauses for dramatic effect before answering. "I could tell you," he says, "but I want you to have some suspense. I don't want you to get to the other side and say, 'Oh, this is what I expected. I am so bored.'"

The audience laughs. I feel cheated, though. I've covered enough news conferences to know when someone has artfully dodged a question.

Now people are shouting questions from the audience. Some of Guru-ji's answers are wise, some merely glib. A few are both.

"How can we stop terrorism?"

"Terrorism is simply a lack of humanism. Every child should learn a little about religion, then they won't think that others are bad."

"How can I know my fate?"

"Life is a combination of freedom and destiny, and the beauty is you don't know which is which."

"When will I get a billion rupees?"

"Ask some fortune-teller. But remember, he will charge you one hundred rupees."

"Expectation leads to disappointment, so what am I to do?"

"Are you expecting an answer from me? Better not to expect."

"When will India be corruption free?"

"When you stand up and fight against corruption."

I like that answer. It was real, and it required action of the asker. Hinduism is a religion of action more than belief. In the *Bhagavad-Gita*, Lord Krishna tells Arjun that his actions, not his beliefs, will set him free. Or, as Guru-ji put it, "When you're in the bathtub, you need to move a little to feel the warmth."

More people are shouting, the questions are infinite, but Guru-ji holds up a hand and says, sorry, that's all the time he has tonight, and just like that he is gone.

People stand to leave. Everyone seems pleased with the evening's performance. I leave feeling like I've just had the spiritual equivalent of popcorn: tasty, easy to swallow, and certainly of some nutritional value, but not particularly filling.

I am unable to separate the message from the messenger. My antennae are on the lookout for even a whiff of hypocrisy and, once detected, negate any wisdom a guru might impart. Not everyone, though, thinks this way.

In the 1980s, a popular guru named Bhagwan Shree Rajneesh, or Osho, attracted a huge following in India and then in the United States. He established an ashram in Oregon, an elaborate, sprawling complex. Osho preached the importance of love and mindfulness. It turns out, though, that Osho had lovingly purchased some ninety-three Rolls-Royces and was then arrested by the authorities on an immigration violation. I had read his teachings, and some of them seemed quite wise and sensible, but the Rolls-Royces were a real turnoff. I couldn't take Osho seriously.

That was not the case, though, with my Indian friend Manju. Manju, a very levelheaded attorney from Delhi, saw no reason to throw out Osho's wisdom with his Rolls-Royces. "I keep the good and discard the bad," she said to me over lunch one day. In other words, Indians don't expect perfection, or even consistency, from their gurus. The guru is wise. The guru is a fraud. Two contradictory thoughts that, for Manju, coexist comfortably in her Indian head.

It's my last day at the ashram. The course is over. I say goodbye to Ami. She beams at me and says, "There's a spiritual revolution coming, maybe not in our lifetime, but it's coming." I say something lame like, "I sure hope so," and then I leave.

I envy people like Ami. Her mind is clear, uncluttered. Her *pranha* is high. Her face glows. I wish I could be like her. What is preventing me? Am I so attached to irony and cleverness? To success? A year of traveling and thinking about happiness has proved fairly conclusively that none of these things leads to happiness, and yet I still can't let them go.

I say goodbye to Eva and Elsa, who are ecstatic about their new guru. They're already making plans to attend the advanced course. Eva gives me a big hug. She says I look different—calmer, and with more energy. I cringe at the mention of that word, but she is right. I do feel more relaxed. I breathe more deeply. I survived three days without coffee, and in fact my headaches have nearly disappeared. The circulation has returned to my legs.

Where did this come from? I can't identify any one moment nor any particular position I twisted my body into. It just snuck up on me. Maybe this is how enlightenment happens. Not with a thunderclap or a bolt of lightning but as a steady drip, drip, drip until one day you realize your bucket is full.


The problem with an Indian ashram is that once you leave it, you're back in India. My taxi is stuck in traffic. My throat burns from the exhaust. My eyes sting. The roads seem even more chaotic than they did just a few days ago, or maybe my mind, serene and caffeine free, is more attuned to the heat and dust and noise. I've always been especially sensitive to noise, a proven detriment to happiness, what essayist Ambrose Bierce called "a stench in the ear."

Finally, we arrive at a plain-looking two-story building in a bustling part of town. One Shanti Road. It's owned by an artist named Suresh. I had heard that he rents out spare rooms and that his house is a sort of revolving salon. Everyone passes through 1 Shanti Road. It seemed like a good way to recover, if that's the

right word, from my ashram experience and get to know Bangalore at the same time.

Suresh designed 1 Shanti Road himself. He built the house
around a large badam tree. He loves that tree so much that his
friends joke that he's married to it.

I stumble up a circular staircase with my bags. The living
room at 1 Shanti Road is chockablock with paintings and books
and Hindu bric-a-brac. Dishes are piled high in the kitchen sink.
Flies hover over the mango rinds and coffee grounds like a fleet
of attack helicopters. "The maid didn't show up today," explains
Suresh. Everyone in India has a maid, even struggling artists.

It's still early in the morning, but Suresh's salon is already hopping. People are sitting around, lounging, smoking cigarettes, and
drinking copious amounts of coffee, deflating their *pranha* to dangerously low levels and not giving a damn. The air is thick with
smoke and irony. I inhale deeply.

"Welcome to the anti-ashram," someone says. I'm introduced
to Harsha, whose name means "happiness," and Vikram and
Arjun and others whose names I can't keep straight.

I've walked into the middle of an Indian bitch session. They're
complaining about Bangalore's exponential growth and what it's
doing to their beloved city. My arrival, fresh from the ashram, has
diverted the conversation from traffic jams to spirituality. It's a
sharp turn, but one this group handles with ease.

"This is a country based on the God syndrome," says Vikram,
or Viki, as his friends call him. He has a gold earring in one ear
and is wearing a saffron shirt and is openly gay in a country that is
not so open about such things. "People need crutches," says Viki,
"and the gurus are crutches."

I feel compelled to defend the gurus, mine in particular, an impulse that surprises me. I tell them about the breathing technique
I learned and my latent relaxation that resulted.

"Someone develops a breathing technique and then you want
all the answers from him," says a beefy sculptor named Vivek.
"You're increasing the oxygen flow to the brain. You get a high

from that," says Roy, who is a doctor and should know. Roy treats many patients, but he's never met one of them. He reads X rays for a hospital in the United States.

Okay, so there is a medical explanation for that giddiness I experienced. Does that make it less real?

"It's a spiritual pedicure," chimes someone else. "You feel better for a while, but nothing has really changed."

"Holy people must renounce," says Viki. "Ultimately, it's about denial and renunciation."

I relay to this group of skeptics how Guru-ji accurately forecasted a lush green ashram, when the ground was rocky and barren and the experts said nothing could grow there.

Classic guru mythology, says someone. They always announce they will build something or grow something even though the experts say it can't be done. These revelations are always in retrospect, though. They are articles of faith, there's no record of them, so they can't be proved or disproved.

"Why can't people just sit and meditate quietly?" says someone else.

"It's too boring," says Viki.

"Can you be genuine and a fraud at the same time?" I ask.

"Apparently, you can," says Suresh. "This is India."

"Everything in India is true, and its opposite is true also," someone else says.

My head is spinning. It feels like it's going to explode. Suresh, sensing my unease, offers me coffee, but I demure. Decaf me has survived three days already. I want to see how much longer I can last.

The conversation ricochets from the petty to the profound and back again. I'm getting spiritual whiplash. The subject of *samsara* comes up. That's the eastern belief that we are born over and over again, until we achieve enlightenment. Then we are liberated and do not return to this earth.

"Personally, I don't mind coming back as a dog or a tree," says Viki. "I'm in no hurry to get off this planet."

"Somewhere in the universe, someone has been given a speck of time. We are that person, it is our speck of time," says Suresh, enigmatically.

Viki's brief burst of optimism has dissipated, and he's griping again. "Do you know what the best business in this country is? Religion. I'm very cynical," says Viki, as if there were any doubt. "If I have a problem I go to see my best friend, not a guru. They are making a mint, these gurus. I don't think there is any such thing as a real *sadhu*. They're all fake."

Someone stands to leave. Someone else enters. In India, a man's home is his castle. It is a porous castle, though, with no moat, and it is prone to invasion by friend and foe alike. At my apartment in Delhi, a perpetual parade of humanity passed: plumbers, electricians, delivery boys, holy men, government clerks, taxi drivers. It can be awfully annoying; sometimes you just want to putter about in your underwear, unmolested. This endlessly flowing river of humanity, though, also means that you are never alone in India.

At 1 Shanti Road, the conversation meanders like the Ganges, sloshing from one subject to another with no discernible pattern. One recurring theme, though, is the change taking place in Bangalore.

"We've become like owls," says Viki. "People stay up all night, working or partying. Why is everybody running around in such a hurry? And the traffic is crazy."

Don't forget the mobile phones, someone says.

"Everyone has one," says Viki, in the same tone of voice he might use for "Everyone has tuberculosis."

"Do you have one, Viki?" I ask.

"Yes, I do," he says, sheepishly, producing a shiny new model from his pocket. "But I growl and snarl at it. I have the right attitude." He makes a snarling expression with his face.

"These people, the cybercoolies, will burn out by thirty, thirty-five," someone says. "They will wake up one day and realize that life has passed them by."

I'm trying to figure out if these are valid concerns or merely sour grapes, when Emma arrives.

She bounds up the stairs carrying two huge suitcases. The flight from London was a nightmare. She's been traveling for twenty-four hours. No, she doesn't need sleep, she needs a ciggie and coffee, stat, and Suresh promptly produces both.

Emma is a hedonic refugee of the first order. When she was five years old, growing up in London, she would tug at women's saris in restaurants. One of the first words she ever spoke was "India."

She finally traveled to India at age twenty-five. She flew into Delhi and hopped into a cab, plunging into the craziness that is an Indian street. Most people find this disconcerting, terrifying, but not Emma. She sat in the backseat of that cab and felt a deep sense of calm wash over her. Maybe she cried, maybe not. She can't remember. One thing she knew for certain, though: She was home.

Properly caffeinated and nicotined, Emma plops down on a chair and joins the conversation. "What do you love so much about India?" I ask.

"I love the sound of horns tooting, the rickshaws, the women balancing pots on their head, the peanut *wallah* calling out, the bells at the temples. I love the Indian accent. It's endless, really. I love everything. "

I can't help but notice that most of the things she listed are aural. India is a feast for the ears. Maybe that will change, as India grows richer because, to be honest, there is nothing more deadly dull than the sound of prosperity. The dull hum of an air conditioner or the muffled clicks on a keyboard simply can't compete with the melodic calls of hawkers at an open-air market or the rhythmic clickity-clack of a sweatshop's sewing machines. Even Third World traffic, with its symphony of honking horns and tinkling bells, beats the monotonous whoosh of a modern freeway.

Emma used to live in Bangalore. That's how she knows Suresh and the gang. Now she's back in London but still returns to India often. A round of Indian geography ensues. They talk of people they know, connections, degrees of separation. A billion souls in India, and the residents of 1 Shanti Road seem to know them all. This country is a chain of infinitely intersecting circles.

Emma opens her suitcases, and I can hardly believe my eyes. Inside are dozens and dozens of bags, each one neatly wrapped in plastic. Emma is in the bag business. She designs them at her studio in London and has them made in Hong Kong and here in Bangalore. I tell her about my bag addiction, and her eyes light up. It is the look of a crack dealer who has just been introduced to a hard-core user.

I ask Emma to analyze my bag addiction. As you recall, I own more bags than most people, including most mental-health professionals, would consider normal. "Hmmm," she says, like a psychoanalyst who's been presented with a particularly challenging case. "It's a safety thing, a security blanket. Plus, you carry things in bags, baggage. So your obsession represents an extension of your emotional baggage. That's it: You need some place to put your emotional baggage."

Not bad, not bad at all.

I'm introduced to Chandra, a roly-poly guy who lives in the apartment downstairs. His bald head is large and bulbous, and he's wearing a green *kurta,* which hangs down to his knees. He reminds me of a friendly Martian. In fact, Chandra is a cultural geographer, which is a perfect thing to be, as far as I'm concerned. He lived in the United States for eighteen years, in places like Waco, Texas, and Fargo, North Dakota. To this day, mere mention of the word "Fargo" is enough to make him shiver. He's also developed an affinity for *Seinfeld* reruns and an unnerving feeling every morning that he needs to be somewhere, anywhere, by 8:30 a.m. "And it's only in the past year that I could take an afternoon nap and not feel guilty," he adds.

I need a break from the conversation, so I step out onto the terrace. Someone once told me that if you want to know India, just stand on a street corner, any street corner, and spin around 360 degrees. You will see it all. The best and worst of humanity. The ridiculous and the sublime. The profane and the profound. Here at 1 Shanti Road you don't even need to spin around. From the terrace, I can see it all. In one direction is a shantytown. A jumble of tin-roofed shacks that, at first glance, looks like a garbage dump. Only when you look more closely do you realize that people live there. Look in another direction and you see a shiny glass building, an office for Cisco Systems.

As I said, in India everything is a sign, especially the signs. Like the one across the street for a company called Sublime Solutions. I have no idea what the company does, probably some sort of software work, but I love the name.

I step back inside and rejoin the conversation, midstream.

"It's all true. And all false," someone is saying, and everyone concurs.

Emma is on her fifth cup of coffee and seventh cigarette. Her eyes have grown big, and she is talking very fast now. Suddenly, the lights go out, and the ceiling fans glide to a halt. I start to sweat almost instantly. No one misses a beat, though.

"Bangalore is the capital of power outages," someone says.

"What about the high-tech companies?" I ask. "How do they do business with all of these power cuts?"

"Oh, come on," says Viki, as if I were terribly naïve, which of course I am. "They have supergenerators, triple redundancy. They're on a separate grid, their own grid."

"The entire IT world is on a separate grid," says Chandra, and he's clearly not talking only about electricity. The high-tech workers, those who have made it big, live in gated communities with names like Dollar Colony. They shop in malls, which also have their own generators. They worship Lakshmi, the goddess of wealth.

Every old building in Bangalore that is torn down is replaced with an office park or a shopping complex. When the term "shopping complex" is translated into the local language, it emerges as, literally, "shopping complicated."

"Yes," says Chandra. "It certainly can be."

I ask Emma for her happiness number.

"I'm a five, not a four. I think, maybe a 3.5."

She's dropping rapidly the more she thinks about it, which, as any Thai will tell you, is precisely her problem.

"I should be happier, but fear has wormed its way inside of me, and my confidence is gone. When I was a painter, when I was younger and had nothing, I was happy."

Researchers have found that happiness forms a U-shaped curve over the course of a lifetime. We're happiest in youth and old age. Emma is at the bottom of the curve, an emotional trough. I don't have the heart to tell her this, though. I fear it might push her happiness score even lower.

Emma tells me that the energy is better here than it is in London. There's that word again, but this time I don't cringe. Spoken here, by a chain-smoking bag-making hedonic refugee, it somehow rings true.

My life at 1 Shanti Road falls into a pleasant routine. I wake up every morning before dawn, a bad habit I picked up at the ashram, and do the *kriya* breathing exercise. Okay, so it's just a hit of oxygen and nothing transcendental. I don't care. It makes me feel good. It gives me energy. (God, now *I'm* using that word.) And since I'm off coffee, I can use all the energy I can get.

Afterward, I step onto the terrace and watch the sun rise over the shantytown next door. The poor live their lives more publicly than the rest of us. A child is squatting, defecating, a woman is giving a man a bath, pouring buckets of water over his head. Another man has a splinter or something stuck in his foot; a small crowd has gathered around him, discussing, I imagine, the best way to remove it. Another man is brushing his teeth. Most of these people have jobs, earning about three dollars a day. They are not at the bottom of the ladder in India, far from it. And that is the beauty of life in India—no matter how low your rung, there is always someone beneath you. An infinite ladder.

Next, Suresh and I drive on his motorcycle to one of Bangalore's parks—Bangalore was known as the Garden City before it was the IT City—and we go for a walk. It's still early, but the park is crowded with people walking, meditating, defecating, doing yoga, laughing. On the way back, we stop to pick up some *idlis* and other spongy items that pass for breakfast in southern India.

The rest of my day unfolds lazily. I sit around reading and thinking about coffee. Mostly, though, I just sit. Indians, and Indian men in particular, are great sitters. World-class. I can't compete with them, but I do my best.

At some point, Chandra, the friendly Martian, will suggest we go to Khoshy's, a coffee shop, and continue our sitting there. Khoshy's is a Bangalore institution. It's been around since 1940, seven years before India gained its independence from Britain.

It's hardly changed since. The walls are mustard yellow and in desperate need of a paint job. Ceiling fans spin but not too quickly. Nothing moves too quickly at Khoshy's. Not the waiters or the chefs or the customers, and that is precisely its appeal. People spend hours and hours here, meeting friends, sipping the ginger punch, and eating Khoshy's signature "smileys," fried potatoes cooked in the shape of smiley faces.

On this day, we're meeting Chandra's friend, Meena. She writes a column for a national newspaper. She has short, grayish hair and a fierce wit.

"Don't get me wrong," Meena says, head tilted at a slight angle. "Gurus have their uses. They're just not for me."

I never thought of it that way before. Gurus have their uses.

Meena once spent six months in the United States, working for the *Baltimore Sun*. She couldn't wait to leave. There's too much distance between people in the United States, and by that she means more than physical distance, though that, too. She found the streets eerily quiet. Where are all the people? she wondered.

"Americans are so busy," she says. "If they're not busy working, they're busy relaxing."

I order a fresh lime soda. Meena does, too, plus the peanut masala, no chili.

"What can Americans learn from India?" I ask Meena.

"You could learn to relax, to live overlapping lives. We are an ad-hoc country. We accept a lot of imperfections. You could be more like that."

If anything, though, India is aping America. Shopping malls, gated communities, fast food. They're all here now. Meena doesn't care for India Shining. She prefers India dull, which was never all that dull, actually.

"The Indian middle class is distancing itself from poverty, and that is dangerous," she says. "The old path you took to God was through suffering and renunciation, the way of the *sanyasi*. That doesn't appeal to the young crowd. Everyone is into the insta-guru now."

Chandra agrees. "There is no sacrifice required with these new gurus."

Chandra offers me a ride back to 1 Shanti Road on his scooter. We are two men of not insignificant heft, and the underpowered scooter wobbles precariously. The traffic is so close I can feel the hot exhaust from the cars on my shins. I had witnessed an accident some days ago and now I see signs of impending danger everywhere. An ambulance passes, sirens blaring, and I realize this is the first time I've ever seen an ambulance in India. Now, we're passing a sign for "Brain and Spine Care." Oh, God, I think, another sign. We're going to crash. But a few minutes later Chandra pulls up to 1 Shanti Road. We're fine.

That evening, I step onto the terrace. The air is soft and cool. I look at the shantytown—it's impossible to avoid—and I see a few kids picking through a pile of trash, looking for something they can sell for a few rupees. A few years in India hardens you to such sights. But there's always something that pierces your armor, no matter how thick it may have grown.

I see a girl, she can't be more than four years old, picking through the trash with one hand and holding something in her other hand. What is it? I squint and see that it is a stuffed animal, a dirty but otherwise intact little bear. My armor dissolves. This is not happy India. This is the country where, as Mark Twain observed, every life is sacred, except human life. Indians may care deeply about their families and circle of friends, but they don't even notice anyone outside that circle. That's why Indian homes are spotless, while just a few feet outside the front door the trash is piled high. It's outside the circle.

Emma has just returned from a visit to her factory. On the floor, she has spread piles of bags. They are everywhere, and they are beautiful. I'm tempted to get naked and roll around in the pile but restrain myself. This is a forgiving place, but even the inhabitants of 1 Shanti Road have their limits.

I walk into the kitchen and notice that the sink is now spotless, the flies have retreated. Suresh's maid, Mona, must be back.

I hear Mona before I see her. The bangles she wears on her wrists and ankles jangle musically. I had heard that Mona was extremely happy, even though she is dirt-poor and lives in one of the shantytowns I see from the terrace. Mona knows only one word of English— "super"—so I ask Suresh to translate.

"Mona, are you happy?"

"Yes, happy."

"And what is the key to happiness?"

"You should not think too much. You should not have anything in your mind. The more you think, the less happy you will be. Live happily, eat happily, die happily." And with that she flings her arms into the air with a flourish. Mona and the Thais would get along beautifully.

"But Mona, don't you have problems? Don't you have money issues?"

She flings her arms again, this time much more forcefully,

indicating that I'm thinking too much. Talking too much, too. The conversation is over. She has work to do. She walks away, her bangles jangling in the soft evening air.

I'm not sure what to make of Mona. I'm well aware of the dangerous myth of the happy, noble savage. They have so little but are so happy. Statistically, that's not true. The poorest countries in the world are also the least happy, and that is certainly true of India. It ranks in the lower end of Ruut Veenhoven's happiness spectrum.

But Mona is not a statistic. She is a person and, she claims, a very happy one. Who am I to disagree? Poverty doesn't guarantee happiness, nor does it deny it.

A few years ago, happiness researcher Robert Biswas-Diener interviewed hundreds of street people in Calcutta, the poorest of the poor, and recorded their happiness levels (again, based on self-reports). Then he did the same with a few hundred homeless people in Fremont, California.

Calcutta's destitute, it turns out, are significantly happier than those in California, even though the Californian homeless had better access to food, shelter, and health services. Biswas-Diener attributed the surprising result to the fact that Calcutta's street people may have little in the way of material wealth, but they do have strong social ties. Family. Friends. I would go a step further and say that no one is really homeless in India. Houseless perhaps, but not homeless.

There's another reason, I think, why Calcutta's poor are happier than America's. If an Indian person is poor, it is because of fate, the gods, or some negative karma accumulated in a previous lifetime. In other words, they are not to blame. If an American is poor, it is seen as a personal failure, a flawed character.


One day, I find myself alone at 1 Shanti Road, a rare occurrence. I'm lounging on the daybed, reading a book, and listening to Hindi pop on the radio when I hear Mona's distinctive jangle. She's balancing a bucket of laundry gracefully on one shoulder. And then we have a conversation, even though we don't share a common language. Not since my pantomimes with Luba in Moldova have I experienced such a thing.

Mona "asks" if I would like some tea. I decline, but she persists. You really should have some tea. Should I turn on the ceiling fan? It's a good idea. It's hot. Maybe that's too high a speed; I'll turn it down. Mona indicates—in her clairvoyant way—that it's best not to do two things at once. She turns off the radio. A few minutes later, she tells me my tea is getting cold, and I really should drink it. She conveys all of this with musical flings of her arms. I decide that, statistics be damned, Mona is happy. Wise, too.


Diwali has arrived. Traditionally, it's known as the Festival of Light, but these days it's the Festival of Loud and Obnoxious Firecrackers. Every street is converted into a free-fire zone. The dogs are traumatized, as am I. For three solid days, my ears are filled with this awful stench. Pop. Boom. And the smoke! It wafts over the city, which now feels like one giant war zone.

On the terrace, Suresh and Emma are preparing for the holiday. Emma is making a Diwali bowl: candles and flowers floating in a pool of water. We light a few sparklers. Mine won't stay lit. Suresh tells me his favorite Hindu god is Shiva, the destroyer, "because you must destroy in order to create."

Emma says she never feels impending doom in India, even though that would be a perfectly rational thing to feel.

"But back in Britain I'm often scared to death."

Suresh puts together a package of cookies for the neighborhood kids and Mona delivers it in a shopping bag. We're sitting under the aging badam tree, which hangs over the terrace like a ceiling.

"Suresh, don't you ever get tired of all these people coming and going constantly? Don't you want to be alone sometimes?"

"No, even when people are around I can be alone. It's a technique that I've mastered."

* * *

My flight leaves soon. I have time for one more trip to Khoshy's, where I've become a regular. I've arranged to meet a professor named Sundar Sarukkai. He wrote an article about happiness that caught my eye. In one short paragraph he managed to capture a paradox that has been nagging me for some time: "Desire is the root cause of sorrow but desire is also the root cause of action. How do we counter the paralysis of action when there is no desire to motivate us?"

Exactly. Hinduism—indeed, most eastern religions—tells us that striving, even striving for happiness, is self-defeating. The moment you try to improve yourself, you've failed. Game over. Yet just lie there like a zombie and you lose, too. What to do?

Sundar seems like he might have some answers. He has advanced degrees in both philosophy and physics. He has shoulder-length hair and, it turns out, is related to Guru-ji.

We grab seats in the corner. I like him immediately. He has Guru-ji's twinkly eyes but not his overt godliness. I'm eager to talk about ambition, the one noun that, more than anything else, has sabotaged my search for happiness. It is the source of my success and my misery. A contradiction that, I figure, only an Indian can wrap his mind around.

"Everyone is ambitious. It's human nature. The question is, what price are we willing to pay for the ambition? Not just an economic price, but a social price." And, he says, the average American is willing to pay a higher price than the average Indian.

"But don't Indians want to succeed?"

"Yes, of course we do, but we deal with disappointment differently. Our attitude is, 'Okay, you've done your best, now let the universe decide.'"

"What do you mean?"

"What some people call chance, we call God. But let's call it unpredictability. You do the same thing ten times, and it doesn't work. On the eleventh time, it works. The entire universe is chance and probability. So we accept everything."

There it is again: that Hindu belief that all of life is *maya*, illusion. Once we see life as a game, no more consequential than a game of chess, then the world seems a lot lighter, a lot happier. Personal failure becomes "as small a cause for concern as playing the role of loser in a summer theater performance," writes Huston Smith in his book *The World's Religions*. If it's all theater, it doesn't matter which role you play, as long as you realize it's only a role. Or, as Alan Watts said: "A genuine person is one who knows he is a big act and does it with complete zip."

We sit there at Khoshy's and talk for a good hour or two. There is no rush, no agenda. It's unpredictable, but in a good way. Time feels expansive. This, I realize, is what I love about India. The hidden little gems amid the grubbiness and the squalor and the greed. I am, dare I say, happy.

"One Shanti Road is the happiest place in India," Emma had said shortly after she arrived. At the time, I didn't know what she was talking about. Now I do. "Shanti," it turns out, is a Sanskrit word that means "inner peace." Maybe 1 Shanti Road isn't the anti-ashram after all. Maybe it's just another kind of ashram.

My flight leaves in a few hours. Bangalore is anything but peaceful. Diwali is in full swing. Firecrackers are going off everywhere. The air is thick with acrid smoke. Suresh hurries me out a side exit to a waiting cab. I feel like I'm boarding the last helicopter out of Saigon. I give him a hug and tell him to be happy. Then the taxi pulls away, and 1 Shanti Road disappears in a cloud of smoke.

I am relieved to be leaving this craziness behind. I want to stay. A contradiction? Yes, but one I can live with and even learn to enjoy.

# Chapter 10

# AMERICA

## Happiness Is Home

Dockominium. The word hung in the air like a perfectly ripe mango. I didn't know what it meant, but it sounded big and juicy, and I couldn't wait to dive in.

The word was uttered by my friend Craig Baggott. Craig was a big, ungainly man with a shaggy flop of grayish hair and eyes that twinkled mischievously when he said things like "dockominium." Which Craig did often.

Craig could make magic with a ribbon of toilet paper, twirling it gracefully in a maneuver he dubbed "the toilet-paper dance." Craig loved cars and Mountain Dew—two passions he often combined in spur-of-the-moment cross-country road trips. He would just grab one of his kids, a few gallons of Dew and hit the road. Craig didn't stop for bathroom breaks. I don't think it was a macho thing but, rather, that Craig, not a conventionally religious man, found some sort of transcendent peace on the open road and didn't want to interrupt it.

Craig was more at ease, more comfortable in his own skin, than anyone I've known. All of the energy that most of us expend worrying about our careers and our marriage and our nasal hair, Craig channeled into just being Craig. This was, I'm sure, a far more efficient and noble use of the energy we call life.

So when Craig uttered the word "dockominium," I paid attention. As you might have guessed by now, a dockominium is a combination of a dock and a condominium. I do not especially care for either docks or condominiums, but somehow I found the combination irresistible. The dock part of "dockominium" sounded frivolous and—let's not mince words here—irresponsible, for what is a dock without a boat, and what is a boat but a floating money pit? But the "ominium" part of "dockominium" anchored the entire enterprise in a bedrock of financial probity, for what is a condominium but an investment, and what is an investment but the exact opposite of a boat? Thus the genius of the dockominium.

I envisioned a carefree, happy life that consisted mainly of sipping drinks with tiny umbrellas in them. The inhabitants of dockominiums, I imagined, tanned easily. They never wore ties and, I bet, rarely felt the need to tuck in their shirts. I desperately wanted to be one of them.

Miami, Craig assured me, is where these dockominiums could be found. Why not? I thought. After a decade bouncing around the world as a foreign correspondent, it was time to come home, and Miami seemed like a good place to reenter America. A baby step back home. Miami had tropical weather, corruption, and political turmoil. All of these things I had grown used to overseas. Miami, along with Hawaii and parts of California, is America's Garden of Eden. Some people (the elderly) come to Miami to die, while others (Cubans) come to be reborn. I wasn't elderly or Cuban, but I wanted to make a fresh start, so I figured that made me the ideal Miami resident.

My wife and I landed at Miami's shabby airport on a reconnaissance visit. We stepped out of the terminal and smack into the delicious heat and humidity. Many languages filled the moist air, not one of them English. Yes, I thought, breathing it all in, I could be happy here.

It was the next day when we got the call. It was from another of Craig's friends. Craig had collapsed while playing a game of Tetris. His teenage daughter had found him on the floor. She did all the right things—calling 911, propping open the door as she ran to the elevator to meet the paramedics—but it was too late. Craig was gone. In his report, the coroner ascribed Craig's death to a massive cardiac infarction. I had my own theory, though. Craig's heart, so big and generous, had simply given out from overuse.

Words spoken by the dead carry a special urgency that render them impossible to ignore. And so it was with Craig's Miami prophecy. I knew then, tears stinging my eyes, that I was moving to Miami. No question about it.

Miami is associated with happiness, if not paradise itself. Beaches. Palm trees. Sunshine. But paradise comes with its own inherent pressures. It screams: "Be happy, God damn it!" I remember driving by a billboard on the way to work one day. There was a photo of a yellow convertible VW Beetle and, underneath, the words, "Woe isn't you. Dare to be happy." What is that ad saying? It's saying, I think, that at the dawn of the twenty-first century, American happiness isn't left to the gods or to fortune, as was the case for most of human history. No, happiness is there for the taking. All we need is enough willpower to summon it, enough gumption to try it in the first place, and of course enough cash to afford a convertible VW Beetle with optional satellite radio and leather interior.

America's current fixation with finding happiness coincides with an era of unprecedented material prosperity. Many commentators have suggested this is not a coincidence. As early as the 1840s, Alexis de Tocqueville observed that America was populated by "so many lucky men, restless in the midst of their abundance." Or, as Kevin Rushby writes in his recent history of paradise, "All talk of paradise only starts when something has been lost." What have we lost? I wonder.

America's place on the happiness spectrum is not as high as you might think, given our superpower status. We are not, by any measure, the happiest nation on earth. One study, by Adrian White at

the University of Leicester in Britain, ranked the United States as
the world's twenty-third happiest nation, behind countries such as
Costa Rica, Malta, and Malaysia. True, most Americans—84 percent, according to one study—describe themselves as either "very"
or "pretty" happy, but it's safe to say that the United States is not
as happy as it is wealthy.

Indeed, there is plenty of evidence that we are less happy
today than ever before, as psychologist David Myers has shown in
his book *The American Paradox: Spiritual Hunger in an Age of
Plenty*. Since 1960, the divorce rate has doubled, the teen-suicide
rate tripled, the violent-crime rate quadrupled, and the prison population quintupled. Then there are the increased rates of depression, anxiety, and other mental-health problems. (There is robust
evidence that what we're witnessing is a genuine increase in these
disorders and not merely a greater willingness to diagnose them.)

What about all that money? We are the wealthiest country in
the world, the wealthiest nation ever. On the one hand, all this cash
is good. Basic survival is not an issue for most Americans. Wealthier Americans are, on average, (slightly) happier than poorer ones.
Yet one fact bedevils the money-equals-happiness argument: As a
nation, we are three times richer than we were in 1950 yet no happier. What is going on?

Clearly, one dynamic at work is rising expectations. We compare ourselves not to the America of 1950 but the America of
today and, more specifically, to our neighbors of today. We give
lip service to the notion that money can't buy happiness but act
as if it does. When asked what would improve the quality of their
lives, Americans' number-one answer was money, according to a
University of Michigan study.

The self-help industrial complex hasn't helped. By telling us
that happiness lives inside us, it's turned us inward just when we
should be looking outward. Not to money but to other people, to
community and to the kind of human bonds that so clearly are the
sources of our happiness.

Americans work longer hours and commute greater distances

than virtually any other people in the world. Commuting, in particular, has been found to be detrimental to our happiness, as well as our physical health. Every minute spent on the road is one less minute that we can spend with family and friends—the kind of activities, in other words, that make us happy.

Political scientist Robert Putnam makes a convincing case in his book *Bowling Alone* that our sense of connection is fraying. We spend less time visiting family and friends; we belong to fewer community groups. Increasingly, we lead fragmented lives. The Internet and other technologies may salve our loneliness, but they have not, I believe, eliminated it.

Americans, like everyone, are notoriously bad at predicting what will make us happy and what will not. This quirk of the human psyche is especially frustrating for Americans because we, more than any other nation, have the means at our disposal to pursue happiness so vigorously. A Bangladeshi farmer might believe that a Mercedes S-Class will make him happy, but he will probably die having never test-driven that belief. Not so with us Americans. We are able to acquire many of the things that we think will make us happy and therefore suffer the confusion and disappointment when they do not.

Over the past fifty years, America's happiness levels have remained remarkably stable, unperturbed by cataclysmic events. After the attacks of September 11, 2001, researchers found no marked decrease in U.S. happiness levels. The 1962 Cuban missile crisis precipitated a brief *increase* in national happiness. Most people of the world derive happiness from the quotidian. Historian Will Durant has said, "History has been too often a picture of the bloody stream. The [real] history of civilization is a record of what happened on the banks."

We remain a profoundly optimistic nation. Two thirds of Americans say they are hopeful about the future. Hopeful, I guess, that we will be happier.

When it comes to thinking about happiness, pondering it, worrying about it, cogitating over it, bemoaning our lack of it, and, of course, pursuing it, the United States is indeed a superpower. Eight out of ten Americans say they think about their happiness at least once a week. The sheer size and scope of the self-help industrial complex is testimony to both our discontent and our belief in the possibility of self-renewal.

No other nation's founding document so prominently celebrates happiness. Of course, the Declaration of Independence only enshrines the right to *pursue* happiness. It's up to us, as Benjamin Franklin once quipped, to catch it. We do this in a number of ways, some legal, some not. Some wise, others not so much.

One way Americans pursue happiness is by physically moving. Indeed, ours is a nation founded on restlessness. What were the pilgrims if not hedonic refugees, searching for happiness someplace else? And what is our much-heralded "frontier spirit" if not a yearning for a happier place? "In America, getting on in the world means getting out of the world we have known before," wrote the editor and teacher Ellery Sedgwick in his autobiography, *The Happy Profession*.

Sedgwick wrote those words in 1946. Since then, we've become even more mobile. Every year, nearly forty million Americans move. Some, no doubt, pick up stakes for job opportunities or to be near a sick relative. But many move simply because they believe they'll be happier somewhere else.

That certainly worked for the hedonic refugees I met on the road—Linda, Lisa, Rob, Jared. Is it the "energy" of these places that attracted these people to them? I'm not so sure. A better explanation, I think, is that they gave themselves permission to be different people in different places.

The ability to choose where we live is, in the scheme of human history, a very recent phenomenon. Over the centuries, most people grew where they were planted. It took some catastrophe—flood or famine or the marauding hordes of Mongols who moved in next door (there goes the neighborhood!)—to prompt a relocation. With the exception of the very rich, who frankly have always been a bit unstable, people didn't move for kicks. Adventure, in the good sense of the word, is a modern concept. For most of history, adventure was something inflicted upon you, not something you sought out and certainly not something you paid for. That old Chinese saying "May you live in interesting times" was actually meant as a curse.

Where is the happiest place in the United States? Here the science of happiness fails me. I could not find one definitive report that answers that question. Christopher Peterson of the University of Michigan told me that people get happier the farther west they move. His theory, though, contradicts the findings of David Schkade of the University of California at San Diego. He and his colleagues surveyed people in California and Michigan and found that they were equally happy (or unhappy, depending on your perspective). The people in Michigan *thought* they would be happier if they moved to California, a belief that Schkade calls a "focusing illusion." Sitting in cold, bleak Michigan, these people imagined a happier life in California, but they failed to take into account the negative side to life there: traffic jams, high real-estate prices, and wildfires, to name a few. "Nothing you focus on will make as much difference as you think," he concludes.

I've seen other reports that the Midwest is the happiest place, or the Ozark region, or small cities with populations of less than one hundred thousand. It's frustratingly inconclusive. One thing is clear though: The differences *within* countries are not nearly as great as the differences *between* countries.


I've tried to like Miami. I really have. I've done my best to fit in. I've gone to the beach. I studied Spanish. I've drunk large quantities of Cuban coffee. I briefly considered getting breast implants. And yet all of the sunshine has left me feeling cold.

Maybe I would like Miami if I were Latino. Latin American nations are unexpectedly happy, given their relative poverty. Some studies suggest that Latinos retain this happiness bonus when they immigrate to the United States. I asked my friend Joe Garcia, a Cuban American, about this. He thinks there's something to it.

Partly it's the Latino focus on family. "It's part of a communal living arrangement. You are part of something much bigger than yourself," said Joe as we lounged, Miami-fashion, at a see-and-be-seen café. "And there's this emphasis on living in the moment. We have an expression in Spanish that translates as 'What you've danced can't be taken away.'"

Nice in theory, but I'm a lousy dancer. No wonder Miami isn't for me.

One man's paradise can be another's hell, and the converse holds true as well. When European missionaries first landed in Greenland several centuries ago, intent on converting the pagan natives to Christianity, they offered the usual carrot-and-stick approach: Convert and you get a shot at heaven; don't, and you will be condemned to an eternity in hell.

"What is this hell like?" asked the curious Greenlanders.

"Oh, it is very, very hot," replied the missionaries. "It is hot all of the time."

The Greenlanders surveyed the frozen Arctic tundra that was their home and replied, "We'll take hell, thank you."

"Paradise gets old," says my neighbor Andy, when I raise this sensitive question. We're sitting in his house in Miami. Andy is preparing to sell it and get out of town. He's had enough.

He moved here twenty-two years ago, not because it was paradise but because he was fresh out of the army and had just landed a job. He was young and single. Life was good. Yet he never felt like he belonged in Miami. It didn't fit him.

Andy is, as he puts it, a "freshwater person, not an ocean person." He says this as if it were a biological predisposition, like body type or cholesterol levels.

The events of August 1992 shed some light on why Andy is so

down on Miami. It's been fifteen years, but Andy can still hear, in his mind's ear, the low rumbling sound, like a freight train; he can still feel the house shake, can still remember waking up and finding boats in his front yard, even though he didn't live near the water. "It was really, really freaky," he says of Hurricane Andrew, now the second-most destructive hurricane in U.S. history, after Hurricane Katrina.

The debris was piled nine feet high outside. There was no electricity for two months. And yet people kept moving to southern Florida, seeking paradise in what was, for Andy, a living hell.

Andy craves a change of seasons. A real change of seasons, not Miami's two seasons: hot and unbearably hot. He wants to feel the gradient of temperatures and the shift in the quality of the air, to experience a natural cycle, to sense the passage of time. In Miami, one month blurs into the next, and life seems painfully eternal.

Andy was never culturally comfortable, as he puts it, in Miami. He doesn't speak Spanish, and that has hurt his prospects as a real-estate agent. He finds the people, no matter their ethnicity, rude.

"I've been here for twenty-two years, and I can't take it any longer."

"When did you snap?" I ask.

"It's been one long snap. I've got to get out of here."

"Is there anything you'll miss about Miami?"

"Not a thing. Not the weather, not the trees, not the beach. Nothing."

Clearly, Andy is a man who should have left Miami a while ago. Staying in a place too long is like staying in a relationship too long. You grow bitter, and the chances of domestic violence increase. Reconciliation becomes impossible.

Andy did his research and fixed his sights on North Carolina. The mountainous western part of the state. Asheville in particular. The small city, population about seventy thousand, fits a lot of his criteria; it has mountains, which he loves. And seasons.

He visited and instantly felt at peace there. It's not quite a spiritual feeling—that's not a word that Andy would use—but Asheville does have a calming, narcotic effect on him. He also likes the scale. Asheville is big enough to have a thriving arts scene and a choice of restaurants yet not so big that it is burdened with big-city problems, such as traffic jams and high crime rates. Andy concedes he probably won't go to many art shows or theater performances, but he likes to know they are there, just in case.

Andy's biggest fear: that he's discovered Asheville too late. "I don't want to get up there and find that the rest of Florida has already moved there."

Cynthia Andros is three years ahead of Andy. She's already moved to Asheville. She grew up in Miami and feels about as affectionately toward the city as Andy does.

We're sitting at a Japanese restaurant in Asheville, eating sushi. "I can eat a lot of sushi," Cynthia warns, so we order extra—heaps of tekka maki, worthy of Tokyo's Tsukiji fish market. For such a small city, Asheville has an inordinate number of Asian restaurants, yoga studios, and "men's ritual gatherings."

Cynthia's a restless soul, having lived in Paris and San Diego, among other places. Three years ago, she decided it was time for a move. She sat down with a map and research material and attempted to calculate—yes, that's the word, calculate—where she would be happiest. It was that deliberate.

Cynthia had her criteria. She wouldn't move someplace flat, either topographically or culturally. She wanted four seasons but a temperate environment. That eliminated Minneapolis, which otherwise scored high. She can't live in places of low humidity; she gets headaches. So that eliminated states such as Arizona and New Mexico. Food was, important, too. She needed regular access to not only feta cheese but "a variety of feta cheeses."

Cynthia is a nature photographer, so she had to be close to the natural world. (Biophilia at work again.) She needed an arts scene and live music and other signs of cultural life.

In the end, though, it wasn't the rational, calculating part of Cynthia's brain that made the decision to move to Asheville but the intuitive part. She was visiting her parents in Sarasota, Florida, and North Carolina began popping up everywhere. She saw billboards for North Carolina. TV commercials for North Carolina. She would pick up a magazine, randomly and—bam!—there would be a story about North Carolina. In particular, the mountains of North Carolina. Cynthia had never been to North Carolina, yet here was the place, insinuating itself into her life.

"It blew me away, and what could I do but laugh? So I laughed."

I'm not sure what to make of her story. At first, I recoil when I hear such fantastic tales. I don't believe in signs—outside of India, that is, where everything is a sign. But then I thought about it. Are Cynthia's signs really so different from my experience with Craig? That was a sign, too, though I didn't think of it that way at the time.

Cynthia looked at a map of North Carolina and discovered that there are mountains only in the western part of the state and there is only one city in the mountains: Asheville. So she visited. A few months later, she moved to Asheville.

Cynthia feels comfortable and accepted, at least within Asheville proper. "Look," she says, sotto voce, "if I step out of Asheville, I'm in hard-core, Bible Belt, southern, small-minded towns. There are people there who don't travel. I've met so many people who haven't been on an airplane. You wouldn't believe it."

It dawns on me that Asheville is an island. A crunchy island of peevish liberalism in a state that is not so liberal. Islands can be places of paradise or self-exile, and I'm not sure which category Asheville falls into.

I ask Cynthia if she is happy in Asheville.

"Yes," she says. She likes the fact that she can get anywhere within a fifteen-minute drive. She likes the mountains, so close and embracing. She likes the fact that she can see the opera or a theater performance. Asheville doesn't meet all of her criteria—there's no large body of water nearby and no major airport—but even paradise requires some compromises.

Cynthia, though, isn't quite ready to call Asheville home. It is home "for now," she says. And that, I realize, is the problem with hedonic floaters like Cynthia and with many of us Americans and our perpetual pursuit of happiness. We may be fairly happy now, but there's always tomorrow and the prospect of a happier place, a happier life. So all options are left on the table. We never fully commit. That is, I think, a dangerous thing. We can't love a place, or a person, if we always have one foot out the door.

Laurey Masterton ended up in Asheville for very different reasons. It was the late 1980s, and Laurey was working in New York as a lighting director for theatrical productions. She needed a break and signed up for an Outward Bound program. At the time, there were five Outward Bound locations in the United States. She chose the one in North Carolina because of the snakes. Laurey was terrified of snakes, and North Carolina had more poisonous snakes than any other location. So she chose that one. She figured if she was going to confront her fears, she might as well do so in a big way.

Laurey fell in love with the Blue Ridge Mountains. She also discovered she had leadership skills. Soon, she enrolled as an Outward Bound instructor, packed her bags, and moved to Asheville. At first, life was difficult. She was used to being in the middle of it all, but in Ashevlle there was no all. She stuck it out, though. "I felt like I was in the right place," she said.

One evening, she was cooking dinner for her landlord, who was holding a party. There were a number of Asheville bigwigs at the party, and one of them said to Laurey, "You're a good cook. You should open a restaurant." She gave Laurey a book about how to do just that and offered some advice.

Laurey calls it the golden thread. A path appears, faint at first, but increasingly clear if you're willing to look closely. And Laurey did look. She opened a catering company, then a restaurant. When I met her recently, on a showery summer day in Asheville, we sat drinking coffee at her expansive new restaurant downtown.

I like Laurey instantly, in a way I haven't felt since I met Karma Ura in Bhutan. So when Laurey tells me that both her parents died, a few months apart, when she was twelve and that she is a two-time cancer survivor, it makes sense. What doesn't kill you not only makes you stronger but also more honest.

Laurey is happy in Asheville. Whenever she returns from a trip, the first thing that strikes her when she gets off the plane is the softness of the air, as if it is caressing her skin. That and the mountains. Laurey feels like they are hugging her. "I respond deeply to a sense of place," she says. A five-minute drive from her house and she is deep in the woods or deep in a Thai restaurant. She's a member of the Chamber of Commerce but can still show up for work wearing shorts and sneakers.

Laurey believes there is something special about Asheville. She's heard so many amazing stories about how people ended up here that she's no longer surprised when she hears another one. "A lot of people spin the globe and their finger stops on Asheville."

She acknowledges that there is tension in Asheville. Tension among the old-timers who don't want anything to change and the newcomers who want everything to change and the people who have been here for ten years and want to lock the door behind them.

When she moved to Asheville, there were literally tumbleweeds blowing down the main street and maybe two restaurants in town. The other day, she went out to dinner and was shocked to find she didn't recognize a single person. That has never happened before.

"Is Asheville home?" I ask.

Again, that slight hesitation. That lack of commitment. "I've been here for twenty years, so I guess this is home. All the parts I care about are here."

Her answer makes me recall something an Icelandic film director had told me. There is one simple question, he said, the answer to which identifies your true home. That question is: "Where do you want to die?"

"Where do you want to die?" I ask Laurey.

"In Vermont, where I grew up," she says. There, not Asheville, is where she wants her ashes scattered.


The problem with finding paradise is that others might find it, too. And that is what's happening with Asheville. Word is out that this is a great place to live. *Money* magazine, *Outside* magazine, and others, they've all said so.

Asheville is on the cusp. It could go either way. Cynthia has seen it happen before. It happened in Destin, Florida. She lived there for several years and watched it change "from a quiet seaside fishing village to a greedy, overpopulated, uptight anywhere." And she's afraid the same thing might happen to Asheville. Paradise is a moving target.

# EPILOGUE

## Are We There Yet?

My search is over. I've logged tens of thousands of miles. I endured the noon darkness of Iceland and the solid heat of Qatar, the persnickety functionality of Switzerland and the utter unpredictability of India. I survived a coup lite, savored minor breakthroughs, and mourned the loss of a Ridiculously Expensive Pen. I may have saved the life of one dumb bug. I smoked Moroccan hash and ate rotten shark. I even quit coffee, for a while.

And now I find myself back in Airport World, in New York, killing time before my flight home to Miami. I've bellied up to the bar and am well into my second Bloody Mary. I love airport bars. Everyone is from someplace else, heading someplace else, and yet there is this unexpected coziness. Everyone is swaddled in the inevitable present moment.

It's all very Buddhist, I'm thinking, when I notice the bartender's name tag. I can hardly believe my eyes. It says "Happy."

"Is that your real name?" I ask.

"Yep. My father was so happy when I was born that's what he named me."

"So, excuse me for asking—I'm sure you get this all the time—but what is it?"

"What is what?"

"The secret—to being you, to being Happy?"

"Just keep on smiling. Even when you're sad. Keep on smiling."

Not the most profound advice, admittedly. But Happy is wise, for only a fool or a philosopher would make sweeping generalizations about the nature of happiness. I am no philosopher, so here goes: Money matters, but less than we think and not in the way that we think. Family is important. So are friends. Envy is toxic. So is excessive thinking. Beaches are optional. Trust is not. Neither is gratitude.

To venture any further, though, is to enter treacherous waters. A slippery seal, happiness is. On the road, I encountered bushels of inconsistencies. The Swiss are uptight and happy. The Thais are laid-back and happy. Icelanders find joy in their binge drinking, Moldovans only misery. Maybe an Indian mind can digest these contradictions, but mine can't. Exasperated, I call one of the leading happiness researchers, John Helliwell. Perhaps he has some answers.

"It's simple," he says. "There's more than one path to happiness."

Of course. How could I have missed it? Tolstoy turned on his head. All miserable countries are alike; happy ones are happy in their own ways.

It's worth considering carbon. We wouldn't be here without it. Carbon is the basis of all life, happy and otherwise. Carbon is also a chameleon atom. Assemble it one way—in tight, interlocking rows—and you have a diamond. Assemble it another way—a disorganized jumble—and you have a handful of soot. The arranging makes all the difference.

Places are the same. It's not the elements that matter so much as how they're arranged and in which proportions. Arrange them one way, and you have Switzerland. Arrange them another way, and you have Moldova. Getting the balance right is important. Qatar has too much money and not enough culture. It has no way of absorbing all that cash.

And then there is Iceland: a country that has no right to be happy yet is. Iceland gets the balance right. A small country but a cosmopolitan one. Dark and light. Efficient and laid-back. American gumption married to European social responsibility. A perfect, happy arrangement. The glue that holds the entire enterprise together is culture. It makes all the difference.

I have some nagging doubts about my journey. I didn't make it everywhere. Yet my doubts extend beyond matters of itinerary. I wonder if happiness is really the highest good, as Aristotle believed. Maybe Guru-ji, Sri Sri Ravi Shankar, is right. Maybe love is more important than happiness. Certainly, there are times when happiness seems beside the point. Ask a single, working mother if she is happy, and she's likely to reply, "You're not asking the right question." Yes, we want to be happy but for the right reasons, and, ultimately, most of us would choose a rich and meaningful life over an empty, happy one, if such a thing is even possible.

"Misery serves a purpose," says psychologist David Myers. He's right. Misery alerts us to dangers. It's what spurs our imagination. As Iceland proves, misery has its own tasty appeal.

A headline on the BBC's website caught my eye the other day. It read: "Dirt Exposure Boosts Happiness." Researchers at Bristol University in Britain treated lung-cancer patients with "friendly" bacteria found in soil, otherwise known as dirt. The patients reported feeling happier and had an improved quality of life. The research, while far from conclusive, points to an essential truth: We thrive on messiness. "The good life...cannot be mere indulgence. It must contain a measure of grit and truth," observed geographer Yi-Fu Tuan.

Tuan is the great unheralded geographer of our time and a man whose writing has accompanied me throughout my journeys. He called one chapter of his autobiography "Salvation by Geography." The title is tongue-in-cheek, but only slightly, for geography can be our salvation. We are shaped by our environment and, if you take this Taoist belief one step further, you might say we *are* our environment. Out there. In here. No difference. Viewed that way, life seems a lot less lonely.

* * *

The word "utopia" has two meanings. It means both "good place" and "nowhere." That's the way it should be. The happiest places, I think, are the ones that reside just this side of paradise. The perfect person would be insufferable to live with; likewise, we wouldn't want to live in the perfect place, either. "A lifetime of happiness! No man could bear it: It would be hell on Earth," wrote George Bernard Shaw, in his play *Man and Superman*.

Ruut Veenhoven, keeper of the database, got it right when he said: "Happiness requires livable conditions, but not paradise." We humans are imminently adaptable. We survived an Ice Age. We can survive anything. We find happiness in a variety of places and, as the residents of frumpy Slough demonstrated, places can change. Any atlas of bliss must be etched in pencil.

My passport is tucked into my desk drawer again. I am relearning the pleasures of home. The simple joys of waking up in the same bed each morning. The pleasant realization that familiarity breeds contentment and not only contempt.

Every now and then, though, my travels resurface and in unexpected ways. My iPod crashed the other day. I lost my entire music collection, nearly two thousand songs. In the past, I would have gone through the roof with rage. This time, though, my anger dissipated like a summer thunderstorm and, to my surprise, I found the Thai words *mai pen lai* on my lips. Never mind. Let it go. I am more aware of the corrosive nature of envy and try my best to squelch it before it grows. I don't take my failures quite so hard anymore. I see beauty in a dark winter sky. I can recognize a genuine smile from twenty yards. I have a newfound appreciation for fresh fruits and vegetables.

Of all the places I visited, of all the people I met, one keeps coming back to me again and again: Karma Ura, the Bhutanese scholar and cancer survivor. "There is no such thing as personal happiness," he told me. "Happiness is one hundred percent relational." At the time, I didn't take him literally. I thought he was exaggerating to make his point: that our relationships with other people are more important than we think.

But now I realize Karma meant exactly what he said. Our happiness is completely and utterly intertwined with other people: family and friends and neighbors and the woman you hardly notice who cleans your office. Happiness is not a noun or verb. It's a conjunction. Connective tissue.

Well, are we there yet? Have I found happiness? I still own an obscene number of bags and am prone to debilitating bouts of hypochondria. But I do experience happy moments. I'm learning, as W. H. Auden counseled, to "dance while you can." He didn't say dance *well*, and for that I am grateful.

I'm not 100 percent happy. Closer to feevty-feevty, I'd say. All things considered, that's not so bad. No, not bad at all.

*Waterford, Virginia, July 2007*

# Acknowledgments

In one of those cruel ironies of human nature, writing a book about happiness turns out to be a trying and, at times, unhappy endeavor—not only for the author but also for those unfortunate enough to cross his grumpy path. I owe a huge debt of gratitude to these people who, despite all common sense and instinct for self-preservation, graciously helped me every step of the way.

My agent, Sloan Harris, believed in the project from the get-go and steered me through the choppy waters of the publishing world with skill and compassion. At TWELVE, Cary Goldstein and Nate Gray provided valuable support, in ways large and small. The eagle-eyed Timothy Mennell nipped, tucked, and polished the manuscript.

Having Jonathan Karp as an editor is enough to make even the most misanthropic writer happy. Jon guided the project from initial inception to final punctuation. He knows when to let a writer write and when to step in and save him from himself.

I owe a debt of appreciation to National Public Radio's foreign desk for their support and collegiality over the years. NPR's vice president of news, Ellen Weiss, was supportive and understanding of my prolonged absence.

Several people provided valuable guidance and encouragement at key stages. David Shenk and Laura Blumenfeld offered indispensable advice about the world of books. Bobbie Roessner provided wise words of encouragement—words that I dipped into during the many difficult twists and bumps on the road to bliss.

It is simply not possible to dive into so many countries, as I did, and not rely heavily on the kindness—and contacts—of others. With apologies to those I've most certainly overlooked, I am indebted to Tony Judge, Karl Blöndal, Odai Sirri, Kaleb Brownlow, Kavita Pillay, Lisa Kirchner, Stokes Jones, Grace Pless, Krista Mahr, Leif Pettersen, Michael Hawley, and Linda Neuman. In Switzerland, my friend Bruno Giussani generously shared his time and insights. In Bhutan, Mark Mancall shared his deep knowledge about that country and put me in touch with all of the right people.

Thank you to Joe Garcia for explaining Miami to a sunburned Anglo, and to the University of Miami in Coral Gables for providing an office and access to their capacious library. Much of the book's early pages were written at Books & Books in Miami, and the store's proprietor, Mitchell Kaplan, was an early supporter. My research assistant, Gretchen Beesing, skillfully mined the dense and surprisingly treacherous world of happiness research, and for that I am extremely grateful. In the Netherlands, the dedicated staff of the World Database of Happiness generously made their files of bliss available to me.

On the road, I am indebted to those who graciously opened their homes to me: Susan Gilman, Scott Neuman, Rob Gifford, Nancy Fraser, and Suresh Jayaram. They offered not only a bed in which to sleep but also a surfeit of insights and suggestions. Sarah Ferguson provided moral support throughout, as well as the world's best writer's retreat.

Several people read early drafts of the book and offered valuable suggestions: Amy Bickers, Chuck Berman, Barbara Brotman, Dan Charles, and Dan Grech. I tip my hat to all of them.

One's family is a great source not only of happiness but also of literary support. I am indebted to my parents and my brother, Paul, for tolerating my grumpiness before, during, and after this project. A big thanks to my daughter, Sonya, one of my greatest sources of happiness, for putting up with my long absences from home. Thanks, too, to my in-laws, and to Marie Jo Paris, for helping take such good care of her while I roamed the world.

Finally, I want to thank my wife, Sharon. This book literally would not exist without her. She courageously and stoically endured the particular brand of misery inflicted on spouses of happiness authors. She never gave up on the project, or on me, and for that I am grateful beyond words. She is my editor, she is my confidante. She is my bliss. This book is dedicated to her.

# About the Author

Eric Weiner spent a decade as a foreign correspondent for National Public Radio. He has been based in New Delhi, Jerusalem, and Tokyo, and has reported from more than 30 countries. He has also served as a correspondent for NPR in New York, Miami, and, currently, Washington, D.C. Weiner is a former reporter for *The New York Times* and was a Knight Journalism Fellow at Stanford University. His commentary has appeared in the *Los Angeles Times*, *Slate*, and *The New Republic*, among other publications. After traveling the world, he has settled, quasi-happily, in the Washington area, where he divides his time between his living room and his kitchen.

www.EricWeinerBooks.com

TWELVE

TWELVE was established in August 2005 with the objective of publishing no more than one book per month. We strive to publish the singular book, by authors who have a unique perspective and compelling authority. Works that explain our culture; that illuminate, inspire, provoke, and entertain. We seek to establish communities of conversation surrounding our books. Talented authors deserve attention not only from publishers but from readers as well. To sell the book is only the beginning of our mission. To build avid audiences of readers who are enriched by these works—that is our ultimate purpose.

For more information about forthcoming TWELVE books, you can visit us at www.twelvebooks.com.